The Economics of Futures Trading

Readings Selected, Edited and Introduced

by

B. A. GOSS
Monash University

and

B. S. YAMEY
The London School of Economics and Political Science
University of London

M

First published 1976 by
THE MACMILLAN PRESS LTD
London and Basingstoke
Associated companies in New York
Dublin Melbourne Johannesburg and Madras

SBN 333 18699 0

Typeset, printed and bound
in Great Britain by
REDWOOD BURN LIMITED
Trowbridge & Esher

Contents

Preface

Several of the major futures markets of today have been established for about a century or longer. Yet the writings of economists on the operation and implications of futures trading were sparse until after the Second World War. It is true that notable publications appeared before 1945 – one thinks, for instance, of the studies by H. C. Emery, C. O. Hardy, J. G. Smith and G. Wright Hoffman. These early works tended to concentrate on descriptions and explanations of futures exchanges, the contracts traded in them and their trading procedures; and in the process they contributed materially towards the formation of analytical ideas about the economics of futures trading and its economic roles and consequences in terms of hedging and speculation. Mainly theoretical contributions came from J. M. Keynes, J. R. Hicks and N. Kaldor.

The volume of publication increased greatly after 1945. The post-war literature on futures trading has covered all aspects of the subject, from chronicles of events in particular markets to the construction and articulation of abstract theories of price behaviour and price relationships. Much of it was inspired (occasionally provoked) by the pioneering inquiries and writings of Holbrook Working, of the Food Research Institute, Stanford University, whose own publications straddle five decades.

In this book we present a selection of papers on futures trading, the majority published since 1945. The main emphasis in the selection is on more theoretical writings, although several mainly empirical studies are included. This bias in the selection reflects nothing more than the impact of two considerations: first, limitations of space tend to work against the inclusion of more empirical papers, which often are necessarily lengthy and also difficult to abridge for reprinting by the omission of whole sections; second, in our long introductory essay which precedes the reprinted papers it has been easier to incorporate briefly the main findings of empirical studies than to include satisfactorily potted versions of primarily theoretical work. Fortunately, analysis and empirical work have tended to go hand in hand in the study of futures markets, so that the distinction between theory and application is not a sharp one.

The first consideration – limitations of space – has a further consequence. It has not been possible to include examples of the work of all the leading contributors to the study of the economics of futures trading.

We trust it is not invidious to name H. Houthakker and L. G. Telser in this context as authors who have made notable contributions to the subject but are not represented in this book.

We are deeply indebted to those authors and publishers (acknowledged individually in the appropriate places) who have allowed us to reprint published material in this book. The publishers have made every effort to trace the copyright-holders but if they have inadvertently overlooked any, they will be pleased to make the necessary arrangements at the first opportunity. We are also in debt to numerous traders and market officials who have, over many years, supplied us with information and answers to our questions. Finally, we gratefully record our thanks to the Wincott Foundation, London, for a research grant which has greatly facilitated our work in preparing our introductory essay as well as the book as a whole.

B. A. Goss
B. S. Yamey

Introduction: The Economics of Futures Trading

The Editors

INTRODUCTORY

Futures trading in an organised commodity market or exchange consists of the sale and purchase of the commodity through the medium of highly standardised futures contracts (called futures) which provide for the delivery of the defined subject-matter at defined future dates. Futures contracts are contracts which provide for the delivery of the contracted goods; but in fact in many futures markets only a small proportion of all contracts are settled by actual delivery. Hence futures markets are sometimes also referred to as paper markets; it is possible to deal in futures without ever actually seeing or handling the physical commodity.

Futures trading has often been controversial, and has increasingly been brought under public control or supervision or been threatened with such measures. Public concern has focused on the supposed effects of futures trading (and of the speculation which it facilitates) on the level and movement of the prices of the traded commodities. Economists have been interested in futures trading for the same reason, and also, in more general terms, because of their interest in the efficiency of the inter-temporal allocation of resources. These markets have been attracting renewed attention because of growing interest in the effects of uncertainty on resource allocation as well as on the nature of information, search and transactions costs and their minimisation by means of special forms of contract and market institution.

Origins of futures trading

It has been claimed that futures trading originated as early as the seventeenth century in Amsterdam, in commodities such as grains, brandy, whale oil and coffee. John Cary, writing of Amsterdam in 1695, said: 'They invent new ways of trade, great quantities of brandy being disposed of every year, which are never intended to be delivered, only the buyer and seller get or lose according to the rates it bears at the time agreed on to make good the bargains.'[1] It has also been claimed that the practice developed independently and more or less contemporaneously in Japan.[2] But it is difficult to judge on the basis of the information now available whether and to what extent the early trading in commodity options and forward contracts resembled what is now understood by trading in futures. Clearing houses for the settlement of contracts do not seem to have existed.

The nineteenth century witnessed the development of the modern futures exchanges in Chicago, New Orleans, New York, Liverpool, London, Berlin and elsewhere. It seems that futures contracts typically evolved from less standardised forward contracts in situations in which merchants (including exporters and importers), processors and manufacturers were exposed to price risks in respect of stocks held or of forward sales commitments undertaken.[3] As futures markets increased in number and range of commodities covered, so futures trading directly or indirectly influenced the production, storage, marketing and processing of larger volumes of domestically and internationally traded commodities and drew more 'outside' capital into these operations.

Present extent of futures trading

Today the great bulk of futures trading takes place in the United States. It has been estimated that in 1968 60 per cent of agricultural commodity production in the United States was of commodities for which there were futures markets.[4] In all markets the volume of business, expressed in number of contracts, more than trebled between 1960 and 1970. About one-third of this increase was represented by trading in commodities for which no futures trading had been available in 1960.[5] There is, or has been at some time since the Second World War, futures trading in the following commodities: aluminium, apples, barley, beef (dressed), beef (frozen boneless), bran, broilers (iced), burlap, butter, cattle (live), cocoa, coconut oil, coffee, copper, corn, cotton, cottonseed meal, cottonseed oil, crude oil, eggs (fresh), eggs (refrigerated), fishmeal, flaxseed, foreign currencies, gold, grain sorghums, hams (skinned), hides, hogs (live), lard, lead, lumber, molasses, mercury, middlings, nickel, oats, onions, orange juice concentrate, palladium, pepper, platinum, plywood, pork bellies (frozen), potatoes, propane, rice, rubber, rye, silver, shorts, shrimps (frozen), silver, silver coins, soybeans, soybean meal, soybean oil, sugar, tallow, tin, tomato paste, turkeys (eviscerated), wheat, wool, wool tops and zinc. The main exchanges are in Chicago and New York.

There is futures trading in a number of countries outside the United States. In Winnipeg there is trading in grain and gold futures. London at present has futures trading in cocoa, coffee, copper, cotton (since the demise of the market in Liverpool), grains, lead, rubber, silver, sugar, tin, wool tops and zinc; there was futures trading in shellac and in various vegetable oils; and a market in soybean meal futures has started recently, in spite of a failed attempt to launch trading in fishmeal futures. Between 1965 and 1973 turnover on the major London exchanges increased from £1,200 million to £15,000 million – a large increase even when allowance is made for changes in the general level of prices.[6] In continental Europe there are (or have been at some period since 1945) futures markets in Antwerp; Amsterdam and Rotterdam; Bremen and Hamburg; Milan; Le Havre, Paris and Roubaix–Tourcoing; and Lisbon. The commodities traded include cocoa, coffee, copra, cotton, grains, linseed oil, pepper, rubber, silk, sugar and wool tops.[7]

There was a cotton exchange in Alexandria, and there is one in Sao Paulo.

In Asia there is futures trading in India, Japan, Malaysia and Singapore, and an exchange has been planned to open in Hong Kong. In India there were in the 1960s a number of exchanges with futures trading covering cotton, groundnuts, various oil seeds, turmeric, copra, raw jute, jute goods and pepper, while futures trading in other commodities (such as cotton yarn and cloth, shellac, wheat and maize) had been banned officially (Natu, 1962). The list of traded commodities has shrunk with further prohibitions. In Japan there are nineteen exchanges, with futures trading in various types of beans, potato starch, sugar, cotton yarn, worsted yarn, rayon filament, rayon yarn, raw silk, dried cocoons and rubber. Futures trading in rice flourished in Japan until it was terminated by government in 1939. It has not been allowed to recommence. In Kuala Lumpur and Singapore there are futures markets in rubber.

Finally, there is a thriving market in greasy wool futures in Sydney, established in 1960.[8]

The establishment since 1945 of futures trading in additional commodities or in additional places reflects the entrepreneurial initiatives of particular exchanges, groups of interested traders or of firms or institutions providing clearing-house facilities. There have been great successes (as in soybeans and pork bellies) and some failures (such as that of the refined sugar market in Paris) as well as the contraction of some traditional markets, notably the cotton futures markets. In the aggregate, futures markets have attained unprecedented volumes of business in recent decades, paradoxically in a political environment which has often been hostile to them or critical of them.

CHARACTERISTICS OF FUTURES CONTRACTS AND MARKETS

Standardisation of futures contract

For each commodity in which there is a futures market there is a parallel market in which the trading in the actual physical commodity takes place.[9] We refer to the latter as the actuals market, which need not be organised or have trading centralised in a particular marketplace. Two main differences between trading in the two types of market may be noted, apart from the fact that a futures market is necessarily an organised market in which trading is confined to members of the market organisation or exchange. First, an actuals market contract and its contract terms can be tailor-made to suit the requirements of the two parties as regards grade of the commodity, quantity, place and time of delivery. In a futures market contracts are highly standardised in each of these respects. Thus, one cocoa futures contract for December delivery in the London market is in all respects interchangeable with another contract of the same delivery month. Second, contracts in an actuals market are settled between the parties in any manner agreed by them. In a futures market settlement of contractual obligations is almost invariably managed by the market or exchange authority or clearing house which interposes itself between the two parties; this settlement procedure is made possible by the standardisation of contracts.

Futures markets are wholesale markets. Individual contracts are for relatively large quantities, for example 5000 bushels of wheat, 27,600 lbs of choice steers, 18,000 dozen fresh eggs, £10,000 sterling, 50,000 lbs of copper, 10 flasks of mercury and 100,000 gallons of propane (all in United States markets).[10] Futures contracts can be entered into for delivery several months ahead, the range being from twenty-one months for rubber in the London market to three months for the non-ferrous metals on the London metal exchange (where, however, there are arrangements available for the extension of a contract). In some markets, such as that for shell eggs in the United States, futures contracts for delivery in each month within the period covered are available for trading. In others, only certain months are delivery months, selected according to the requirements of the trade. In United States markets there are the same five delivery months for wheat, corn and oats, and seven for soybeans. The New York platinum futures contract is quoted for January, April, July and October, and the Sydney greasy wool contract for March, May, July, October and December delivery – in both markets up to eighteen months ahead.

Seller's options

A third major difference between contracts in an actuals market and contracts in a futures market is that in the latter the seller typically is given some options as to delivery, exercisable at his discretion. The presence of these options does not derogate from the standardisation of futures contracts, since all contracts of the same class have the same set of options. The options relate to grade, place and date of delivery.

Many futures contracts allow the seller to deliver either the specified contract grade (sometimes called the basis grade) or any one of a prescribed list of deliverable or substitutable grades. For example, the Chicago wheat contract allows over twenty-five deliverable grades, the soybeans four and the corn three. The subject-matter of the present London copper wirebars contract is either electrolytic copper wirebars or high conductivity fire refined copper wirebars. But not all futures contracts allow substitutions, and most of the metals futures in fact are single-grade contracts. The New York nickel contract, for instance, relates to one grade only – new electrolytic nickel cathodes of a defined standard (though even here the seller can deliver the material in any one of a number of sizes).

Contracts usually give the seller a choice of delivery in one of a number of exchange-licensed warehouses or depositories either in a single locality or in several localities. The New York palladium and platinum contracts allow delivery in approved depositories in the New York metropolitan area within a radius of 50 miles from Columbus Circle. The nickel contract allows delivery in New York or Chicago. The two London tin contracts (high grade tin and standard tin) provide for delivery in an approved warehouse in 'either London, Birmingham, Manchester, Liverpool, Birkenhead, Hull, Newcastle-on-Tyne, Glasgow, Avonmouth, Swansea, Rotterdam, Hamburg (free port area) and Antwerp in seller's option'. Some sugar contracts include delivery points throughout the world. At the other extreme, the newly introduced New York crude oil contract specifies delivery in Rotterdam alone.

The typical futures contract refers to a particular month of delivery; and the seller is at liberty to make delivery on any day within the delivery month or a specified part of it, subject to giving appropriate notice of intention to deliver. Exceptionally a longer period of delivery is sometimes specified. When trading on the Liverpool cotton market was reopened after the Second World War, the futures contract allowed delivery within a two-month (instead of the pre-war one-month) period in recognition of the expected slow building-up of cotton stocks in the United Kingdom (Yamey, 1959). At the other extreme, the London contracts in the four non-ferrous metals now stipulate delivery on a single specified day (the 'prompt').[11] The Chicago foreign currency futures also require delivery on a single day (the third Wednesday of the chosen month), whilst, in contrast, the corresponding New York contracts allow delivery at any time within the delivery month.

Difference systems

Futures contracts allow the seller to exercise his choice of date of delivery within the permitted period without attracting any contractual premium or penalty. This is also true of most contracts as regards choice of precise place of delivery, although some contracts specify discounts payable to the buyer if certain of the permitted delivery locations are chosen. An example of the latter is the Chicago live cattle contract: the contact delivery point is Chicago, but delivery in Omaha or Kansas City is optional, at discounts of 75 cents and $1 per hundredweight. However, where options as to deliverable grade are allowed, contracts almost invariably prescribe the receipt of premia from the buyer, or the payment of discounts to the buyer, according to the grade actually tendered.

The contract rules regulating grade of delivery mainly fall into one of two categories: the commercial difference system and the fixed difference system. The latter is by far the more common.

The commercial difference system is used in some cotton futures contracts.[12] The contract grade is deliverable at par. Other deliverable grades are deliverable at premia or discounts, determined daily according to the inter-grade price differences prevailing in the market for physical cotton (the actuals market). The premia and discounts fluctuate, therefore, according to changes in conditions in the actuals market. Drawbacks of the system are that the differences payable or receivable are not known in advance, and that the market authorities have to determine grade price differences in the actuals market, a determination which may lead to abuse and in any case may be difficult when activity in the actuals market is meagre and discontinuous or the market is not organised.[13]

A contract which incorporates the fixed difference system itself specifies the exact amounts to be paid on the delivery of the various non-basis grades. Thus the Chicago wheat contract lists eight grades deliverable at par, ten at a premium of 1 cent, one at a premium of .5 cents, and six at a discount of 1 cent a lb. The soybean contract has one grade at par, one at a 3 cent premium, and one at a discount of 2 cents or 5 cents according to whether the moisture content is below or above 14 per cent. The London copper wirebar contract makes electrolytic copper deliverable at par and the alternative high conductivity fire refined copper at a discount of £20 per ton.[14] The first post-war Amsterdam cocoa contract named defined cocoas of several countries of origin as the basis of contract, specified a premium of 5 gulden per 100 kilos for superior types, and allowed delivery of two groups of inferior cocoas at discounts of 5 and 10 gulden respectively.

The fixed differences governing delivery of different grades are reviewed from time to time, so as not to become too far out of line with prevailing average relative prices in the actuals market. The rules of the post-war coffee futures market organisation in Hamburg provided for an annual review of the permitted grades and the applicable differences. In some markets the fixed differences are changed more frequently in the light of prevailing actuals market prices. Thus on the Sydney greasy wool market the differences governing delivery within a particular month are fixed on the first day of that month; the same practice is followed for the London wool tops contract. The more frequent the revision of differences, the more closely does the fixed difference system in its effects approximate the commercial difference system.

Hybrid difference systems are to be found in some futures contracts. In the earlier Chicago eggs futures contract differences allowable to the buyer on the delivery of non-basis grades or descriptions were expressed in terms of specified numbers of eggs per case. The New York hides contract provides for percentage premia and discounts according to the average weight of delivered hides, modified to take account of the season of off-take. These premia and discounts are used to determine the total weight of hides to be delivered (i.e. a smaller net weight of superior hides and a larger net weight of inferior hides has to be delivered as compared with the 40,000 lbs of basis grade hides).

Implications of seller's options

A futures contract in which the seller has no options as to grade, place or date of delivery is considered undesirable because it would facilitate corners and squeezes. A buyer could accumulate a large holding of contracts of a particular maturity and at the same time gain control of the major part of the physical commodity eligible for delivery. He would then be able to squeeze the sellers of the contracts as the delivery date drew near. The resulting increase in actuals and futures prices would disrupt the market and serve no economic purpose. The broader the contract is based in terms of its seller's options, the more difficult it is for such manipulation to be feasible, since the volume of eligible supplies is increased.[15] Historically, the introduction of grade and place of delivery options seems to have been designed primarily to reduce the risk of corners and of the development unintentionally of similar tight-supply situations. However, the range of deliverable grades in some modern futures contracts is almost certainly wider than is necessary to preclude such undesirable developments; and some apparently narrow-based contracts do not experience the apprehended difficulties.[16] Moreover, in most futures exchanges the governing bodies have wide powers of intervention when manipulations or other untoward developments in the market are suspected or experienced. Thus, the rules of the London Wool Terminal Market Association allow sellers to deliver otherwise non-tenderable grades of wool tops or to defer delivery for one or two months (on terms announced) whenever the appropriate authority decides 'that a "corner" is in existence or threatened'.

The inclusion of seller's options, by reducing the risk of deliberate manipulation or of unintended technically tight delivery situations, serves directly to increase the attractiveness of dealing in futures contracts. Indirectly, a broadly drawn contract also widens the market in futures by making it less likely that contracts will be settled by the delivery of the physical commodity. Since the buyer is subject to the risk that he may be delivered an unwanted grade of the commodity at an inconvenient time or place, a futures contract is ordinarily not suitable as an instrument for the acquisition of desired supplies of the commodity, and is not used for that purpose. Rather, it is used primarily by operators known as hedgers and speculators who are not interested in making or taking delivery in settlement of their commitments on futures contracts. Typically, obligations on one contract are discharged by means of a subsequent off-setting contract (a purchase being followed by a sale), price differences being dealt with by an appropriate monetary settlement. The availability and low cost of this latter alternative method of settlement, itself made possible by the standardisation of contracts and facilitated by the operation of clearing houses, attract hedgers and speculators interested in the futures market for enabling them to 'trade in price changes' and not for enabling them to dispose of or to acquire supplies of the physical commodity.

In most large-volume futures markets only a small proportion of futures contracts are settled by delivery of the actual commodity. Percentages below 1 per cent are recorded for commodities such as wheat, soybeans, cotton, potatoes, cattle, pork bellies and eggs in the United States. In the Sydney wool futures market deliveries are generally less than 2 per cent of total contracts made (Snape, 1968, p. 169); and low percentages have been reported in Indian markets.[17] On the other hand, some futures contracts contain such limited seller's options that they approximate quite closely to actuals contracts and consequentially are used relatively more frequently as vehicles for the disposal and acquisition of physical supplies, especially as the rules of the exchanges or their clearing houses provide virtually cast-iron guarantees of contract fulfilment.[18] Futures contracts in metals provide examples, although the range of delivery points included in the London non-ferrous metals contracts is some discouragement to buyers. Deliveries are relatively more frequent on the wool tops contracts on the Antwerp and Roubaix-Tourcoing exchanges than on the London exchange; this difference has been attributed to the narrower range of deliverable grades on the former contracts.

Settlement of contracts

Standardisation of futures contracts makes possible the use of economical methods for the transaction of business. No inspection of the subject-matter is necessary, and the individual buyer or seller need not seek out the trading partner most appropriate to his particular needs. Dealing is centralised in the exchange, and further economy is achieved by limiting hours of dealing. Trading normally proceeds on the basis of open outcry[19] so that the market is sensitively responsive to changing market views, and bids and offers are quickly brought into equilibrium.

Transaction prices, as well as bid and asked prices, can be recorded publicly and transmitted readily.

In the typical futures markets there are arrangements which reduce the risks of default. Trading on the floor of the exchange is limited to members of the exchange, which can require general financial guarantees or otherwise screen new members for financial strength. Risks of default are further reduced, indeed virtually eliminated, by the operation of clearing houses. Most futures markets require futures contracts to be handled by a clearing house, whether owned and operated by the exchange itself or by an independent company.[20] In effect, the clearing house interposes itself between the seller and buyer of the futures contract, assuming the opposite position to each of the two parties. By requiring initial deposits from each party, and by requiring additional margins from the losing party to the extent that price changes adversely, the clearing house is protected against loss by subsequent default of either party; and each party need not concern himself with the financial reliability of the other party. At the same time the arrangements serve to minimise members' capital locked up in respect of uncompleted (i.e. open) contracts. Further, the clearing house is able to arrange the monetary settlement of price differences on off-setting transactions in contracts of the same delivery month. It is also well placed to organise physical deliveries on those expiring contracts which remain open at the end of the delivery period. The clearing-house mechanism therefore serves not only to facilitate the settlement of contracts by the making of off-setting contracts but also to facilitate the settlement of the minority of contracts where delivery is made.

Members of an exchange can trade on behalf of non-members, but they act as principals *vis-à-vis* the exchange and its members. Subject to the rules of the exchange and any government regulation, it is for the member (broker) to decide whether he should require deposits and additional margins from his various clients.

The standardisation of the futures contract, the method of trading in futures and the operations of the clearing house all contribute to economy in the performance of business[21] and to impersonality in the making and settlement of transactions. Entry into the ranks of the users of futures markets, both hedgers and speculators, is thus facilitated. A well-functioning futures market is perhaps the closest real-world counterpart to the abstract model of a perfectly competitive market.

Design of futures contracts

In designing a futures contract choices have to be made in respect of the various terms of the contract. The choices made affect the market price of the futures contract relative to the prices of the various grades of the commodity in different actuals-market locations. Such price relationships and changes in them are of critical importance to the practice of hedging; and the volume of hedging is of critical importance to the health of a futures market. Care has to be taken, therefore, in the initial design of a futures contract and its subsequent modification to meet changes in market requirements.[22]

RELATION BETWEEN ACTUALS AND FUTURES PRICES

Three types of basis or futures–actuals price differences

The term 'basis' is used for the difference between the price of a futures contract and the price of the commodity in the related actuals market. Three types of basis or futures–actuals price differences may be distinguished: the price of the futures contract in its delivery month *less* the price of the commodity for immediate delivery (the so-called spot price) in the actuals market (here called the maturity basis); the price of a futures contract stipulating delivery in a future month *less* the spot price of the commodity in the actuals market (here called simply the basis); and the price of a futures contract stipulating delivery in a future month *less* the price in the actuals market of the commodity for forward delivery in that same month. If f is price in the futures market, and a is price in the actuals market, and the first sub-script refers to the date of delivery and the second the date of the price, the three types of basis are:

$$\begin{array}{ll} \text{(i)} & f_{0,0} - a_{0,0} \\ \text{(ii)} & f_{i,0} - a_{0,0} \\ \text{(iii)} & f_{i,0} - a_{i,0} \end{array}$$

where i is a future date and 0 the present date.

It follows that at any time there are as many values of the second and third types of basis as there are different months for which futures contracts are quoted; and it is necessary to stipulate which forward month is being considered.

It follows also that, for each of the three types of basis, there is a separate value of basis for every grade of the commodity in every actuals-market location. Except where the opposite is indicated, we adopt the usual simplification of defining the actuals price a as being the price of the basis grade at the contract delivery point (that is, the grade and location which involve neither premium nor discount under the contract).

The maturity basis

In its delivery month the price of a futures contract tends to be approximately the same as the spot price of the underlying commodity in the actuals market. This tendency to equality is a consequence of the right of a seller of a futures contract to make delivery of the commodity and of the buyer (unless held by the exchange authorities to be engaged in manipulation) to hold open his futures contract until delivery is due on it. Any material discrepancy between the two prices would cause parties to unsettled (open) futures contracts either to make delivery or to hold for delivery, according to the nature of the discrepancy. Arbitrage operations involving virtually simultaneous off-setting transactions in the two markets would also be profitable. These actions keep the prices in the two markets together: although delivery is relatively rare, as has been noted, the possibility of settlement by delivery binds together the two market prices. Nevertheless, for various reasons minor discrepancies are common.

Take the case of a single-grade futures contract. As compared with the spot price in the actuals market, the price of the matured futures contract is likely to be at some discount, which reflects the uncertainty, for the buyer, of the exact place and exact day on which delivery will be made to him if he elects to take delivery. Even where, as in the London non-ferrous metals futures contracts, the precise day is stipulated in advance, the seller's option as to place of delivery (from Bristol to Hamburg) is often likely to cause sellers of actuals metal in London to a London-based customer to command a premium over the futures price on its 'prompt' day. However, although a negative maturity basis will ordinarily be present, it may sometimes happen to be positive. There are costs (and minor risks) involved in arbitrage transactions; and the maturity basis can lie within a range of positive and negative values within which arbitrage is unprofitable.

The factors affecting maturity basis are much the same for multi-grade futures contracts incorporating the commercial difference system as for single-grade contracts. There will be a close connection between the spot price of the basis grade in the actuals market and the price of the futures contract in its delivery month. The deliverability of non-basis grades does not affect the maturity basis directly. This is so because, in principle, delivery of any non-basis grade puts the deliverer in the same position as if he delivers the basis grade: the difference receivable or payable on delivery is the difference between the spot price of the non-basis grade and the basis grade in the actuals market. The basis grade is always the grade whose spot price can be said to govern the price of the futures contract. Indirectly, however, the deliverability of non-basis grades does affect the maturity basis since it increases the uncertainty as to what the buyer receives on taking delivery.

The determination of the maturity basis is more complex where the fixed difference system is used in respect of the delivery of non-basis grades. The seller is not indifferent as to the grade to be delivered because, in terms of the fixed differences, at any time one or other of the deliverable grades is the cheapest to deliver on the contract. A sort of Gresham's law operates: for purposes of delivery on the futures contract one grade displaces the other deliverable grades.[23] The cheapest grade in this sense is that grade for which the spot actuals price plus the fixed discount (or less the fixed premium) is the lowest at the particular time. It is the discount-adjusted price of the cheapest grade which governs the price of the matured futures. (Assume that B is the basis grade, S a superior, and I an inferior deliverable grade, and that there is a fixed premium of 3p. for S and a fixed discount of 5p for I per bushel. Suppose that on a particular day the spot actuals prices are: $B = 90$p, $S = 94$p, and $I = 82$p. Grade I will be the cheapest grade to deliver on the futures contract, and the price of the matured futures will approximate 87p, i.e. 82 plus 5).

Thus, the basis grade need not be the governing grade; and the same grade is not always the governing grade. The grade preferred for delivery changes according to changes in the relative prices of the deliverable grades in the actuals market.[24] It follows that the gap between the spot actuals price of the basis grade and the price of the matured futures contract will be greater than under a regime of commercial differences whenever the futures price is governed by a non-basis grade: even more than otherwise, like is not being compared with like.

Whilst it is usual and convenient in theoretical work on futures markets, and sometimes also in empirical studies, to treat the price of the matured futures contract as if it were the corresponding spot actuals price, in fact, for the reasons given above, the maturity basis generally is negative and also varies. However, the tendency for there to be a negative maturity basis is known to those operating in the market[25]; and some of the variations in the size of the basis (those arising for example from seasonal influences on the governing grade) are also reasonably predictable.[26] Moreover, the frequency of changes in the identity of governing grade is reduced in some markets by deliberately fixing the premia for superior grades on the low side and the discounts for inferior grades on the high side. Such adjustments strengthen the basis-grade character of a multi-grade futures contract with fixed differences; the availability of other eligible grades nevertheless serves to reduce market disturbances which might otherwise occur whenever the actuals price of the basis grade became seriously out of line with the prices of other grades, for example because of supply conditions peculiarly affecting the basis grade.

Some idea of the size and variability of maturity basis is given by the following statistics for the Liverpool middling cotton contract (a commercial differences contract) for the period 1924–5 to 1938–9. The average annual maturity basis, based on Friday closing prices, ranged from −0.17d per pound in 1937–8 to −0.49 in 1927–8.[27]

The basis

The influences which bear upon the level of the price of the matured futures relative to that of the spot actuals price also affect the level of the prices of forward futures contracts relative to the spot actuals price. But it is convenient as well as customary to abstract from these influences when considering the determination of the forward basis.

There is an upper limit to the extent by which the price of a *forward* futures contract can exceed the spot price of the commodity in the actuals market. The maximum positive value of the basis – or the maximum value of the contango or forward premium as it is sometimes called – is the marginal cost of holding a unit of the physical commodity from the present date until the maturity of the futures contract (storage, interest, insurance, etc.) and of effecting delivery. Any larger basis would be short-lived. Its presence offers a riskless profit to arbitrage operations: the arbitrageurs buy actuals and simultaneously sell futures. Such arbitrage raises the actuals price and reduces the futures price, and thereby reduces the basis. The operation of this constraint on the basis is independent of the size of the stocks of the commodity, of their ownership and of market expectations when the temporary disequilibrium occurs. Whatever is the marginal carrying and delivery cost of the commodity at the time, that is the upper limit of the contango. (It may be observed, in passing, that there is no upper limit to the basis in a market in which there is some discontinuity in economically feasible storage – as for potatoes – and when the basis relates to a delivery month falling within the next storage period. This is so because carrying costs between two successive storage periods are infinitely large.)

The basis can, however, be below this maximum. In fact, it can be negative, a situation sometimes referred to as an inverted market, with a backwardation or spot premium in evidence. There is no process of riskless and profitable dealing which necessarily restores the basis to its maximum. Arbitrage in a situation of a backwardation involves the simultaneous sale of actuals and purchase of futures. At any time the maximum volume of such *riskless* trading depends upon the volume of physical stocks held by certain categories of trader who alone can take advantage, with profit and without risk, of the prevailing intermarket price relationship. These traders include firms who hold stocks against their own forward sales commitments in actuals. They can sell their stocks now, replace them by the purchase of suitably dated futures contracts, and hold the latter to their maturity (unless an even more favourable opportunity were to arise before then). At the postulated relative actuals and futures prices, this course of action enables them to reduce their carrying costs and so to increase their profits without involving them in additional risks (other than the risk of an unpredictable change in the maturity basis). Similarly, firms who hold stocks and have hedged them by sales of futures can also take advantage of the prevailing backwardation by selling their stocks and closing out their position in the futures market by buying futures. However, there is at any time only a given volume of potential arbitrage because the stocks held in the appropriate trading contexts are limited. This volume of arbitrage may be insufficient to bring about increases in the price of the futures and reductions in the price of spot actuals to bring the basis up to its maximum value.[28] In fact, large backwardations have been present in some markets for periods of several months.

Thus, the basis can take values within a wide range; and the basis can change materially over the life of a given futures contract. It will be seen in the next section ('Hedging') that the value of the basis and changes in the value of the basis are of central importance in the practice of hedging. At any time the particular level of the basis (with respect to a particular futures contract) depends upon a variety of circumstances and influences. These include the preferences of holders of stocks of the commodity for the security provided by hedging relative to the prevailing cost of hedging, expectations about changes in the basis which may affect hedging decisions (which in turn affect the supply of futures), and the expectations of speculators as well as stockholders about future supply and demand conditions (which affect the demand for and supply of futures). Various attempts have been made to construct theories of price determination in the futures market and its related actuals market, incorporating in various ways what are considered to be the relevant determinants and the method and form of their operation.[29]

Digression on carrying costs

It is convenient to digress briefly at this point for some consideration of the marginal carrying cost associated with the holding of physical stocks.

The carrying costs consist of the cost of storage facilities and such other costs as interest charges, insurance and loss by wastage. At any given time these carrying costs per unit of the commodity are likely to be at a constant level for a wide range of total stocks of the commodity. However, for unusually high levels of total stocks, marginal carrying costs are likely to rise progressively as recourse is had to less satisfactory or more expensive storage facilities.

At the other end of the scale, for unusually low levels of stocks *net* carrying costs are likely to be lower than for the more normal range of stocks. This is so because of the so-called convenience yield on physical stocks. A merchant, processor or manufacturer is likely to hold some stocks even when he confidently expects that the price of the commodity will fall. He holds some stocks in order to maintain his goodwill by being able to meet the uncertain demands of his more valued customers or in order to facilitate cost-saving continuity in his own processing or manufacturing operations. The marginal value of the convenience of being open to sell or supply is likely to be significantly large for very low levels of stocks and, *ceteris paribus*, to decline rather rapidly for progressively larger stocks.

Putting together the convenience yield of stocks and the costs incurred or involved in carrying stocks, at any given time the marginal *net* carrying cost is likely to be negative for very low levels of total stocks of a commodity, to increase quite sharply for progressively larger levels, to reach a plateau, and then to increase again for unusually large levels (although it must be recognised that the precise form of the relationship may differ from one commodity to another or from one period to another).

Of course, even if the general shape of the curve of marginal net carrying costs for a particular product may persist, the level of net carrying costs for a given level of total stocks of the commodity will change with changes in the prices of the inputs in the storage and stock-carrying operations: the price of storage facilities (which depends in part on the demand for storage facilities for other commodities), the rate of interest, insurance premiums and the like.[30] Other things being equal, an increase in the rate of interest can be expected to reduce the volume of stocks, raise the forward futures price and reduce the current actuals price (and so increase the basis).

Some characteristic patterns of basis

Examination of prices on the boards in futures exchanges or as reported in the newspapers discloses certain characteristic patterns of price relationships, i.e. of basis. These patterns relate to the prices, at a given time, of futures contracts of different maturities or delivery months.

A common – one might almost say typical – pattern is for the basis to be progressively higher for the more distant contract months, reflecting the incidence of increases in carrying costs for longer periods of stock-holding. The carrying charges so reflected in the pattern of basis may be more or less close to the maximum possible contango (see p. 13 above).

This pattern of increasing basis often extends further ahead and includes contracts with delivery months falling within the next season. Such a pattern is likely to be found when the market expects there to be a need for an above-normal carry-over of stocks of the commodity from the present season to the next in the light of expectations about the size of the next crop or harvest relative to expected demand conditions.

Where such a pattern prevails, a change in market expectations occasioned, for instance, by an upsurge or expected upsurge in general business activity or by some reassessment of the size of the next crop or harvest, is apt to affect the prices of contracts of all maturities more or less equally. This is so because the continuity of stock-holding binds together, as it were, the prices of the various maturities, so that they all move broadly in harmony in response to changes in market expectations. It may be noted further that the pattern of futures prices cannot register differences in expected demand conditions at different times within the same crop year. Suppose the crop year coincides with the calendar year. If in January it is expected that demand in May will be well below demand in March, the May contract price in January will nevertheless tend to exceed the March contract price by an amount approximating the additional carrying costs from March to May.[31]

A different pattern occurs when the market expects the next crop or harvest to be unusually large, or large relative to the current crop. In such circumstances the price board at any time during the present season may well show a pattern of increasing contangoes for maturities within that season, but (possibly marked) backwardations for the early delivery months falling within the period when the next season's crop will have become available. These backwardations are sometimes called new-season or new-crop discounts. They appropriately discourage the holding of stocks for carrying over from the present to the next season. However, contangoes relative to the price of the earliest new-season contracts are likely to be recorded for later contracts within the next season.

Backwardations occur in other circumstances also: a situation of new-crop discounts is merely one example of a more general category of situations in which current supplies are relatively tight and cannot be augmented in the short run and in which the market expects supplies to become relatively easier in the future. Such situations occur, for example, when there are strikes or threats of strikes affecting the production or shipping of new supplies, for instance, of metals or rubber. They may also occur when the market believes that a dominant holder of stocks, such as a governmental or inter-governmental price-supporting agency, will be forced to dispose of its stocks in the near future, or a dominant supplying country will devalue its currency. Uncertainty as to the precise date and extent of the anticipated change may cause the backwardations to extend progressively into the future, especially as the market for distant futures is likely to be thin in these circumstances.[32] Yet another example is when the market expects prices to break after a period of high prices brought about by what are considered to be temporary or once-for-all factors. At the height of the boom in commodity prices early in 1974 the price of three-month copper wirebars stood at a discount of almost £100 a metric ton below the spot actuals (= matured futures) price of almost £1400; the discount on standard tin was almost £200, the spot actuals price being over £4000.

Relation between forward futures and forward actuals prices

We now turn to the third type of basis – the difference between the price of a forward futures contract and the price in the actuals market for forward delivery of the commodity at the same forward date.

The prices of similarly dated forward actuals and forward futures are closely related for the same reason that the spot price in the actuals market is kept closely in line with the price of the matured futures. A backwardation in the forward futures price would tend to be matched, by virtue of opportunities for arbitrage otherwise, by a discount on forward sales in the actuals market; and conversely for contangoes. Differences between forward futures and forward actuals prices would also occur for the same reasons as in the case of prices relating to current delivery. However, since the market in forward actuals is likely to be less active than that in spot supplies, larger variations in the third type of basis may be expected than in the maturity basis.[33]

HEDGING

Critics of futures markets generally concede that these institutions serve a useful purpose in making it possible for those who handle commodities to engage in the practice known as hedging. Speculation on these markets, while frequently the subject of heavy strictures, is nevertheless often excused by their critics on the ground that socially useful hedging would not be possible unless speculators were willing to trade in futures.

Hedging and hedging outcomes

In its usual meaning in the context of futures trading, hedging involves concomitant opposite transactions in the related actuals and futures markets. A trader who acquires an unsold stock of soybeans hedges it by selling soybean futures. He is 'long' in actuals and 'short' in futures, and is called a 'short hedger'. A trader who sells soybeans for delivery at some future date, and does not have a stock of them, hedges his forward commitment in the actuals market by buying futures. He is short in actuals and long in futures, and is called a 'long hedger'. In each case an open position in the actuals market is off-set by an opposite position in the futures market. When the open position in actuals is terminated, the hedge is closed out by a reversing transaction in futures.

The nature of short hedging and the determinants of hedging outcomes can be illustrated by means of an example. For simplification, it is assumed that the opposite positions taken in the two markets are equal in quantity; and costs of making transactions and of holding stocks are ignored. (Long hedging is dealt with later). Suppose a merchant acquires a stock of a commodity at time t_0 and eventually sells it at t_1; and suppose he hedges it by selling a futures contract maturing at t_1. Using the notation introduced earlier, and letting the minus sign represent purchases and the plus sign sales, the outcome of the hedged transaction is:

$$-a_{0,0} + a_{1,1} + f_{1,0} - f_{1,1}, \text{ i.e. } (f_{1,0} - a_{0,0}) - (f_{1,1} - a_{1,1}),$$

i.e. the opening basis *less* the closing basis.

There is a profit if the basis narrows between the opening and the closing of the hedge; a loss if it widens; and neither profit nor loss if it remains unchanged. In the last-mentioned case, the profit (loss) in the actuals market is exactly matched by the loss (profit) in the futures market. Of course, in all cases the profit may be greater or the loss smaller if the basis is more favourable to the hedger at some intermediate date between t_0 and t_1 and the hedger avails himself of the opportunity by closing out at that date.

If the hedge is intended to be carried to the maturity month of the futures contract (as in the example), the hedger has a reasonably precise idea of what the basis at the closing date will be – it is the maturity basis which, as explained on pp. 11–12, typically varies to only a limited extent around some known average level. Thus the hedger knows with some degree of assurance, though not with certainty, what the outcome of his hedged transaction will be. And he knows, too, that there may be more satisfactory outcomes available to him during the currency of the futures contract in which he hedges. On the other hand, if the merchant does not hedge, the outcome of his unhedged transactions will be $(-a_{0,0} + a_{n,n})$, where n is the date at which he eventually sells; and at the time of entering his commitment to be long in actuals, the likely value of $a_{n,n}$ is a matter of expectation.

It may be asked why a merchant or processor hedging a long position in the actuals market does not make the off-setting transaction also in the *actuals* market in the form of a forward sale (and, *mutatis mutandis*, for a short seller in actuals). This can be done. But where there is an efficient futures market in the commodity, there are cost and other advantages in hedging in futures. An efficient futures market is a continuous market with a considerable capacity, by its special attraction for speculators, to absorb buying and selling from hedgers. Moreover, since the commitment on a futures contract can readily be extinguished by reversing the transaction rather than by actual delivery, the short hedger who uses the futures market can secure for himself the convenience yield on his stock of actuals: it is not earmarked for delivery to meet a specific commitment, but can be used at the hedger's discretion to his maximum advantage.[34] Finally, because futures contracts are standardised, trading in them allows the hedger to avoid the costs he would otherwise have to incur to find the appropriate dealers in actuals whose forward requirements or supplies (in terms of grade, time, and place) mesh in with the hedger's own specific position and plans in actuals.

Types of hedging

Hedging is usually seen as a practice which enables the hedger to shed a risk of a price change he would otherwise carry. The risk of loss of an adverse change of price in the actuals market is avoided or reduced by hedging. An uncertain outcome is replaced by a more certain one. This entails, naturally, that, when hedging, the chance is foregone of gaining from a favourable price change in the actuals market.

The view that hedging is primarily or solely concerned with the risks of price changes is dominant in public discussions, in much of the literature and also in the information brochures issued by futures exchanges and brokers. For example, a recent brochure of the London Sugar Terminal Market begins its section on hedging as follows: 'The most important use of the Terminal Market for all participants in the international sugar trade is for the hedging of their price risks.' According to the leading pre-war monograph on futures trading, 'hedging may then be defined as the practice of buying or selling futures to counterbalance an existing position in the trade market and thus avoid the risk of unforeseen major movements in price' (Hoffman, 1932, p. 382). The analogy with insurance has often been drawn, and sometimes pressed too far.

The common tendency to associate hedging with price risks has had the unfortunate effect of obscuring the presence of hedging operations which have little or nothing to do with risk avoidance or risk reduction. It is due to Working that a more complete and balanced view of hedging has developed in the last twenty years.[35] A discussion of three of the types of hedging referred to in the literature will illustrate the elaboration of the concept.

It would be possible to express each of these types of hedging in a more general but unified form, namely in terms of a hedger's objective of maximising his expected utility subject to a risk-reduction constraint. However, such a formulation has not been used in the literature in descriptive accounts of hedging practices and situations. (Thus it is not used in Working's discussions of hedging 'motivation': for example, Working, 1962.) In this part of our Introduction we follow the more usual approach.

For simplicity of exposition, we concentrate our discussion on short hedging. Much of the discussion relates also to long hedging, although there are differences to be noted later.

The first type of hedging concerns the hedging of price risks and involves the routine 'covering' of the trader's position in actuals by the making of equivalent off-setting transactions in futures. Routine hedging of this kind has been said to be common in the grain and cotton trades in the United States. According to Working, writing in 1962, in these trades 'routine hedging is accepted as standard practice in most parts of the country' (Working, 1962, p. 440).[36]

Routine short hedging is attractive to a trader, processor or manufacturer whose main business activities require the holding of stocks but who finds it inexpedient or costly to study the market or who is unwilling to trust his judgement about prospective price movements.[37]

Routine hedging 'assumes no need for forming judgment on price prospects' (Gray, 1960*b*, p. 302). Moreover, routine hedging is encouraged where banks require or prefer that a borrower's stocks be hedged so that his solvency is not impaired by a drastic fall in market price (Wilson, 1966, p. 188).

Where the variability of the basis (strictly, basis change over the hedge period) is less than that of the commodity's price, routine hedging reduces the variability of returns as compared with the corresponding situation without hedging: the flow of profits over time is smoother. The necessary condition for the reduction in variability of profit or loss is generally satisfied in well-established and active commodity markets. Routine hedging on these markets reduces or avoids risk in this sense. A trader who prefers less to more risk in this sense would engage in routine hedging in such a market provided he did not expect to have to pay too high a price for the anticipated improvement in his situation. This 'price' would be represented by any reduction in the *average* return (profit or loss) over time with routine hedging as compared with the corresponding situation without hedging. Studies of price relationships in active commodity markets suggest that this price may be zero or low.[38] The matter is considered more fully in our discussion below of the theory of normal backwardation.

Selective hedging or discretionary hedging is distinguished from routine hedging by the exercise of judgement about price changes by the trader. A selective short hedger hedges only when he expects a fall (or a small rise) in the price, but he nevertheless finds it necessary to carry some stock of the commodity for his business purposes. He hedges on such occasions to reduce the expected loss or to avoid the risk of making a loss. According to such circumstances as his confidence in his particular market judgement, the extent of his actuals commitment, his ability to withstand losses and the likely cost of hedging, he may hedge the whole or only part of his actuals commitment. As Gray has noted, 'hedging which depends so heavily upon price and market considerations seems to fit the usual definition of speculation' (Gray, 1960*b*, p. 302). The selective hedger, that is to say, sometimes takes hedging action to reduce his exposure to risk and sometimes does not – his decision when and how much to hedge depends heavily on his own price expectations in the actuals market.

Both routine and selective hedging are responses to uncertainty about price changes in the actuals market. The third type of hedging, carrying-charge or arbitrage hedging, most fully first explored by Working, differs from these two types in that it is not a response to such uncertainty. Whilst futures markets may be said to serve the *needs* of hedgers when they engage in routine or selective hedging, these markets may be said to provide *opportunities* for hedging when the third type of hedging is involved.

Carrying-charge or arbitrage hedging is done to take advantage of expected favourable changes in the basis. Short hedging of this type is engaged in by those who at the relevant date expect the basis to narrow to such an extent that the overall result of the hedged transaction would be profitable. A profitable overall outcome can be anticipated when the hedger expects the favourable change in the basis to exceed his costs of carrying stock over the period as well as the transactions costs involved. As the basis is known to converge towards the maturity basis with the passage of time, the main source of uncertainty is, as we noted earlier, the generally limited (but in some markets not negligible) variability of the maturity basis around a reasonably predictable average value. Moreover, before the month of maturity the basis may conceivably take on values even more favourable to the short hedger. Skill at forecasting changes in basis is evidently developed by many hedgers.[39]

It may be noted that, strictly, in carrying-charge or arbitrage hedging the hedger acts on his judgement of prospective change in the basis, and not on his expectation of changes in the actuals or the futures price. It may be noted, further, that a short hedger may be regarded as being simultaneously a selective hedger and a carrying-charge hedger when he is acting on his expectation that the actuals price will fall and that the basis will narrow profitably. He may, of course, in this situation 'over-hedge', that is, sell more futures than necessary to cover his optimal long position in actuals. It may be noted, finally, that the same individual or firm may sometimes engage in selective hedging and sometimes in carrying-charge hedging.

The term carrying-charge hedging derives from the consideration that the expected change in the basis may be likened to the price or remuneration (which at times may be negative) received by those carrying hedged stocks through time. The carrying-charge hedger hedges when the carrying charge is expected to be profitable. The alternative term, arbitrage hedging, derives from Working's remark that our third type of hedging 'is a sort of arbitrage' (Working, 1953*a*, p. 325). This type of hedging is attractive when the basis is high relative to carrying costs. And then hedging activities, by taking advantage of the existing inter-market price relationship, serve to affect the relationship by simultaneously adding to the demand for actuals and increasing the supply of futures. This is seen most clearly in the behaviour of certain market operators who do not ordinarily carry on the business of stocking and supplying the commodity but move in as simultaneous buyers of actuals and sellers of futures whenever the basis is favourably high. Arbitrage hedging thus serves to keep prices in the two markets in line. In the process it brings about a rational distribution of supplies over time – rational, that is, in relation to the whole market's assessment of future market conditions – by encouraging or discouraging the holding of stocks.[40]

Working also introduced other types of hedging into the literature. One of these is 'anticipatory' hedging. Here the sale or purchase of futures is made before the actuals market commitment is entered into: 'the anticipatory hedge serves as a temporary substitute for a merchandising contract that will be made later' (Working, 1962, p. 441). However, since there is no simultaneity or near-simultaneity between the futures and actuals transactions, it may be better not to describe this use of the futures markets by traders as a form of hedging. It may be nearer the mark to regard it, with Hoffman, as an 'open speculation' which may 'ultimately prove to be a wise policy' (Hoffman, 1932, p. 399); '. . . it is essentially speculation upon the price level' (Gray, 1967, p. 180). It is fair to add, however, that each of the three types of hedging discussed above involves the hedger in *some* residual uncertainty, and to that more limited extent can also be said to be speculative. What Working calls anticipatory hedging is in any case an example of the varied use of futures markets made by firms engaged in the marketing or processing of the physical commodity.

The volume of short hedging

Although some formulations in the literature may suggest otherwise (Hoffman, 1932, p. 382), the decision of the merchant, processor or manufacturer as to the size of his long commitment in actuals is not made independently of his decision as to whether and to what extent he should hedge it. The decisions are interrelated and are affected, as one would expect, by the terms on which hedging is available at the relevant time.

The interrelatedness of the two decisions is self-evident in carrying-charge or arbitrage hedging. As Working has put it, the decision made by the carrying-charge hedger 'is not primarily whether to hedge or not, but whether to store or not' (Working, 1962, p. 438). A carrying-charge hedger adjusts his stocks according to the 'price' he expects to obtain for performing the service of carrying it for the period. Other things (including the costs of stock-holding) being equal, the higher the value of the basis – the larger the contango – the larger the stock he is prepared to acquire and to carry. Thus, one would expect the total volume of stocks held and the total volume of short hedging entered into by carrying-charge hedgers to be positively related to the value of the basis.

To a selective hedger who expects the actuals price to fall, the size of his stock may be supposed to depend in part on his expectations of the change in the basis, which is part of his cost of avoiding the apprehended loss without hedging. Again, other things (including price-expectations) being equal, the total volume of stocks and that of short hedging of selective hedgers may be expected to be positively related to the value of the basis.

The volume of stock held by routine hedgers, and hence the volume of their hedging, may seem to be unresponsive to the basis when hedges are placed. Such lack of responsiveness may well be true for those routine hedgers whose stock-holding operations are closely geared to their major activity, such as processing or manufacturing. But even they might be expected to have regard to the existence in the market at times of large contangoes or large backwardations.

Although it is obviously difficult to allow fully for the effects of changes in such other factors as expectations, the cost of storage facilities and the rate of interest, a few empirical studies have disclosed a positive relationship between the volume of short hedging and the value of the basis.[41]

The market is especially unfavourable for short hedging when the value of the basis is low. But even when the market is inverted with a large backwardation, some risk-averse traders may be prepared to hedge at a high cost if they find it desirable to carrying some stock and are fearful of the prospect of large losses if unhedged. During the period 1953–5 millers in the United States hedged in an inverted market: 'in essence the loss expected by millers in the face of inverse carrying charges must have been less than expectations of loss on stocks kept unhedged' (Ehrich, 1966, p. 322). Further, there may be traders who expect that an inverted market may become yet more inverted, so that a short hedge could be profitable if closed out before the futures contract's maturity: 'it is . . . possible that cash [current actuals] . . . prices may advance to a still larger premium [over futures] but there is a large element of chance in such an assumption' (Hoffman, 1932, p. 406).

Since in any futures market there are different futures contracts with different maturity months, there may also be several different values of basis. This allows the hedger some choice of contract in which to hedge (Wilson, 1966, pp. 178–9). But this feature complicates research, because available statistical sources do not disclose the distribution of the total volume of hedging among the various futures contracts (maturities) available at the relevant time.

Tests of the effectiveness of futures markets for short hedging

A number of studies have been published of attempts to determine empirically whether particular futures markets were effective for hedging purposes. Following the notion that hedging is practised to avoid or reduce risk, a common test has been to ascertain the outcomes of a series of hypothetical hedged transactions generated according to a selected standardised programme as to choice of futures contract-month and period of hedge. Outcomes have been classified variously, according to the extent of parallelism in the movements of actuals and futures prices and the size and direction of deviations from parallelism. Parallel movements, meaning stability in the value of the basis over the hedge period, have been said to give the hedger 'perfect' cover; and for imperfect hedges the extent of the cover has been expressed in various ways. The studies have shown differences among the markets studied, with a tendency being disclosed for marked deviations from stability of basis to be unusual.[42]

The stability-of-basis test is evidently most applicable to routine hedging; and its critics have objected to it partly because the earlier studies implied that the test was relevant for hedging in general. Even for routine hedging the test has its limitations; for example, studies using the test have proceeded on the basis that the hedger has a constant long position in actuals. The limitation is not especially damaging to the general finding that the variability of hedged outcomes is smaller than the variability of the corresponding unhedged outcomes. But it does reduce the significance of exercises showing the difference between the hypothetical aggregated results over a period of time with routine hedging and without any hedging. The studies also suffer from the drawback that the costs of making the futures transactions are omitted.

It is difficult to see how a test can be devised to assess the effectiveness of a futures market for selective hedging, since the making of such hedges depends critically on the individual hedger's price expectations. One approach might be to calculate the outcomes of hypothetical hedges for selected hedge periods in which relatively large price declines were experienced. The effectiveness of loss reduction through hedging could then be judged. But one would be proceeding on the heroic assumption that selective hedgers successfully predict large price declines and do not hedge otherwise.

Similar difficulties beset the design of a test of a market's effectiveness for carrying-charge hedging. Such hedging depends critically on the individual hedger's expectations about changes in the basis. One approach might be to determine the frequency with which the basis has high positive values, which, other things being equal, create opportunities for carrying-charge hedging.[43] Another might be simply to classify the outcomes of a series of hypothetical hedges, generated routinely according to a selected programme, in terms of the observed change in basis. A limitation in both cases would be that carrying costs incurred in the holding of stock would be omitted. Because costs change, and also differ among traders, it is difficult to see how the limitation can be removed.[44]

Long hedging

Long hedging, as has been explained, is the purchase of futures in association with a forward sale in the actuals market of the commodity or a product of it. As with short hedging, long hedging can be of the routine, selective or arbitrage variety.

Short hedging involves the purchase of actuals and the sale of futures, and long hedging the sale of actuals and the purchase of futures. It may look, therefore, as if long hedging is the reverse of short hedging and that in otherwise similar conditions the outcome of long hedging must be the opposite of the outcome of short hedging per unit of trade. This is the usual way in which long hedging has been treated.

However, although it is true that in the expression on p. 17 above, the signs have to be reversed for long hedging, the expressions are not otherwise identical because the term $a_{0,0}$ in the short-hedging expression is replaced by $a_{1,0}$ in the corresponding long-hedging expression. If the hedge is held to the maturity of the futures contract, the outcome is:

$$-(f_{1,0} - a_{1,0}) + (f_{1,1} - a_{1,1}),$$

where the *a*s now refer, when appropriate, to the commodity content of whatever is being sold forward in the actuals market (for example, if it is flour, the *a*s refer to the price of wheat less the cost of converting the wheat into flour). It has been shown above (p. 17) that the basis $(f_{1,0} - a_{0,0})$ may differ materially from the expression $(f_{1,0} - a_{1,0})$; further, that $f_{1,0}$ will tend to approximate closely to $a_{1,0}$; and, finally, that the average value of $(f_{1,0} - a_{1,0})$ can be expected to be the same as that of $(f_{1,1} - a_{1,1})$.

Two inferences may be drawn. First, the value of the basis $(f_{1,0} - a_{0,0})$, which is crucial to the outcome of short hedging, is irrelevant to the outcome of long hedging. Second, the outcomes of individual long hedging transactions are likely to show little variability and will be close to zero (showing neither gain nor loss).[45] As for the first conclusion, empirical studies have not revealed any systematic relationship between the value of basis and the volume of long hedging. It follows also that the stability-of-basis test is not appropriate for routine long hedging. As for the second, it suggests that arbitrage hedging (that is, hedging to take advantages of opportunities for gain) is likely to be far less significant for long than for short hedging.[46]

Limitations of hedging facilities

In the preceding discussion of hedging it has been assumed that the hedger's commitment in the actuals market is of the same grade as the grade effectively governing the prices of the futures contract. In the case of a single-grade futures contract, the actuals commitment has been assumed to be in the contract grade itself. It follows that hedging outcomes for actuals-market positions in any other grade will differ from those for the contract grade to the extent that the difference between the prices in the actuals market of that grade and the contract grade changes over the hedge period. Moreover, additional uncertainty is introduced into hedging. These same considerations apply, *mutatis mutandis*, to hedging in multi-grade contracts, whether with commercial difference or fixed difference systems. They apply also to differences in the location of actuals commitments.

The practical difficulties posed by these considerations – in the older literature referred to as the horizontal limitations of hedging – could in principle be overcome by having several different futures contracts for each of the main grades and for each of the main trading or processing locations of the commodity. But a multiplicity of futures contracts for the same commodity in the same country is usually not practicable. The splitting-up of the speculative interest in a commodity would narrow the futures market for each contract, thus adversely affecting the liquidity of each market and its ability to absorb, with minimal reactions in price, the sales or purchases of futures made by hedgers when they need to enter the market.

There is considerable evidence that hedging takes place in respect of grades and locations in the actuals market which differ from the grades and locations stipulated in single-grade futures contracts or typically 'governing' the prices of multi-grade futures contracts. This suggests that inter-grade or inter-locational actuals price differences are reasonably stable, or that it is costly, in terms of price reactions, to hedge in thin markets. Again, the introduction of a second or third specially differentiated futures contract in an attempt to cater specifically for the need of hedgers interested in particular grades or locations has frequently failed.[47] However, there are instances where the horizontal limitation can be seen to have reduced the volume of hedging[48]; and in some markets, for example in wheat in the United States, more than one futures contract is traded successfully.[49]

Besides the so-called horizontal limitations of hedging there are vertical limitations. In so far as the actuals prices of calves and dressed meat do not move in harmony with the price of cattle, a cattle futures contract has disadvantages as a hedging medium for those with interests in the earlier and later stages of production. The same considerations and observations apply as for horizontal limitations.[50]

It has been suggested that the hedging needs of traders in the various grades of a commodity are best served by a multi-grade futures contract with 'effective deliverability of a broad range of grades and locations' because, *inter alia*, 'it widens the range of spot prices with which the futures price is correlated through the delivery mechanism. . .' (Houthakker, 1959, p. 150).[51] However, this suggestion is incorrect in so far as it postulates a multi-grade contract. This is so because, as we have seen, at any given time the price of a multi-grade futures contract can be 'governed' by the actuals price of one grade only (see p. 12, above); and the delivery provisions of a futures contract cannot affect the relative prices of different grades in the actuals market.[52] 'The presumption . . . that a broader contract engenders broader hedging interest and thereby contributes to a larger volume of futures trading is not persuasive' (Johnson, 1957, p. 317). The moral is that, where only one contract is feasible for a commodity, the interests of hedgers are best served by basing that contract on the commercially most important grade and location, and by modifying it when necessary to accommodate changes in the trade.

Excess of volume of short hedging over volume of long hedging

It is characteristic of most futures market at most times that short hedging exceeds long hedging in volume: typically, hedgers in the aggregate are net short. It is this feature which provided a foundation for the theory of normal backwardation which is referred to below.

Various attempts have been made to explain this phenomenon of net short hedging. The most common explanation is that the seasonality of agricultural output as well as other technological considerations dictate that stocks be held, and that, on the other hand, there is no technological or other imperative requiring traders, processors or manufacturers to make forward sales in the actuals market. Thus, there is necessarily a large potential demand for short hedging but not for long hedging facilities. Although the formulation of this explanation can be criticised (Houthakker, 1968), it nevertheless refers to what is likely to be the main element in any satisfactory full explanation, which will be elusive so long as little is known about the economics of forward contracts in actuals markets.

Two other attempts have been made to explain the characteristic that hedging generally is net short; both run in terms of an asymmetry between short hedging and long hedging. Telser's explanation is largely to the effect that short hedgers derive some convenience yield from their hedged stocks, while long hedgers do not derive such a yield from their hedged forward sales (Telser, 1967, pp. 134–6). Houthakker's explanation is largely to the effect that the residual risk associated with short hedging is less than that with long hedging – a difference which derives from the fact noted earlier (pp. 13–14 above) that while there is no lower limit to the size of a backwardation there is an upper limit to the size of a contango (Houthakker, 1968, pp. 196–7). Yamey has suggested that both these explanations are not acceptable in the forms in which they are expressed, but may nevertheless point to factors which may contribute towards a full explanation (Yamey, 1971).[53]

The fact that short hedging typically is not matched in volume by long hedging implies that speculators typically are net long. It is more important, however, that any imbalance between the two sorts of hedging necessitates the presence and activities of speculators in an efficiently functioning futures market.

The treatment of hedging in the theoretical literature

In his *A Treatise on Money*, Keynes develops his analysis of price relationships on the basis of short hedgers who hedge their stocks fully so that they 'can go ahead and produce . . . running no risk' (Keynes, 1930, p. 142). In the 'normal' case (where the spot actuals price is expected to remain unchanged) the futures price is below the speculators' expected price by the amount hedgers are willing to sacrifice to achieve certainty for themselves. This gives rise to the hypothesis of normal backwardation of which more is said below.

Kaldor's analysis gives more precision to the theory sketched by Keynes. It retains the assumption that hedgers are net short in the futures market. The conclusion is derived that in Keynes' 'normal' case the actuals price exceeds the forward futures price by the marginal risk premium (Kaldor, 1939).

The analysis of Keynes and Kaldor requires that there is a substantial measure of uniformity in the expectations held by speculators. Kaldor noted that the backwardation relationship did not hold if 'there is a marked divergence in individual expectations' (Kaldor, 1940, p. 201). The analysis is further limited in that it deals only with the situation in which speculators are net long in futures – a common but not invariable situation in practice. The analysis also implies that hedgers are routine hedgers who do not have expectations about price movements or that, if they do, they do not act on them.[54]

More recent theoretical work has attempted to take account of hedgers' expectations and the action taken in their light. In particular, attention has been directed to the question of the determination by the hedger of the proportion of his stock to be hedged. Models in which expected returns and risk are key variables have been developed to throw light on this matter and on other questions.

Stein's model (Stein, 1961*a*; correction in Stein, 1964) is concerned with the optimal proportion of stock to be hedged by an individual. It is postulated that the hedger aims to maximise his expected utility, and that this is based on his expected return and on risk. Expected return and risk are treated as a function of the hedger's price expectations and the proportion of stock which is hedged. While the model allows for the adjustment of the optimum proportion of stock to be hedged in response to a change in current actuals price, in futures price and in price expectations, it has some limitations.[55] First, it does not embrace the size of the hedger's actuals position. Second, while it can explain why a hedger may under-hedge (i.e. not cover his stock fully, but carry a portion of the risk himself), it does not encompass the possibility of over-hedging (i.e. where the trader hedges his stock fully and in addition takes a further short position in futures in the expectation that prices will fall). Third, it cannot explain why a trader may carry a stock unhedged and in addition take a long position in futures – in the expectation that both actuals and futures prices will rise.[56]

Johnson's model (Johnson, 1960) is developed to explain the individual's market position in both actuals and futures markets and incorporates both hedging and speculative elements; it can explain types of situations which are beyond the reach of Stein's model. It is assumed that the hedger aims at the optimum combination of expected return and risk, subject to the constraint of risk minimisation in the actuals market. It may be noted that in this model the effectiveness of hedging is made to depend on the closeness of the expected correlation of movements in the actuals and futures prices.[57]

McKinnon has developed a model (McKinnon, 1967) to explain how a farmer can use the futures market so as to minimise the variance over time of his income, taking account of the fact that when he makes his planting decision he is uncertain both as to the size of his eventual crop and also as to the actuals price at harvesting. McKinnon shows that the model 'does not preclude the rather strange probability of a negative optimal hedge', that is, the possibility that at planting time the farmer *buys* futures (McKinnon, 1967, pp. 849–50).[58]

SPECULATION, PRICES AND PRICE MOVEMENTS

Speculation and futures markets

Speculation is ubiquitous in any economy, however organised, in which economic decisions have to be made in the face of uncertainties. Speculation in commodities – taking the form of the assumption of risks by 'speculators' who hold stocks or sell forward – does not depend upon the existence of futures markets.

Futures markets contribute distinctively towards speculative activities by making it possible for individuals to engage in speculation without having to become engaged in the production, handling or processing of the commodity: specialisation of speculation is facilitated by the standardisation of the futures contract. The organisation of a futures market further enables the specialist speculator to economise in his operations: transactions costs and capital commitments are minimised. Finally, the standardisation of the futures contract enables the speculator with equal ease to take up either a long position or a short position in the market, according as to whether he expects price to rise or to fall. He can thus take advantage of market situations whether he judges the current price to be too low or too high, a possibility which is not matched in markets without futures trading, such as the markets for houses, works of art or tea. In this way, too, speculators through their transactions can influence the market equally readily in either direction.

It is indeed the efficiency of futures markets in relation to speculative transactions that gives rise to much criticism of futures trading. Because of the ease of trading in these markets, inexpert amateur speculators can place their bets and influence the market as easily as the professionals; and waves of speculative buying or selling both by professionals and amateurs can influence the price levels and price movements of commodities with serious effects on the fortunes of those who perforce are engaged in their production, distribution and processing.

In principle, futures markets are neutral as to the effects of speculation on prices and price movements. Careful analysis and examination of the evidence are necessary to establish its effects in particular markets. Neither approach may be conclusive, although both serve to place the issues in perspective. A particular difficulty is that the prices which obtain in a market are the results of a myriad of buying and selling decisions, actuated by many diverse expectations. The market activities of the so-called speculators who deal in futures but do not handle the commodity as well as those of many others who handle the commodity (and may deal in futures) are speculative and influence prices. It is not easy to isolate the effects of the activities of the former category of traders, and, *a fortiori*, of any segment of it.

The classical view of speculation

In the writings of many economists since (at least) Adam Smith there is a line of reasoning which concludes that speculation is beneficent. It brings about a better allocation of supplies over time and reduces fluctuations in price. Speculators are seen as buying when the commodity is relatively abundant and selling when it is relatively scarce. They thereby help to husband supplies in fat periods and to augment them in lean periods, improving the inter-temporal distribution of supplies and stabilising prices.[59]

The classical view of speculation is well expressed by John Stuart Mill (Mill, 1848, bk 4, ch. 2, sections 4 and 5). He noted that improvements in communications had enabled local gluts and deficiencies to be ameliorated, rendering 'the fluctuations of prices much less extreme than formerly'. He added:

> This effect is much promoted by the existence of large capitals, belonging to what are called speculative merchants whose business it is to buy goods in order to resell them at a profit. These dealers naturally buying things when they are cheapest, and storing them up to be brought again into the market when the price has become unusually high; the tendency of their operations is to equalize price, or at least to moderate its inequalities. The prices of things are neither so much depressed at one time, nor so much raised at another, as they would be if speculative dealers did not exist.
>
> Speculators, therefore, have a highly useful office in the economy of society; and (contrary to common opinion) the most useful portion of the class are those who speculate in commodities affected by the vissicitudes of seasons. If there were no corn-dealers, not only would the price of corn be liable to variations much more extreme

> than at present, but in a deficient season the necessary supplies might not be forthcoming at all. Unless there were speculators in corn, or unless, in default of dealers, the farmers became speculators, the price in a season of abundance would fall without any limit or check, except the wasteful consumption that would invariably follow. That any part of the surplus of one year remains to supply the deficiency of another, is owing either to farmers who withhold corn from the market, or to dealers who buy it when at the cheapest and lay it up in store.

There are two main elements in the theory of what Marshall termed 'constructive speculation' (Marshall, 1932, bk II, ch. V). The first is that it is in the interests of speculators to inform themselves of market conditions and prospects, because wrong decisions lead to losses: 'therefore they are in their own interest contributing to the public the best judgment of minds that are generally alert, well-informed and capable' (Marshall, 1932, p. 262). The second element is that inefficient speculators, that is those who tend to make wrong forecasts, lose money and are eliminated from the market, while efficient speculators are enabled to engage in increased trading. The theory, which was developed before futures trading began to flourish, is applicable to speculation in actuals as well as to speculation in futures.

According to this theory speculators engage in market forecasting and they gain according to their skill at it.[60] This feature distinguishes the theory from the Keynes-inspired theory of normal backwardation. For in the latter theory the speculators' role in the futures market seems to be that of passively taking up the opposite position to that of the hedgers, a process which somehow on the average is supposed to work so as to yield a satisfactory and necessary level of profit to the speculators which is acceptable to the hedgers (the price the latter are willing to pay for the shifting of risk). It is difficult to see, however, how speculators would take up long positions in futures simply to accommodate hedgers and without having regard to their own price forecasts or expectations. Further, there is evidence in Rockwell's study which suggests that in major American futures markets a speculator who did no more than take up the opposite position to that of hedgers (in the aggregate) would have made only insignificant gains. The major part of the gains of large speculators came from their taking up, from time to time, positions not in accordance with the theory of normal backwardation; and these gains can be interpreted as the fruits of forecasting skill. Rockwell was led to 'the conclusion that a tendency toward normal backwardation is neither a consistent nor an important characteristic of futures markets' (Rockwell, 1967, p. 126). Other studies confirm the absence of any consistent tendency toward normal backwardation. There is no general tendency for the prices of a particular futures contract consistently to rise (or fall) over the period from the commencement of trading in the contract to the month of its maturity.[61]

Several published studies concern attempts to measure the accuracy with which prices have been forecast in markets with futures trading. These studies generally show relatively large forecasting 'errors' for long forecast periods, with diminishing errors for shorter periods.[62] However, forecasting errors tend to be randomly distributed: the forecasts are unbiassed in the sense that in wide active markets there is no tendency for the forecasts (the forward futures prices) consistently either to under-shoot or to over-shoot the eventual price at maturity. This is borne out by the results of the tests of the effectiveness of futures markets for hedging purposes, and is an aspect of the failure to find evidence in support of the hypothesis of normal backwardation. In thin markets, on the other hand, bias in one or other direction has been found. Price forecasts embodied in futures prices in these markets show some tendency to be persistently optimistic or pessimistic. Such markets have been described as lopsided or unbalanced (Gray, 1960*b*).[63]

It is evident, however, that measurements of forecasting accuracy in futures markets, while interesting in themselves and also for raising the question of differences in accuracy among commodities, do not throw light on the issue whether futures trading is stabilising or otherwise. For they cannot disclose what would have happened had there not been futures trading and the same exogenous changes in economic and political conditions – both general and also local to the particular commodity – had occurred.

Destabilising speculation: general considerations

The hypothesis that speculation tends to stabilise prices over time, i.e. to reduce the frequency and amplitude of price fluctuations, is not accepted by critics of speculation, especially critics of speculation in futures markets. The contrary view is frequently expressed that speculation tends to bring about unjustified levels of price and unnecessary and undesirable price fluctuations. Indeed, as Lerner has put it, 'the extraordinary usefulness of speculation . . . goes ill with the hostility which people who have to work hard for their living often develop against the mysterious gains that speculators make in offices while dealing in goods which they would not even recognize' (Lerner, 1944, p. 94).

Attempts to explain why speculation has undesirable effects on prices range from the crude to the more sophisticated. Crude explanations include the assertion that, since the annual volume of business on an active futures exchange exceeds several-fold the volume of the annual physical supply of the commodity in question, prices therefore must be depressed artificially because the supply on the price-forming market is magnified. The emptiness of this explanation is evident from the fact that the opposite assertion can be made equally improperly: because the crop is bought several times over, demand is inflated and therefore speculation raises prices artificially.[64] Nothing can be inferred from the mere volume of futures trading.

A large part of the volume of transactions on an efficient futures market is made by hedgers. Another large part is made by so-called scalpers or floor-traders who, by their willingness to buy or sell, add greatly to the liquidity of the market, and reduce the costs of hedging (and speculative) operations by improving the ability of the market to absorb bursts of selling or buying.[65] A large part of the trading of scalpers is balanced within the day (each scalper balancing his purchases and his sales), and so it cannot affect prices or price movements except for very short periods. Its most likely effect is to smooth short-period movements of prices by reducing the amplitude of the price dips and bulges occasioned by the placing and lifting of hedges (Working, 1967, p. 44). Yet another body of transactions is made up of spreads or straddles – arbitrage transactions which keep in alignment the prices of different futures maturities of the same commodity or the prices of the same commodity's futures in different markets, nationally or internationally.

This is not to argue, of course, that speculation does not affect prices and price movements, but only that statistics of volumes of futures transactions can provide no guidance as to the likely magnitude or direction of the effects of speculation.

A more significant statistic is that of the 'open interest' of speculators (or sub-categories of speculators), i.e. the aggregated market position of speculators who individually are net long and that of those who individually are net short. The open interest and changes in it are more realistic indicators of the price-influencing weight of speculative activity. It has been established that by and large the open position of, say, long speculators tends to be related to the open position of short hedgers. The available statistics, adjusted for known deficiencies, show

> that the amount of long speculation, measured in dollar value of open speculative contracts, has differed greatly between commodities, some commodities having ten, twenty, or as much as several hundred times as much speculation as others; and that these differences in amounts of speculation depend primarily on the amounts of hedging in the markets (Working, 1960*b*, p. 213).

Similarly, short-period changes in the speculative open interest tend to be correlated positively with changes in hedgers' open interest. Working adduces evidence from the experiences of various markets to show that the volume of speculative open interest tends to respond quite closely to the volume of hedging, rather than that the causation runs in the other direction.[66]

It would be surprising, however, to find that the aggregated open interest of speculators with long positions exactly equalled the *net* short open position of hedgers. One would not expect such a degree of 'balance' because of discontinuities in trading by both hedgers and speculators (reduced, it is true, by the activities of scalpers) and because of differences in market expectations among speculators which would cause some to be net long and others net short at any given time. To our knowledge only one study, itself limited in scope, has been made of the relationship between the varying extent of the excess of aggregated speculative open interest (over the net hedging open position) and price. A study by Ward of the New York futures market in frozen concentrated orange juice shows an index of excess speculation to be inversely related to the spread between the prices of the near-month futures contract and the estimated price of the corresponding actuals. The results suggest that, by increasing the liquidity of the market, speculation in excess of hedging requirements tended to reduce price distortion (Ward, 1974).

Thus, superficially appealing as it may be to liken an organised futures exchange to a gambling casino, the economic rationale of the great bulk of transactions in futures contracts is evident.

Destabilising speculation: movement trading

In an article published in 1937, H. S. Irwin argued that much of the trading activity of *professional* speculators on commodity and stock exchanges did not correspond with the activities subsumed in the classical theory of speculation; and that this type of trading, called movement trading, was destabilising. Movement trading was 'detrimental to the public interest' because it tended to drive 'prices away from the levels warranted by existing conditions' and to 'increase the fluctuations of prices'.[67] In movement trading, according to Irwin, the professional speculators, including the largest, go with the market; that is, when a price movement has started for whatever reason, professionals follow the movement, thereby reinforcing it. They do not act on the basis of their assessments of underlying supply and demand conditions or of prospective changes in them; instead, they depend upon 'their market intuition and market agility to close out their holdings at once' when the price movement is about to come to an end or to be reversed. This type of trading is said to be made possible and profitable by 'technical conditions of the market' and especially by 'the ways in which the public enters and leaves the market' (*ibid.*, p. 269). The major ingredient in the technical conditions is 'the inertia or momentum in the price movements which arises mainly from the large number of traders operating in these markets' (*ibid.*, p. 270), and another is that most of the large number of traders, while each is acting for himself, 'are likely to act as a crowd, especially since they form a compact group so that most of them are subject to mass psychology' (*ibid.*, p. 275). Irwin noted that movement trading could apply to price movements ranging from those within a single day to the 'longer price swings which may extend over several days or sometimes over several weeks' (*ibid.*, p. 269).

This theory of movement trading, in which professional speculators do not fulfill their classical role, is one which may well articulate the common belief that speculation is destabilising: it certainly gives prominence to the participation in trading on organised markets by 'amateurs'[68] and to 'mass psychology'.[69] It should be noted, however, that this theory does not imply that speculators *as a whole* make profits from their destabilising activities: it implies no more than that one important category of speculators – the professionals, and then only the agile ones – makes profits in the circumstances.

Since Irwin's paper was published, statistical techniques have been developed and applied to test whether and to what extent particular commodity (or security) prices over time display 'dependence', that is, whether and to what extent successive prices are correlated so that segments of price series exhibit continuity. If Irwin's contentions were valid, price series in futures markets would exhibit marked evidence of price dependence for varying spans of time.

It would be inappropriate to attempt an explanation of the nature of the various statistical tests which have been used or a detailed listing of the results of the various studies. A recent paper by Praetz (1975), reprinted in this book, uses a number of the tests in his investigation of price series for the Sydney wool futures market, and also considers some earlier published studies. The findings of the various empirical studies can be summarised to the effect that there is little evidence in support of price dependence. Price series exhibit the characteristics of a random walk in that the increments or decrements linking successive prices tend to be randomly distributed. This feature is consistent with the view that futures markets are 'efficient' markets in the sense that each price tends fully to reflect available market information. Such evidence as there is of price dependence over short periods is best explained in terms of the non-instantaneous diffusion of new information which becomes available to a market rather than in terms of trading practices such as movement trading.[70] Referring to the results of such enquiries, Samuelson (1972, pp. 16–17) has commented:

> Many scholars have been confirming the statistical finding of Working that price changes of commodity futures very nearly mimic purely random numbers – a result that would deal a lethal blow to all chartists, but would be confirmatory of the hypothesis that keen and intelligent speculation has already made proper allowances for everything but the unknowables of chance.

The evidence summarised above is consistent with the view that efficient professional speculators tend to gain at the expense of other traders, including amateurs: but their gains reflect more rapid gathering and more successful interpretation of information about changing market conditions, and not greater agility at climbing on and getting off market bandwagons. Observed fluctuations of prices over time are, on this evidence, the consequences of the presence of uncertainty and the impact of chance influences which are outside the control of those trading in the market.

Price fluctuations with and without futures trading

The question remains, however, whether futures trading and the speculation facilitated by it improve the process of price formation as compared with the alternative without futures trading. Even if movement trading and other destabilising practices such as deliberate manipulation can be excluded, the question remains whether the quality of price forecasting by those in the market is better with futures trading than without it.[71] General reasoning suggests that in this respect market performance will be improved. Futures trading encourages specialisation in the activities of assembling and interpreting market information, and so can be expected to improve their performance. Commodity exchange organisations themselves also commonly provide for the gathering and dissemination of market data. Again, because it enables those who deal in the physical commodity to adjust more readily their stock-holdings and their market positions in the light of their own expectations and their own attitudes towards risk, futures trading may be expected to damp down intra-seasonal and inter-seasonal price movements.

Attempts to test directly from historical price data whether futures trading has reduced the amplitude of price fluctuations run up against the familiar difficulty that the test period, with futures trading, cannot in all other relevant respects be the same as the control period, without futures trading. Changes in conditions of production, transport, marketing, storage and use of the commodity make it difficult if not impossible to infer with confidence whether the availability of futures trading was responsible for any observed change in the amplitude and frequency of price fluctuations. The difficulties are particularly severe when the two contrasted periods both are lengthy, and when the control period is the earlier.[72]

Although they also cannot be conclusive, special interest attaches to a few studies which have examined the variability of prices in periods with futures trading as well as in both earlier and later periods without futures trading. These situations have arisen because of the permanent or temporary prohibition of futures trading in certain markets. Thus Working has examined intra-seasonal price variations in the United

States onion market in periods with and without futures trading (Working, 1963).[73] In India Naik has investigated the record of price behaviour in the market for groundnuts, in which years without futures trading precede, are interspersed with, and succeed the observed years with futures trading (Naik, 1970).[74] The general statistical findings of these studies as well as most of the others are of lower price variability in the periods with futures trading.

Can destabilising speculation be profitable?

In the classical theory of speculation the basic proposition is that speculators make profits if and only if their activities stabilise prices.[75] This notion is intuitively appealing. Some economic theorists have, however, tried to construct theoretical counter-examples, while others have tried to establish the necessary validity of the basic proposition. In these demonstrations and counter-demonstrations, which are not specifically related to futures markets, theorists have had, among other things, to choose a criterion of stabilisation and to adopt some uneasy classification of operators into 'speculators' and 'non-speculators'. We need not review the various interesting contributions and the discussion of the main issues.[76] In an important paper Farrell succeeded in showing that the basic proposition 'is too strong to hold with any great generality'. It was critically dependent for its *general* validity upon certain conditions (for example that the non-speculative demand function and the reigning price in any period are independent of speculative activity in earlier periods, and that the excess demand function of non-speculators is linear). However, the introduction of speculators' transactions costs 'led to less stringent sufficient conditions' (Farrell, 1966, p. 192).[77] Farrell concludes that 'our search for reasonably simple and plausible sufficient conditions for the validity of our basic proposition seems to have been in vain' (*ibid.*, p. 192). It should not, of course, be inferred from this that in a market where these conditions were not satisfied (which would obviously be difficult to determine empirically), profitable speculation would be destabilising.

To our knowledge only one attempt has been made to determine for a particular futures market whether speculative activity which demonstrably was destabilising was also profitable. Aliber developed an ingenious test to identify short periods within which speculators (as classified in official statistics) could be said to have been bullish (bearish) and within which prices could be said to have reached an upper (lower) turning-point. He applied this test to two sample periods of prices and trading on the United States cotton futures market. Using other data for the profits and losses of speculators, derived from official statistics, he claimed that profits had been made by speculators when, on his test, their activities unjustifiably had been reinforcing price movements.[78] Yamey showed that the test was not altogether conclusive in identifying periods of destabilising speculation. He also pointed out that the statistics of speculators' profits related to the total of all activities in a given period, while the identified periods of destabilisation were certain shorter sub-periods within the longer trading-results period.[79]

Expectations, attitudes to risk and their treatment in the theoretical literature

By an expectation we mean, following De Morgan in his *Formal Logic* of 1847, the view of a person, or group of persons, of a coming event or any other matter on which absolute knowledge does not necessarily exist.[80] De Morgan used the term 'state of mind' rather than 'view'; but as Georgescu-Roegen pointed out all aspects of the state of mind (for example, gloom, joy) are not relevant here: in particular we wish to keep separate the individual's behaviour consequent upon this view (Georgescu-Roegen, 1958).

It is helpful to identify an expectation by three objective elements:[81] the individual by whom it is held; the evidence (or total knowledge of the individual) at the time it is held; and the individual's prediction of the coming event. The study of the individual is relevant, for different individuals may perceive different evidence from given facts, and, moreover, may reach different predictions from given evidence.

Expectations may be compared with respect to their objective elements, and an individual may be able to say which prediction he thinks more desirable. Yet a unique ordinal ranking may not be possible. Suppose an individual compares his price expectations at two different times, each expectation being in the form of a subjective probability density function. Suppose that at the later time the mean expectation is greater, but the variance is also greater. The expectations may be ranked by reference to a single number, the probability ratio. Yet such an ordering is not unique: the individual may adjust to the mean expectation or the probability.[82]

Clearly all expectations held by traders in commodity exchanges are not capable of numerical representation: some expectations will take the form of a vague notion that at some imprecisely defined future date the price of a certain commodity will rise or fall.[83] Other expectations may be capable of more precise representation, although for the support of such an hypothesis the methodology of positive economics does not require that traders actually form such precise expectations, but merely that they behave as if they do. In a pilot study of sixteen ring dealers on the London Metal Exchange and a further study of twenty-five floor members and associate members of the Sydney wool futures market, Goss found that almost every respondent interviewed claimed to form expectations about spot and futures prices and the price spread on those exchanges, but only about ten per cent of respondents claimed to form expectations in terms of probabilities (Goss, 1972*b*).

Because of the nature of the problem, objective probabilities of price changes in commodity markets are not defined, and precise representation of expectations in the literature on futures markets has usually taken the form of an implicit or explicit assumption of a subjective probability density function. In the early theoretical work, reference was made to the expected value only, although the use of a marginal risk premium indicates that these expectations were held with uncertainty.[84] In some cases multi-valued expectations are implied, and a central value is referred to as 'the expected price [of an individual]' (Keynes, 1930; Hicks, 1939; Peston and Yamey, 1960).

Subsequently, it has been explicitly assumed that individuals' expectations take the form of a subjective probability distribution, with the mean of that distribution used as a measure of expected return and with the variance as a measure of risk (Johnson, 1960; Stein, 1961*a*). No attempt has been made, in the futures market context, to estimate individual subjective probabilities by means of a 'Jevonsian Operation' (Ozga, 1965, pp. 84f.). In this operation of interrogation the individual is asked to nominate events with zero and unit probabilities, and then to nominate, successively, events with probabilities falling in the middle of the resulting intervals.

In the early literature concerned with the hypothesis of normal backwardation, uniformity of mean expectation among individuals was assumed, although derivation of that hypothesis required only approximate uniformity of expectations.[85] Market equilibrium in the speculative stock-holding models of Brennan and Telser, which are based on Kaldor, requires identical mean expectations. Expectations of basis change form the cornerstone of papers by Working and Gray, although no formal representation of those expectations is made (Working, 1953*a*; Gray, 1961*a*). The implication, however, is that those expectations are held with uncertainty and are heterogeneous as between individuals. Peston and Yamey made 'no special assumption' about expectations, but their downward-sloping demand functions for speculators in actuals and futures would seem to require either uncertain and/or heterogeneous expectations and/or diversity in attitude to risk.

Little is known about the factors which cause traders in organised commodity exchanges to revise their price expectations, although Klein has referred to 'direct measurement' in the Wharton School Project (Klein, 1972, pp. 184–8). Some attention has been given to the theoretical consequences of the revision of traders' expectations, although again factual information is scarce. In the London Metal Exchange pilot study and the Sydney Wool Futures survey, Goss asked respondents whether they revised their price expectations, what factors led to such a revision, and what adjustments to their market positions followed such a revision. Of the sixteen London respondents and twenty-five Sydney respondents, all except two (one respondent in each survey) claimed to revise their price expectations (one respondent in each survey claimed to hedge in a routine manner). The factors suggested as leading to such revisions were, in order of frequency, a change in the state of the market, new information on the commodities traded, and new information on the state of the economy in general. These respondents were also asked how they would adjust their market positions if their expectation of 'the most likely price' increased. Most traders claimed that if they were sellers, they would sell less, and that, if buyers, they would buy more. These results are perhaps intuitively obvious for a risk-averter, although one-third of the respondents claimed that in each case they would leave their market positions unchanged (Goss, 1972*b*).

This result may mean that futures trading is a fruitful field for application of Simon's distinction between habitual and non-habitual behaviour. The former occurs where, in terms of the three elements of an expectation discussed above, a change in 'evidence' leads to no change in 'prediction' or an automatic change along predetermined lines, while the latter means that a change in 'evidence' leads to a discretionary change in 'predictions' (Simon, 1958; Ozga, 1965).

An hypothesis of revision of expectations popular with economists is that of adaptive expectations, developed by Nerlove and others (Nerlove, 1958). This model assumes that expectations in the current period are revised in proportion to the error in expectations in the preceding period. This model implies that the current expected price is a weighted average of past actual prices. This hypothesis was used by Brennan in his estimation of the supply of storage function (Brennan, 1958). However, while it permits separate estimation of the expectations function, and allows prices to be predicted temporally, it suffers from the disadvantage that if expectations in the current period are correct no revision is permitted even if relevant new information comes to hand.

This last criticism does not apply to Mills's concept of the 'implicit expectation', which permits all relevant information to be incorporated in the estimates (Mills, 1962). To our knowledge, Mills's technique has not been used in the study of futures markets.

The technique, *inter alia*, does not yield a separate estimate of the expectations function: it joins together the decision function and the expectations function. This is a disadvantage if one accepts that different individuals may arrive at different decisions from given expectations, or that a group of individuals may arrive at different decisions from given expectations at different times (e.g. because their evaluation of the risk has changed).

The individual's attitude toward risk is based on his preference for risk as compared with certainty, and is expressed in his market decision, given his expectations and current prices. Risk here means risk of loss from some particular market situation, and the risk is relevant because no one can predict with certainty the price which will rule at a particular later date. Normally the prospect of increased returns is accompanied by an increased risk. If the trader is a risk-averter, the question of trade-off arises; while if the trader prefers risk, his decision may be contrained by other factors (e.g. availability of capital). The term risk-averter means that the trader, while willing to take some risk, shows in some average or marginal sense a tendency to prefer less risk to more, although the precise definition will depend on the measure of risk used and the way in which the individual's preferences are expressed.

For an individual to make a decision about the level of risk he is willing to accept *inter alia* in a given situation, there must be available to him an estimate, either objective or subjective, of the amount of risk involved at various market positions. In the context of futures trading, because of the nature of the problem, no objective estimates of the risks involved in various market positions can be made.

In the literature on futures trading the subjective estimate of the risk of loss per unit is, of course, derived from the individual's uncertain expectations about the actuals and futures prices. Risk aversion, which has almost always been assumed in the literature, has been expressed in two main ways. In the first it has been expressed as the requirement of a marginal risk premium in an expected-revenue function. For example, before taking a position in their respective markets, Kaldor's long speculators in actuals (and in futures) require a marginal risk premium as a component of their expected return. Their expectations are held with uncertainty, and they will not buy unless the current actuals or futures price is less than their expected price by at least the marginal risk premium.[86] Keynes in *A Treatise on Money* paid little attention to speculation in actuals; but his long speculators in futures are risk averters in the same sense as Kaldor's. Risk aversion is treated in the same way in Brennan's and Telser's models of speculative stock-holding; in them the expected-revenue function is based upon Kaldor's expected revenue for speculators in actuals.

The second main way in which risk aversion has been expressed in the theory of futures trading is in the form of the rising marginal rate of substitution of risk for expected return in the individual's expected-utility contours. This notion has its counterpart in general economics in the assumption of a falling marginal utility of income which depresses the expected utility in a von Neumann–Morgenstern hypothesis (linear in the probabilities) below the utility of a sure prospect of the same monetary amount. In Stein's model of the hedger–speculator, risk aversion at the margin is assumed in the rising marginal rate of substitution of risk for expected return, and risk aversion in an average sense is assumed in the *positive* marginal rate of substitution. In Johnson's model of the hedger–speculator there is a positive and falling marginal rate of substitution of expected return for risk, and risk aversion is further assumed in the form in which the opportunity locus is defined.[87]

Goss has defined risk aversion as an individual's willingness to take a smaller risk of loss as his market commitment increases (Goss, 1972*a*, ch. 7). Another aspect of risk aversion in that model is that the individual may be unwilling to take a market position unless the subjective probability of gain is in his favour (Goss, 1972*b*). (This definition can easily be modified to incorporate a conventional risk premium.)

The question is then whether speculators are risk-averters in practice. Goss asked forty-one respondents in the London Metal and Sydney Wool surveys whether they were willing to take an increasing, decreasing or constant risk of loss as their market commitments increased, and whether they were willing to take a market position if the subjective probability of loss was against them (that is, greater than 0.5). Respondents divided themselves about 60–40 between decreasing and constant willingness-to-take-risk functions, none claiming to take an increasing risk as market commitment increased. Nevertheless, about 20 per cent of these traders claimed to take market positions when they believed the subjective probability of loss to be against them. Respondents were also asked whether they revised their attitude to risk, and if so, what were the main reasons for this revision. Affirmative answers to this question were given by 60 per cent of traders interviewed, the main factors suggested being the current state of the market and their recent history of profits and losses, with 'psychological factors' being the next most important (Goss, 1972*b*).

For several agricultural commodities, Brennan estimated as a residual the compound subjective variable, marginal risk premium less marginal convenience yield, as a function of stocks held. The estimates are consistent with the requirement of a positive marginal risk premium and with a positive marginal convenience yield which varies inversely with stocks.

What, then, are the predicted implications of risk aversion? Let us consider the effect of an increase in the individual's expected actuals price for a risk-averse trader: we shall find that the predictions from various models are in substantial agreement. In the Kaldor model an increase in the expected price would mean an increase in the speculator's holdings. It would also mean an increase in the speculator's purchases of futures. In the Johnson hedger–speculator model, it would mean an increase in the individual's long position in actuals, and an increase in his short position in futures as a hedge against the additional holding of actuals. In the Stein hedger–speculator model it would mean an increase in the proportion of stock unhedged. Since expected utility had increased, the individual's total stock-holding and hence the quantity of unhedged stock would increase: the quantity of hedged stock might go either way. In the Goss speculator model, for (say) a long speculator it would mean a decrease in the subjective probability of loss, and equating this to his willingness to take risk, would result in an increased market commitment.[88]

Finally, what decision rules are speculators and hedger–speculators assumed to follow in determining their actuals and futures market positions in the various models discussed here?

Long speculators in Kaldor's model, in effect, equate their expected net marginal return on actuals with the marginal cost of acquiring actuals (the current actuals price), the latter assumed constant for each individual. They behave, in effect, as if they are maximising expected net profit. With the uniformity assumption of Kaldor's, the description of market behaviour serves as a description of individual behaviour, except that the actuals price declines as long speculators in the aggregate expand their positions. Such a maximising assumption is explicitly made by Brennan and Telser, whose individual stock-holders maximise expected net revenue by equating the net marginal cost of storage with the expected price change in the actuals market. The behaviour of Kaldor's long speculators in futures is also consistent with a maximising assumption, although here the expected marginal net return (the expected actuals price less the marginal risk premium) is equated to the marginal cost of acquiring futures (the futures price) for an individual.[89]

In the discussion of their model of market price determination, Peston and Yamey express a wish that their supply and demand functions should not be slave to any particular theory of uncertainty. Their speculative holding of unhedged stocks by merchants is a decreasing function of the current actuals price, and can be seen as consistent with maximisation of expected net return by individuals, in the same way as the similar functions of Kaldor, Brennan and Telser (although it may well be consistent with other assumptions). Although no specific assumptions are made about expectations or risk aversion, it is unlikely that this function could be obtained except for risk-averse individuals, although it would not seem to require heterogeneity of attitude to risk. Similar comments apply to the demand for futures by long speculators in the Peston–Yamey model: demand is a decreasing function of the futures price, but is unresponsive to changes in the spot price.

In the models of Stein and Johnson, hedger–speculators determine their market commitments through maximisation of expected utility. But Goss's model of speculation is not a maximising model. Speculators determine their market position by equating their willingness to take (total) risk with their subjective estimate of the risk of loss as given by their expectations. It is shown explicitly that an inverse relation between quantity and price for *long* speculators can be found only if speculators are risk-averse. Risk preference by long speculators in that model results in a positively sloped demand function. Similarly, a conventionally shaped supply function is derived for risk-averse speculators only. Risk preference on the short side results in a negative price–quantity relationship. Hence, it enables some obvious inferences about static stability and risk aversion to be made.[90]

CONDITIONS FAVOURABLE TO FUTURES TRADING

Futures trading appears to develop only when there is a need for hedging facilities by those producing, handling, merchanting or processing the commodity. Hedging need arises when there are, or are expected to be, material fluctuations in the price of the commodity. It is therefore not surprising that there is no successful futures trading in commodities of which the supply is concentrated in a small number of sources and of which prices are kept unchanged for longish periods (possibly accompanied by price guarantees to buyers from major sellers). But even in such instances the demand for futures trading is heard on occasions when prices tend to become 'unstable', for example, when there is heavy excess capacity or when unusual sources of supply become available temporarily (for example, from Communist countries which are not normally exporters). Aluminium and certain chemicals have provided instances in the post-war period. Governmental and inter-governmental price control or price support schemes are another source of price stability which is adverse to futures trading. Trading in cotton futures, which flourished before the Second World War, has been greatly affected by post-war developments of this kind (Brand, 1964; Yamey, 1959). Moreover, 'informed speculators tend to avoid dealing in a commodity whose price is subject to a substantial degree of control. . .' (Working, 1960*b*, p. 202).[91]

It has usually been said that storability and storage of the commodity are necessary for futures trading. The connection of storage with the need for hedging facilities is apparent. The development of refrigeration has greatly increased the scope for futures trading.[92] However, futures trading in live cattle and futures-like trading in share-price indexes in Amsterdam suggest that storability in the strict sense is not a necessary condition.

The need for hedging facilities is not sufficient to generate futures trading. It is also necessary that it is possible to specify a standard grade or description for the commodity and to measure deviations from it. Without this possibility, which is said to be absent for a commodity such as tea – although there was futures trading in tea for a few years in the late nineteenth century and a new tea contract is under consideration (Rees and Jones, 1975, pp. 244, 252) – trading without inspection is difficult if not impossible, and successful trading in standardised futures contracts inconceivable. Again, it is necessary that contract terms and conditions can be devised which are satisfactory both from the point of view of hedgers as well as from the point of view of speculators, without whose adequate presence and activity a futures market is apt to languish, as the studies of Working and Gray have demonstrated.[93]

It is necessary that the market for the commodity is extensive enough to attract and sustain a large body of non-hedging traders (scalpers and other speculators) so that the liquidity of the market and continuity of trading can be maintained. In their absence, the cost of placing and lifting hedges and of making speculative trades is so high as to reduce the volume of hedging and speculation. The smaller the market, the greater are hedgers' 'execution costs', to use Working's term (Working, 1967), or, put differently, the wider the gap between a market trader's bid and asked prices. As has been noted earlier, these same considerations explain the tendency for futures trading to be concentrated in a single contract and a single market for each commodity, even in an economy as large as the United States. They also help to explain why an already successful futures exchange is at an advantage in introducing futures trading for additional commodities (Working, 1970, pp. 27–8), or why primary producing countries, unless they have well developed commercial and financial sectors, are at a disadvantage in the local establishment of futures markets in the primary products they produce.

It must be remembered also that there sometimes are feasible alternatives to hedging and that those with interests in the actuals market may be accustomed to or prefer other marketing arrangements which dispense with the need for futures markets. Vertical integration and long-term supply contracts (including contract farming) are examples of the former. As an example of the latter, Australian wool-growers are accustomed to sale by auction through a broker and have made little use of the Sydney wool futures market for hedging purposes, even during the 1960s when wool prices were falling. Much may depend, moreover, on the initiative taken by individuals, trade associations and exchanges themselves in the establishment and promotion of new futures markets.[94]

One could broadly account, along the preceding lines, for the presence or absence of futures trading in different commodities or in different places, or for the varying degrees of success of different markets. But we are conscious that we have not provided a systematic analysis or analytical framework from which the necessary conditions for the feasibility and success of futures trading can be derived. This lack of such a firm framework is a deficiency in the theory of futures trading. It is possible that the burgeoning interest among economists in the economics of transactions costs, of contracts and of property rights might provoke the insights and produce the research to make good the deficiency.[95]

REGULATION OF FUTURES MARKETS

Official intervention in, or regulation of, futures markets has in its timing been associated with the prevalence among politically influential groups of the view that particular commodity prices were either 'too high' or 'too low' or 'too unstable' and that the blame lay with futures trading and the 'gambling' that took place in futures exchanges. Thus, the first strong pressure for official control (even prohibition) of futures trading in the United States occurred in the 1890s in the period of generally low agricultural prices.[96] Organised futures trading in Berlin was subjected to severe official handicaps in the same period (Smith, 1922, pp. 134–7). In Canada an official enquiry into grain futures trading was initiated early in 1931.[97] In the United Kingdom early in 1974 official concern over futures markets was sparked off by influential suggestions that futures trading was responsible for the large increases in the prices of the various commodities traded in them.

In many of these instances easily available evidence would have shown up the emptiness of the charges levelled against futures trading: other commodities not traded on futures markets were undergoing broadly the same price experience as commodities for which there were futures contracts. General deflation was the underlying explanation of the earlier phenomena. In more recent decades it has been general inflation, the effects of which on the prices of particular internationally traded commodities have sometimes been enhanced by anticipations of further inflation or of the devaluation of certain currencies.[98]

Intervention or regulation as practised or proposed has taken a variety of forms. These range from outright prohibition of futures trading in certain commodities[99] to the mere requirement that commodity exchanges be registered. Between these extremes there are many other forms: regulations relating to the membership and organisation of exchanges; prescription of rules such as rules for investigating and dealing with irregularities, suspected manipulation and so on; prescription of contract terms; prescription of margins payable by members or their clients; limitation of daily or sessional price movements; limitation of open positions of individual traders; requirements to furnish information on open positions; and provisions for the initiation and conduct of official enquiries into cases of suspected malpractice. Except where it does no more than codify and generalise common practice, most forms of regulation, however well intentioned, are apt to increase the costs of those using the markets. They do this directly, and also indirectly by adversely affecting the volume of transactions and thereby reducing the liquidity of the contracts and the capacity of the markets to absorb surges of trading (for example when hedges are placed). Regulation of the limits of price movements within the day or the trading session has the additional disadvantage that the market and its hedging facilities can be made inaccessible at times when they are most needed.[100] Further, regulations which restrict trading by members of an exchange or of the public may serve to affect price movements; but such effects are as likely to be unfavourable as favourable, since the regulations are as likely to affect those who would be making economically justified decisions as those who would not. Regulation is not a sharply and accurately discriminating instrument.[101]

The ease with which futures trading can be made the scapegoat for price levels and price movements considered to be against the public interest explains much ill-considered official intervention and regulation. But instances can be cited where legislatures have resisted the introduction of such measures or have made desirable changes. We conclude our survey of the economics of futures trading with a short account of an instance of the latter kind. In 1938, on the advice of the official Commodities Exchange Commission, the United States Congress repealed a transactions tax on futures trading first imposed in 1926. 'The Commission argued that the markets' three hundred scalpers were necessary to the hedging process and their livelihood was being endangered by the tax.' The repeal was carried through in spite of the strong canvassing of the familiar allegations against the markets (Cowing, 1965, pp. 255–6). It is of special interest that the reasoning of the Commission has been borne out by recent work (already referred to) of Holbrook Working, the doyen of the study of futures trading.

POSTSCRIPT (referring to publications noted after completion of the foregoing text)

1. The portfolio-theory approach to hedging—in which both expected profits and expected variability of profits are assumed to affect the hedging decision—has been incorporated in several theoretical papers (e.g. Johnson, 1960; Ward and Fletcher, 1971). Two recent studies specifically employ the portfolio-theory approach to derive estimates of what would have been the optimal proportion of a primary producer's production commitments to have hedged in two markets, cattle and eggs. (R. G. Heifner, 'Optimal Hedging Levels and Hedging Effectiveness in Cattle Feeding', *Agricultural Economics Research*, vol. 24, 1972; A. E. Peck, 'Hedging and Income Stability: Concepts, Implications, and an Example', *American Journal of Agricultural Economics*, vol. 57, 1975.) Although the two studies incorporate materially different assumptions—for example, in the first case the hedger's 'risk' relates to the variability of the 'error' in his price forecasts—both suggest that it would have been optimal for the hypothetical hedger, given his defined characteristics and circumstances, to have hedged well over half of his actuals

(production) commitments on the average over the selected period. Rutledge, 1972, also makes use of the portfolio-theory approach, but incorporates its implications less directly in his study of a different question: the determinants of hedging volume in the complex of soybean markets.

2. Following Johnson, 1960, Heifner, *op. cit.*, defines a measure of hedging effectiveness as the proportional reduction in the variance of profits achieved through hedging. He presents estimates of the hedging effectiveness of the optimal hedging positions, derived on the simplifying assumptions of zero hedging costs and of absence of bias in futures prices against short hedging. For the period studied, hedging effectiveness was estimated to be around 50 per cent, with minor differences according to the various combinations of specification and location of the actuals commitment examined in the study. (The study shows also the sensitivity of the results to relaxation of the simplifying assumptions.) One conclusion is that 'location, grade and sex of cattle fed have little effect on optimal hedging levels and hedging effectiveness. This suggests that one slaughter cattle futures contract may be sufficient to serve cattle feeders' hedging needs throughout the United States'.

3. A recent paper by Cargill and Rausser presents the findings of a wide-ranging analysis of futures prices in seven markets to test whether 'futures price increments are independent and thus uncorrelated over time'. The commodities studied were corn, oats, soybeans, wheat, copper, live cattle and pork bellies. Daily prices of 464 futures contracts [i.e. maturities] within the period 1960 to 1972 were examined. The authors report that 'although a large number of contracts [studied] appear random for each statistical test [six were applied], there are a significant number of contracts that are judged non-random by at least one test'. However, drawing attention to work of Mandelbrot and Samuelson, they point out that a market may be 'efficient' even if prices in it do not form a random walk. (T. F. Cargill and G. C. Rausser, 'Temporal Price Behavior in Futures Markets', *Journal of Finance*, vol. 30, 1975.)

4. It may be noted, incidentally, that limitations on the daily movement of futures prices, imposed by regulatory agencies or by exchanges, can introduce 'trends' in recorded futures prices: what might otherwise have been a single large increase (decrease) in the price of a futures can be transformed into a succession of smaller increases (decreases) in the recorded prices. Neither the frequency of impact of such restrictions nor the duration of their distorting effects in the markets studied by Cargill and Rausser is known. Typically, the imposed constraints on daily price movements do not operate for contracts in their delivery month. It may be noted further that statistics of values of basis may include observations which reflect artificial situations brought about by limits placed on daily price movements: the observed basis could be large, yet

no short hedging might have occurred if no one had been willing to buy futures at the constrained price.

5. Black has argued recently that the major benefit to society of futures trading is its 'side effect': 'futures prices provide a wealth of valuable information for those who produce, store, and use commodities', even if they do not take positions in the relevant futures markets. While in his view 'futures markets exist because in some situations they provide an inexpensive way to transfer risk', there are other methods for 'diversifying away' price risks, including pervasively the spreading of risk through the corporation (joint stock company). He infers that companies 'do a better job for most commodities, because organised futures markets don't even exist for most commodities'. (F. Black, 'The Pricing of Commodity Contracts', *Journal of Financial Economics*, vol. 3, 1976.)

6. H. G. Johnson has made an interesting contribution to the question whether destabilising speculators must lose money. He considers the question in both partial-equilibrium and general-equilibrium frameworks. He stresses the difficulties and ambiguities involved in attempts to distinguish between 'speculators' and others. (H. G. Johnson, 'Destabilizing Speculation: A General Equilibrium Approach', *Journal of Political Economy*, vol. 84, 1976.)

7. For a detailed study of futures trading in grains in London, see G. L. Rees, D. W. Colenutt and C. J. Redston, *The London Grain Futures Market*, Home-Grown Cereals Authority, London, 1976.

NOTES

1 Quoted in Glamann, 1974, p. 512. See also Haccoû, 1947, ch. 2. (References in the text and notes are listed in the Bibliography, pp. 225–32.)
2 See, for example, Hauser, 1974, esp. pp. 145–8, 184–5.
3 Information on the origins and development of various futures markets is to be found in: Dumbell, 1927; Dantwala, 1937; Irwin, 1954; Liverpool Cotton Association, 1957, pp. 107–304, 1958, pp. 135–291; London Metal Exchange, 1958; Radi, 1957; Snape, 1962; Rees, 1972; Vicziany, 1975.
4 Estimate by Gunnelson, quoted in Kofi, 1973, p. 584.
5 Sandor, 1973, p. 119. Comprehensive statistics relating to those futures markets in the United States subject to regulation by the Commodity Exchange Authority are published annually by the Authority. No similar source is available for other markets in the United States or elsewhere.
6 R. J. Gare, letter in *The Times*, 14 Feb. 1975.
7 The list is based in part on International Chamber of Commerce, 1956.
8 For location of futures markets throughout the world before 1939, see Haccoû, 1947, *passim*.
9 This condition is not true of forward contracting in stock market indexes, facilities for which are provided by the Forward Contract Exchange Company Ltd of Amsterdam. Such forward contracting has several features in common with futures trading in commodities, including the use of a clearing system. At present contracting facilities are available for the New York and Tokyo Dow–Jones indexes and for the *Financial Times* Industrial Ordinary Share Index. The reader will be able to make the necessary adjustments in the text to accommodate such forward contracting, which might well be extended to include insurance premiums, for example.
10 Weight or volume tolerances within prescribed limits are generally allowed, as in most other commodity contracts.
11 Earlier, lead and zinc contracts stipulated delivery within half-months, i.e. first half or second half of month.
12 See Hoffman, 1932, pp. 284–5, for the development of difference systems in cotton futures contracts in the United States. In the so-called mixed contract introduced in Liverpool in 1956, fixed premia and discounts were specified for different growths of American-type cotton. The contract was designed to minimise the impact of the United States government's cotton price policy. See Yamey, 1959. The East India Jute and Hessian Exchange in 1958 adopted a form of the commercial difference system for its various contracts.
13 The premia and discounts applicable to cotton futures in the United States are based on official spot prices in various designated actuals markets.
14 When trading in copper futures re-commenced in 1953 after the Second World War, there was a single standard copper contract. Wirebars, electrolytic or fire refined, were deliverable at par; two other categories of copper were deliverable at fixed discounts of £3 and £10 per ton, that on the former reduced to £1 in 1960. In 1963 the single

contract was replaced by three separate contracts: wirebars, cathodes and fire refined (the last-named allowing delivery of a lower grade at a fixed discount of £7 per ton). These contracts were in due course replaced by a wirebars contract (as in the text) and a cathodes contract. The changes in the arrangements and the terms were designed to meet changing needs of the trade and changes in the (average) relative prices of different types of copper on the actuals market.

15 The development in 1916 of an unintended corner in the Winnipeg grain market is described in Sharp, 1940.

16 Johnson carried out statistical tests on actuals price movements to see whether a rather narrow-base coffee contract was responsible for the kind of price movements associated with deliberate or accidental squeezes. He concluded that it was not. Johnson, 1957, pp. 307–10. Islam repeated these tests for a narrow-base cotton contract in use in India in the 1930s. He also found no evidence of squeeze effects. Islam, 1966, pp. 60–4.

17 See Natu, 1962, pp. 71–4, for data on Indian exchanges. Haccoû, 1949, appendix 1, has data on deliveries on markets in several countries before the Second World War.

18 For an example in the cocoa market where purchases of multi-grade futures contracts were used to secure delivery of actuals, because importers lacked confidence in the ability of certain exporters to fulfil forward actuals contracts, see Yamey, 1954, pp. 35–6. See also Dominion of Canada, 1931, p. 37.

19 In the London rubber market sale of futures by open outcry was introduced only in 1974. Before then sales were by private treaty on the floor of the exchange.

20 Until 1974 the London rubber market did not use a clearing house. The London Metal Exchange does not use a clearing house. It relies on its selection of members and the limited term of forward trading (i.e. no more than three months ahead) to avoid risks of default. The now defunct London shellac futures market also did not use a clearing house.

21 Rates of commission payable by non-members on a purchase and sale for selected futures contracts on United States exchanges in 1969 worked out as follows: 0.44 cents per bushel, wheat; 0.12 cents per pound, pork bellies; 0.3 cents per pound, orange juice; 0.05 cents per pound, potatoes; .10 cents per pound, copper. Source: Teweles *et al.*, 1969, pp. 18–20.

22 For studies of the design and modification of contract terms, see Federal Trade Commission, 1954 (coffee); Powers, 1967 (pork bellies); Ward, 1971 (orange juice); and Sandor, 1973 (plywood). Several of the matters considered in the preceding pages are illustrated by a recent development in the London Terminal Sugar Market, in which the main futures contract is for raw sugar (the terms of which have been changed from time to time to accommodate changes in the marketing of sugar: see Snape, 1962, and Rees, 1972, ch. 10). The Paris white (refined) sugar market ceased operations in December 1974. There was an unsatisfied need for hedging facilities, and the London exchange decided to meet it by means of an ingenious innovation. A new contract,

known as the white sugar conversion, has been traded since the middle of July 1975. It relates to the conversion of raw sugar into refined sugar, and therefore by itself does not correspond to anything which can be delivered in an actuals market. Delivery of the appropriate refined sugar can be effected only where the seller has sold an equal amount of raw contracts and conversions.

23 The analogy was used in Emery, 1896, pp. 136–7. See also Houthakker, 1959, p. 149.

24 For the illuminating discussion of an example of a change in the governing grade and its consequences, see Working, 1954. See also Johnson, 1957.

25 A commonly quoted actuals price for Maine potatoes is for potatoes at Presque Isle, Maine, while the potato futures contract in New York is for delivery in New York City. As is well known to those concerned the maturity basis is positive in this market because of the transport costs included in the actuals price. See United States Department of Agriculture, 1958, pp. 38–42.

26 The direction of movement of wheat into or out of storage affects the relation of the spot actuals price to the matured futures price in Chicago when the former is quoted on an 'on track' basis and the latter on an ex-warehouse basis. Such changes in maturity basis are reasonably forseeable. See Working, 1953*a*, p. 322, n. 17.

27 The post-war Bombay cotton contract has undergone a number of changes in its provisions regarding premia and discounts. Some of these changes have been required by government, and have been designed, ineffectively, to moderate increases in the price of cotton in the actuals market. The provisions have frequently caused a large negative value in the maturity basis. On the development of the provisions and on their implications, see Natu, 1962, ch. IV; Pavaskar, 1969, ch. VI; Islam, 1973.

28 See, for example, Blau, 1944, p. 10.

29 Examples in the present volume are the papers of Kaldor, 1939; Peston and Yamey, 1960; and Stein, 1961. See also Telser, 1958. For reviews of theories, see Venkataramanan, 1965, and Goss, 1972*a*.

30 For a theoretical and empirical study of the short-run supply price of grain storage, see Paul, 1970. See also Brennan, 1958, and Telser, 1958. The costs of feeding and maintaining feeder cattle to produce beef cattle, or the costs of processing soybeans into soybean products, are analogous to the costs of carrying a commodity physically unchanged over a period of time. In each case value is added (subject to uncertainty) in the course of the activity. For relevant analyses, and their implications for futures trading, see Paul and Wesson, 1966 (soybeans); and Ehrich, 1969 (cattle).

31 See Working, 1948, esp. p. 14: 'The idea that a futures market *should* quote different prices for different future dates in accordance with developments anticipated between them cannot be valid when stocks must be carried from one date to another.' See also, Samuelson, 1957.

32 For examples, see Yamey, 1959 (cotton in Liverpool) and Johnson, 1957, pp. 319–20, esp. p. 320, n. 33 (coffee in New York).

33 For more detailed discussion, see Yamey, 1971, pp. 423–4.

34 On convenience yield, see Telser, 1967, pp. 135–6, and Yamey, 1971, pp. 418–19.

35 Working, 1953*a* and *b*. Although credit should be given to Working for drawing attention to the carrying-charge or arbitrage type of hedging (described in the text), the essential point was made in Hoffman, 1932, p. 405.

36 See also Hoffman, 1932, p. 413; and Gray, 1960*b*, p. 301.

37 Working's category of 'operational hedging' seems to be similar to routine hedging, except that the typical duration of the hedge is short (Working, 1962, p. 439).

38 For a discussion of the potentialities for routine hedging in potato futures, whether before or after harvest, see Gray, 1972, pp. 328–37. That vertical integration in certain circumstances can reduce the variability of profits in a manner analogous to routine hedging is discussed in Oi and Hurter, 1965, pp. 57–67.

39 See, for example, Heifner, 1966.

40 Working and Gray, in developing the concept of carrying-charge hedging, tended at first to stress the importance of this type of hedging and to diminish that of the hedging of price risks (Working, 1953*b*, p. 561; Gray, 1960*a*, p. 77). Thus, Gray wrote in 1960 that 'most hedgers are arbitragers trying to get ahead in the world,' and not 'a queer sort of conservative commercial idiot striving always and only to break even' (Gray, 1960*a*, p. 77). However, in 1967 he wrote: 'Hedgers value futures markets chiefly for their convenience, . . . and are undoubtedly willing to pay something over the mere cost of market operation . . . in order to have this convenience' (Gray, 1967, p. 181). It is difficult to reconcile this latter statement with the earlier statement about the ubiquity of arbitrage hedging (with its accent on profit). Specific examples of hedging in connection with market risks are to be found in Gray, 1960*a*, p. 76 (coffee, wheat); and Working, 1970, p. 36 (onions, by growers).

41 See Ehrich, 1966 (wheat, 1953–63); Telser, 1967 (wheat, corn, soybeans, 1952–63). Both studies allow for the volume of stocks held commercially, and Telser allows for the rate of interest. Rutledge introduces in his regression analysis an explanatory variable the 'expected basis change'. This is proxied by the basis change actually experienced. He obtains a coefficient of the expected sign for soybeans (Rutledge, 1972). It is likely that the actual basis change is highly positively correlated with the opening basis. He also introduces, analogously, the expected change in the actuals price as an explanatory variable, and finds a negative association. This is interesting in the context of selective hedging, provided it is appropriate to treat the change in price which actually occurred during a period as the price change *expected* by traders at the beginning of the period.

42 Studies of this type include: Howell and Watson, 1938 (cotton); Howell, 1948 (grain); Yamey, 1951 (cotton); Graf, 1953 (wheat, corn and oats); Snape, 1962 (sugar); Venkataramanan, 1965 (cotton); Islam, 1966 (cotton); Snape, 1968 (wool); and Pavaskar, 1969 (cotton). Pavaskar's

study allows for estimated carrying costs in the calculation of hedging outcomes.

43 This approach would be a modified form of Gray's 'buy premiums' programme which he developed in another context (Gray, 1961*a*, p. 255).

44 Gray presented a test for 'expectational bias', which purported to assess the effectiveness of a market for arbitrage hedging (Gray, 1960*a*). While the concept of expectational bias and the test itself are of interest in the context of the theory of normal backwardation, it has been shown that the test is not an appropriate test of the effectiveness of a market in relation to arbitrage hedging: Snape and Yamey, 1965; Yamey, 1968.

45 Yamey shows that these conclusions are not affected materially by the possibility that more favourable opportunities may occur for closing out the hedge before the futures contract has matured (a corollary of the upper limit to the value of a contango), or by the possibility that the volume of forward sales commitments eligible for long hedging may be influenced by the basis (Yamey, 1971).

46 This conclusion should strictly be modified to allow for long hedging of actuals commitments in grades other than that 'governing' the prices of the futures contract. The modification would not materially alter the conclusion.

47 The failure of alternative futures contracts to attract sufficient business can be illustrated for cotton in pre-war India (Dantwala, 1937), and for wool tops in the United Kingdom. In the United States, a Western cattle contract, providing for delivery in California, failed (Minger, 1970, pp. 148–51). In the United States, trading in the smaller markets in Memphis (soybean meal) and New York (soybean oil) ceased in the early 1960s as hedgers shifted their business to the larger Chicago market (Gray, 1961*b*, p. 22).

48 See, for example, Working, 1970, p. 39 (onions), and Futrell, 1970, p. 74 (cattle).

49 An interesting example is that of wheat, with futures markets in Chicago, Kansas City and Minneapolis. Gray explains that the contracts in the latter two markets allow 'closer' hedges both in the geographical sense and also in the sense that the contracts specify classes of wheat 'that more nearly represent the needs' of the hedgers than the Chicago contract. The narrowness of the two markets, which otherwise would be a disadvantage to hedgers, is off-set by the ability for unexpected volumes of hedging to be absorbed by traders who shift them to the more active Chicago market (Gray, 1961*b*). The existence of futures markets for the same commodity in different countries provides further examples.

50 Gray conjectured that a successful flour futures market was not established in the United States because there was a successful wheat futures market and 'wheat and flour prices correlate closely.' He noted that trading in wool tops futures was waning as trading in greasy wool futures was waxing. He observed that futures trading in processed products flourishes only where product prices are not closely correlated with the prices of the commodities themselves, for example cotton and

cottonseed products, soybeans and soybean products. He expressed doubts whether the relatively new live hogs contract would flourish in the face of the thriving pork belly futures market. Gray, 1970, p. 131.

51 But see the qualification made in Houthakker, 1959, pp. 157–8.

52 For fuller treatment of this matter, see Johnson, 1957, pp. 310–18, and Yamey, 1971, pp. 416–17.

53 It will be noted that Houthakker's explanation hinges on the erroneous premise that the outcome of a long hedge depends in part on the value of the opening basis.

54 For a full discussion of the treatment of hedging by Keynes, Hicks and Kaldor, see Goss, 1972*a*, ch. 1.

55 For a more extensive discussion, see Goss, 1972*a*, pp. 61–7.

56 Goss shows that while the measure of risk used by Stein (and also by Johnson) is an efficient measure of risk for dealing with changes in expectations (with given current actuals and futures prices), it is not an efficient measure for dealing with changes in current actuals and futures prices (with given expectations) (Goss, 1972*a*, pp. 66–7).

57 For a full discussion, see Goss, 1972*a*, ch. 6. He shows (pp. 83–4) that, while Johnson's paper does not develop the individual's demand and supply functions for actuals and futures nor deal with price determination in either market, the model could be extended appropriately. He shows also that the model is not suitable for adaptation to the situation of a trader who prefers risk.

58 For other treatments of hedging in economic models, see Telser, 1955; Ward and Fletcher, 1971; Rutledge, 1972.

59 See, for example, Smith, 1776, bk. 4, ch. 5, Digression concerning the Corn Trade; Mill, 1848, bk. 4, ch. 2, secs 4, 5; Marshall, 1932, p. 262; Lerner, 1944, ch. 8; Friedman, 1953, pp. 175–7. The (Canadian) report on Trading in Grain Futures noted: 'It was brought to our attention by Professor Boyle that in a case before the Supreme Court in 1922, twenty-two economists declared their belief, by affidavit, and eleven more were cited in evidence as teaching, that with infrequent and minor exceptions, futures trading has a marked tendency to stabilize prices. . . Dr. Boyle's view was that economists generally would stand one hundred to one in favour of the view that futures trading stabilizes prices' (Dominion of Canada, 1931, p. 20).

60 McKinnon has suggested that in futures markets speculators are either not able or not willing to take up speculative positions far ahead in time, and that this reduces the social value of futures trading. He argues the case for government intervention to remedy the defect by supplementing the activities of speculators (McKinnon, 1967). For a commentary on McKinnon's article, see Poole, 1970. For a view somewhat similar to McKinnon's, see Houthakker, 1967; for a commentary on his specific proposal, see Richardson and Farris, 1973. It is evident that government intervention will stabilize prices only if the government authority is more accurate at price forecasting than the unaided market.

61 See the controversy between Telser and Cootner: Telser, 1958; Cootner, 1960; Telser, 1960. See also Gray, 1961*a*, and Dusak, 1973, esp. sec. 5. Houthakker, 1957, reports on a more limited study than Rockwell's,

and with different conclusions. For a critique, see Gray, 1961*a*, pp. 251–3. In 1967 Working put forward the view that speculators as a group *do* tend to gain from hedgers, and that they do so by meeting the needs of hedgers. 'The income flow from hedgers to speculators is much larger than has previously been estimated, and has been positive and substantial even in markets in which the seasonal trend of futures prices by itself has afforded no income, or has been a source of loss, to speculators as a group.' The additional source of gain is the 'execution cost' of hedging – the effects on prices of hedging orders to sell or buy (Working, 1967). These effects tend to be obscured in calculations of speculators' profits based on reported prices (for example, the closing prices on particular days) rather than on transactions prices. Working once again has drawn attention to an important issue. But it is fair to say that the quantitative significance of execution costs in the present context has not yet been demonstrated conclusively, although it is plausible. See also Gray, 1972, pp. 334–7.

62 Studies of forecasting accuracy, based on the observed difference between forward futures prices and the eventual actuals or matured futures prices include: Emery, 1896, p. 132; Smith, 1922, p. 142; Dow, 1941; Pavaskar, 1965. The following studies measure forecasting accuracy by means of regressions of the eventual matured futures price on the forward futures price: Tomek and Gray, 1970; Kofi, 1973. For an exchange on the former, see Heifner, 1971, and Gray and Tomek, 1971.

63 Three futures markets in India, cotton, castorseed and groundnuts, for periods of about ten years up to the mid-1960s, showed a strong tendency towards under-estimation of the eventual price. Prices generally rose during the period. Pavaskar, 1966.

64 'It is not so many years ago since a large and representative meeting of western American farmers passed a resolution against options [a form of futures] on the score that they tended to unfairly reduce the price of wheat, and it was just three weeks after that meeting that a convention of the National Association of American Millers, attended by some 500 members, was held in Minneapolis, and passed a resolution condemning options, on the ground that they unfairly raised the price of wheat.' *Bradstreet's*, 22 Aug. 1896; quoted in Emery, 1896, p. 118.

65 'Evidence was adduced to show that both spreading and scalping operations greatly assisted the market in making it more liquid so that those requiring hedges were able to obtain them on a more satisfactory basis' (Dominion of Canada, 1931, p. 32). See also Working, 1967.

66 Working, 1960*b*. See also Irwin, 1935, referred to by Working. The need for adjustment of the published statistics of open positions by categories of traders is explained in Working, 1960*b*, pp. 191–4, and Larson, 1961. The history of the futures market in refrigerated eggs in Chicago from 1947 to 1961 'appears to be a direct refutation of the well-supported hypothesis that the size of a futures market is related to the amount of hedging business that it attracts'. Hedging use declined while speculative open positions increased. Miracle, 1972.

67 Irwin, 1937, p. 267. Irwin's (p. 268 n.) general assessment of futures trading is of interest: 'The writer's view is that they have a considerable

net social value as things are, but that this net value may be increased greatly by bringing the undesirable kinds of trading under control.'

68 On 'amateur' speculators and speculation on futures markets, see Stewart, 1949; Smidt, 1965; Johnson, 1972. Johnson's study of the potato market suggests that 'the role of uninformed traders is minor in the total process' (*ibid.*, p. 309).

69 Irwin's views are somewhat similar to Keynes's views of professional speculators in the stock market 'who are more concerned with forecasting the next shift of market sentiment than with a reasonable estimate of the future yield of capital-assets'. Keynes also stressed the 'influence of purchasers largely ignorant of what they are buying' (Keynes, 1936, p. 316). It may be noted that in two important respects commodity futures markets differ from stock markets. First, on the former a speculator can both 'go with the market' when he thinks it is wrong and also simultaneously back his market assessment by taking an opposite position in a futures contract maturing further ahead. He thus, if correct, gains twice. But the second gain arises from 'correct' behaviour which tends to off-set the results of the 'incorrect' behaviour. Facilities for forward buying and selling are limited on stock markets. Secondly, in commodity markets there is a continuous stream of relevant market information (about stocks, current rates of usage, crop forecasts and so on). This makes it difficult for inappropriate price levels to persist for long. There is no corresponding stream of information about individual securities.

70 Praetz, 1975, lists and discusses a number of studies. See also Brinegar, 1970. Brinegar applied a statistical test for continuity, devised by Working, to futures prices of wheat, corn and rye in several periods. His general conclusion (pp. 53–4) is that 'our statistical results have strengthened the belief that speculative prices reflect rational appraisals of all available information and that they do provide a valid economic function.' More generally, see Cootner, 1964, esp. the editor's introductions to the various sections; also Labys and Granger, 1970.

71 Larson concludes his study (Larson, 1960, p. 324) by observing that the absence of market continuity in price series and the evidence of limited price movements could be consistent with the operation as dominant price-forming influences of misinformation or pure guesses!

72 For a review of some of these studies, see Brinegar, 1970, ch. 2. See also Powers, 1970.

73 See also Gray, 1963.

74 Naik, 1970, also includes studies of linseed and hessian prices. Pavaskar, 1968, also deals with groundnut prices in India.

75 According to John Stuart Mill: 'The operations . . . of speculative dealers are useful to the public whenever profitable to themselves; and though they are sometimes injurious to the public, by heightening the fluctuations which their more usual office is to alleviate, yet whenever this happens the speculators are the greatest losers. The interest, in short, of the speculators as a body, coincides with the interest of the public. . .' Mill, 1848, bk. 4, ch. 2, sec. 5.

76 The earlier contributions include: Baumol, 1957; Telser, 1959; Baumol, 1959; Stein, 1961*b*; Kemp, 1963; Glahe, 1966. For an instructive exposition and analysis of the literature, see Steinmann, 1970, pp. 44–59.

77 For the importance of the level of transactions costs, see also Schimmler, 1974, pp. 75, 77, 79.

78 Aliber, 1964. The analysis concerns the two periods 1937–41 and 1957–62.

79 Yamey, 1966; with a reply, Aliber, 1966.

80 Quoted in Georgescu-Roegen, 1958, p. 12.

81 See Georgescu-Roegen, 1958, and Ozga, 1965, pp. 78 ff.

82 See also Georgescu-Roegen, 1958, p. 13.

83 See Hawtrey, 1940.

84 E.g. Kaldor, 1939, and also Brennan, 1958, and Telser, 1958.

85 Kaldor, 1939; Dow, 1940. The old adage that 'with identical expectations there can be no [inter-speculator] trading' (for example, Hawtrey, 1940, p. 205) is easily seen to be unfounded, as such trading can occur with heterogeneity of expectations and/or attitudes to risk (Goss, 1972*a*).

86 Kaldor, 1939. Other costs have to be covered for speculation in actuals.

87 See Goss, 1972*a*, pp. 77, 83–4.

88 In the Johnson model, the result depends upon $u_j = 0$. (For u_j see p. 88.)

89 Working's carrying-charge hedgers who buy actuals and sell futures in anticipation of a decrease in the basis are not assumed to fulfil any particular equilibrium condition in deciding their market positions. The description of their behaviour, however, is consistent with maximisation of an expected gain, and it would be a simple matter to formalise a model by introducing an explicit basis expectation and placing appropriate restrictions on risk and storage-cost variables. The same comment applies to Gray's speculators who 'buy discounts' and 'sell premiums' (Gray, 1961*a*). These individuals are also speculating on the expected basis change, although no actuals counterpart is involved.

90 In the models considered above, the speculating individual is concerned only with expected return and uncertainty in relation to the actuals and futures of the commodity in question. Dusak, on the other hand, applies the portfolio approach which places emphasis on a particular asset's contribution – positive, negative or zero – to the risk of a large and well diversified portfolio of assets (in fact, all assets, in principle). She presents estimates of the 'systematic risk' for a sample of wheat, corn and soybean futures contracts over the period 1952–67. Dusak, 1973.

91 'Belief that the price was subject to a degree of producer control led the Chicago Mercantile Exchange, a few years ago, to reject a proposal for establishment of a futures market in concentrated orange juice, a commodity for which producers desired hedging facilities' (Working, 1960*b*, p. 202, n. 21). A successful futures market was eventually established in New York. In 1960 Gray (1960*b*, p. 309) wrote the following about the New York coffee futures market at a time when the

Brazilian government's policies greatly affected coffee prices: 'But because speculators tend, wisely, to avoid a market where the price is subject to arbitrary change by any group (or government) that holds dominant influence, the coffee market was left with little ability to carry the load of risk that some private holders of coffee stocks wished to shift to it.'

92 The development of refrigeration has, of course, eliminated futures trading in such commodities as mess pork which were superseded by refrigerated products (Working, 1960*b*, p. 189).

93 On detailed studies of the determination of contract terms, see references in note 22 above; also Working, 1954.

94 See Sandor, 1973.

95 The general economics literature using the property-rights approach includes Demsetz, 1967 and 1968; Cheung, 1969; Furubotn and Pejovich, 1972.

96 See Cowing, 1965, ch. 1. This book traces the history of regulation and pressures for regulation up to 1936.

97 The report of the enquiry, largely favourable to futures trading, is Dominion of Canada, 1931.

98 For a study of certain aspects of the relation between devaluation and futures trading, see Dominguez, 1972.

99 In the United States, trading in onion futures was prohibited by law in 1958. For discussions of the background to, and effects of, the prohibition, see Working, 1960*a* and 1963. Attacks on potato futures trading are analysed in Gray, 1964. For prohibition of futures trading in certain commodities in India, see Natu, 1962. In Japan, rice futures trading was terminated shortly before the Second World War, as part of the introduction of national economic planning arrangements. Its revival has not been permitted. The re-commencement of futures trading in cotton in Liverpool after the closure during the Second World War was prohibited by legislation which established the statutory cotton-trading monopoly, the Raw Cotton Commission. Traditional hostile sentiments to futures trading contributed to this legislation. The Commission's monopoly powers were terminated in 1952. See Wiseman and Yamey, 1956.

100 Some exchanges have themselves introduced limits to daily price movements. Such limitations serve to protect the clearing house (and hence members) from defaults which might be caused by large changes in price if they occur too rapidly for clearing-house margins to be adjusted in time.

101 On the prescription of margins, see Telser and Yamey, 1965, pp. 656–7.

Section One

Hedging, Stock-holding and Inter-Temporal Price Relationships

1 Forward Trading as a Means of Overcoming Disequilibrium

J. R. HICKS

This is an extract from J. R. Hicks, Value and Capital, *2nd ed., Oxford: Oxford University Press, 1946, reprinted by permission of the publisher. It is the fourth section (pp. 135–9) of Chapter* X, *'Equilibrium and Disequilibrium'. In the preceeding section four causes of disequilibrium are distinguished. The first (and 'perhaps the least important') arises 'when different people's price-expectations are inconsistent'. The second, 'perhaps the most interesting cause of all', arises when different people's plans are inconsistent. The third arises when people 'foresee their own wants incorrectly, or make wrong estimates of the results of the technical processes of production'. The fourth arises when 'their sense of risk may have prevented entrepreneurs from producing those quantities of output, or those sorts of output, which they would have produced if they had been more confident that their anticipations were right'.*

This classification of the causes of disequilibrium has a distinct bearing upon the great dispute about the relative efficiency of different types of economic organization. The third and fourth sources of waste must be found in every conceivable economic system, Capitalist or Socialist, Liberal or Authoritarian. Even Robinson Crusoe would not be free of them; he could not foresee when he might be ill, or when his crops might fail; and he would be troubled in his search for the most perfect adjustment of means to ends by the uncertainty of such events in the future. Even the most perfectly organized economic system (whatever that may be) will be thrown out of its stride by harvest fluctuations, inventions, or political upheavals. It would appear at first sight, on the other hand, that the first and second sources are peculiar to a system of private enterprise. In a completely centralized system they would be removed. But a completely centralized system is a mere figment of the imagination; every government delegates its authority to some extent. Thus in practice the different parts of a State machine can get out of step, just as entrepreneurs can get out of step. Whether capitalism is less or more efficient than socialism depends very much upon the efficiency of socialism. That is still rather an open question.

It is often supposed that capitalism is entirely devoid of any organization for the co-ordination of plans; but that is not altogether the case. A way does exist, within the orbit of private enterprise, whereby expectations and plans can be (at least partially) co-ordinated. This is the device of forward trading (including not only dealings in forward markets, commonly so called, but also all orders given in advance, and all long-term contracts). It is very instructive, even at this stage, to pay some attention to the working of this sort of co-ordination, and to examine why it is not more efficient, and its range more extensive, than it is in fact.

A system of private enterprise is perfectly conceivable, in which there would be no forward trading, all transactions being for immediate delivery ('Spot'). In such a 'Spot Economy', nothing would be fixed up in advance, and co-ordination would be left very much to chance. Only current demands and supplies would be matched on the market; people would have to base their expectations of future prices, as best they were able, upon these current prices, and any other information available. Of course, even so, the amount of disequilibrium likely to arise need not be very considerable. If plans are mostly of a fairly stationary type, so that most people are planning to buy and sell much the same quantities in future periods as in the current period, not much disequilibrium due to inconsistency will arise, so long as they merely expect a continuance of current prices. Even if plans are not stationary, but the quantities people plan to buy or sell have some tendency to increase or diminish with futurity, this will not necessarily lead to inconsistency disequilibrium, if people can make good guesses at the relevant plans of other people. This is a good deal more to ask, but still observation of the current conduct of business men does give some clue to their plans, so that something of this sort probably does take place to some extent. When firms are planning a large extension of their operations, it is impossible to keep it dark altogether. Yet this is not much to go on. When conditions are at all disturbed, a spot economy must be expected to get out of equilibrium to a considerable extent.

It is possible, at the other extreme, to conceive of an economy in which, for a considerable period ahead, everything was fixed up in advance. If all goods were bought and sold forward, not only would current demands and supplies be matched, but also planned demands and supplies. In such a 'Futures Economy', the first two kinds of disequilibrium would be absent. Plans would be co-ordinated; and, for practical purposes, expectations would be co-ordinated too. (The price which would govern a firm's planned output for a particular future week would be the futures price, and not its own individual price-expectation.) Thus inconsistency disequilibrium would be removed; but the possibility of disequilibrium due to unexpected changes in wants or resources would not be removed. People would be under contract to buy or sell certain goods on the second Monday. But when the second Monday arrived, they might be unwilling or unable to buy or sell the amounts of goods contracted for. They would then be obliged to make additional spot sales or purchases, or to offset their contracts by spot transactions. Thus a spot market would come into existence, and the spot price established in that market would probably be different from the futures price which had previously been established for that Monday.

Now people know that they cannot escape the third kind of disequilibrium by forward trading; and this it is, in the end, which limits the extent to which forward trading can be carried on in practice. They know that the demands and supplies which can be fixed up in advance for any particular date may have little relation to the demands and supplies which will actually be forthcoming at that date; and, in particular, they know that they cannot foretell at all exactly what quantities they will themselves desire to buy or sell at a future period. Consequently the ordinary business man only enters into a forward contract if by so doing he can 'hedge' – that is to say, if the forward transaction lessens the riskiness of his position. And this will only happen in those cases where he is somehow otherwise committed to making a sale or purchase at the date in question; if he has already planned such a sale or purchase, and if he has already done something which will make it difficult for him to alter his plan. Now there are quite sufficient technical rigidities in the process of production to make it certain that a number of entrepreneurs will want to hedge their sales for this reason; supplies in the near future are largely governed by decisions taken in the past, so that if these planned supplies can be covered by forward sales, risk is reduced. But although the same thing sometimes happens with planned purchases as well, it is almost inevitably rarer; technical conditions give the entrepreneur a much freer hand about the acquisition of inputs (which are largely needed to start new processes) than about the completion of outputs (whose process of production – in the ordinary business sense – may be already begun). Thus, while there is likely to be some desire to hedge planned purchases, it tends to be less insistent than the desire to hedge planned sales. If forward markets consisted entirely of hedgers, there would always be a tendency for a relative weakness on the demand side; a smaller proportion of planned purchases than of planned sales would be covered by forward contracts.[1]

But for this very reason forward markets rarely consist entirely of hedgers. The futures price (say, for one month's delivery) which would be made by the transactions of hedgers alone would be determined by causes that have nothing to do with the causes ordinarily determining market price; it would therefore be widely different from the spot price which any sensible person would expect to rule in a month's time, and would ordinarily be much below that expected price. Futures prices are therefore nearly always made partly by *speculators*, who seek a profit by buying futures when the futures price is below the spot price they expect to rule on the corresponding date; their action tends to raise the futures price to a more reasonable level. But it is of the essence of speculation, as opposed to hedging, that the speculator puts himself into a more risky position as a result of his forward trading – he need not have ventured into forward dealing at all, and would have been safer if he had not done so. He will therefore only be willing to go on buying futures so long as the futures price remains definitely below the spot price he expects; for it is the difference between these prices which he can expect to receive as a return for his risk-bearing, and it will not be worth his while to undertake the risk if the prospective return is too small.

Mr. Keynes has pointed out the consequences of this in an important passage of his *Treatise on Money*. In 'normal' conditions, when demand and supply conditions are expected to remain unchanged, and therefore the spot price is expected to be about the same in a month's time as it is to-day, the futures price for one month's delivery is bound to be below the spot price now ruling. The difference between these two prices (the current spot price and the currently fixed futures price) is called by Mr. Keynes 'normal backwardation'.[2] It measures the amount which hedgers have to hand over to speculators in order to persuade the speculators to take over the risks of the price-fluctuations in question. Ultimately, therefore, it measures the cost of the co-ordination achieved by forward trading; if the cost is very heavy, potential hedgers will prefer not to hedge.

The same sorts of considerations limit those other kinds of transactions which we have classified as types of forward trading, although they are not usually so regarded. For example, it is usually to the interest of an employee to 'hedge' future sales of his labour – as he would do, if he could secure engagement for a long period. But it is not to the interest of his employer to make such contracts, unless he derives some particular advantage from so doing – as he would do, if this particular employee were difficult to replace. In this way we can fit into our analysis that particular type of long-term contract which distinguishes (more or less) the salary-earner from the wage-earner.[3]

NOTES

1 This congenital weakness of the demand side of course applies only to forward markets in commodities, and will not apply (for instance) to

forward markets in foreign exchange. However, in all forward markets there is likely to be a tendency for hedgers to predominate on one side or the other over long periods. No forward market can do without the speculative element.

2 Keynes, *Treatise on Money*, vol. ii, pp. 142–4. In market language, there is said to be a 'backwardation' if the futures price is below the spot price, a 'contango' in the reverse case. It will be evident that a contango can only arise when spot prices are expected to rise sharply in the future; this usually means that spot prices are *abnormally* low.

3 Both in this case of labour contracts, and in the case of ordinary forward markets in commodities, there is another kind of uncertainty which limits forward dealing. This is uncertainty about the exact quality of the goods promised to be supplied at the future date. Organized produce markets adopt elaborate devices to mitigate this uncertainty, but all such devices are costly, and the cost easily becomes prohibitive.

2 Futures Trading and Hedging

HOLBROOK WORKING

A good deal of difference of opinion on the utility of futures trading persists even among economists who have studied the subject rather closely. Some, at least, of this disagreement is traceable to imperfect concepts that emerged in connection with early academic studies of futures trading. Such concepts have tended to survive on the strength of their partial validity, despite shortcomings evident to the well-informed. Businessmen and others who are intimately acquainted with futures trading and its consequences tend to realize (often unconsciously) the defects of such imperfect concepts, to employ the concepts so far as they are valid and useful, and to avoid drawing any seriously mistaken conclusions from them. People who have little direct knowledge of futures trading and its observable results have no such protection against false inferences. If, like most economists, they are accustomed to rely on deductions from what seem to be well-established premises, they are especially vulnerable to the imperfections of basic concepts.

ORIGIN AND NATURE OF FUTURES TRADING

Much of the popular suspicion of futures trading stems from a sense of mystery associated with it. It is in this respect, and some others, rather like bank credit. Futures trading, like banking, is an institution that developed as a contribution to efficiency of a relatively free competitive economy. A primitive form of futures trading emerged spontaneously in various market centers at least as early as 1850. Only in the grain trade at Chicago, however, was the demand for a means of hedging commercial risks then strong and persistent enough to permit this unconventional form of trade to survive the fluctuations in speculative interest, overcome conservative opposition, and live through the stormy period of experimentation necessary to put it on a firm footing. When that had been accomplished at Chicago, the new form of trading

* From *American Economic Review*, vol. LXIII, 1953, pp. 314–43. (Only the first three sections are reprinted here.) Reprinted by permission.

was soon adopted at other market centers and for other commodities than grains.[1]

Futures trading in commodities may be defined as *trading conducted under special regulations and conventions, more restrictive than those applied to any other class of commodity transactions, which serve primarily to facilitate hedging and speculation by promoting exceptional convenience and economy of the transactions.*

This may seem to some an inadequate definition. It does not say that futures trading is buying and selling for deferred delivery; it draws only a slender line of distinction between futures transactions and 'cash' transactions (dealings in the 'actual commodity'); and it makes the distinction between futures trading and other sorts of trading turn primarily on *purpose* rather than on more easily and objectively recognizable criteria. All of these characteristics are in fact merits of the definition.

It would be inaccurate to define futures trading as always involving purchase and sale for deferred delivery. Trading in the September wheat future, for example, is done in the month of September as well as in earlier months, and in that month if often happens that some sellers of September wheat intend to make immediate delivery, and the purchaser knows that he may expect to receive immediate delivery. The price of the future is then in fact a spot price. One might, of course, qualify the statement by saying that *most* futures trading is for deferred delivery. The statement would then be true, but objectionable in a definition because it would focus attention on a characteristic (deferred delivery) that has little distinguishing value. A great deal of buying and selling that is *not* futures trading involves delivery at some later time. In international commodity trade in staples, purchases calling for delivery two or three months or more in the future are commonplace, quite apart from true futures trading, and independently of whether or not futures trading exists in the commodity. Much of the trade in manufactured products as diverse as flour, steel rails, and machine tools (none of which has futures trading) involves purchase on contracts entered into several months in advance of the specified delivery date; in the case of machine tools, the interval may sometimes be measured in years. Because the people who turn for enlightenment to a definition of futures trading are often unaware of the wide prevalence of forward purchases (except in retail trade), the characterization 'usually for deferred delivery' would fail to be generally recognized as only slightly narrowing the area of reference, and would divert attention from more sharply distinguishing characteristics.

The definition given above does in fact distinguish clearly between futures transactions and other transactions – so clearly that there need never be any problem of identification except in such cases as appeared when futures trading was taking its first steps in evolution from other trading and was not yet clearly differentiated. The definition lacks sharpness only in the sense that it does not make futures trading appear very different from other trading. That is a merit, because futures trading in fact has no distinguishing economic characteristics except those stated in the definition, or resulting from them (such as exceptional volume of trading, frequency of transactions, and publicity of quotations).

If a reader feels that the foregoing definition does not distinguish strongly enough between futures trading and other trading in commodities, it may be either because he underestimates the remarkable convenience and economy which are the primary distinguishing characteristics of futures trading, or because he mistakenly believes it to have peculiar characteristics that it does not have. Its extraordinary economy is illustrated by data cited below, in another connection, indicating that a trader in cotton futures could make a very satisfactory net income on the basis of a *gross* profit margin of about 23 cents per thousand dollars worth of transactions – a gross profit of one-fortieth of one per cent.

Mistaken impressions of the difference between futures trading and other trading have been furthered by a language difficulty that arises in connection with the frequent need to speak collectively of all-other-sorts of trading, as against futures trading. There is no good and convenient word for the purpose – and perhaps there cannot be, simply because the need is to designate all of a heterogeneous category except one special, narrow segment of it. 'Nonfutures' would be an accurate and transparent term for the purpose, but an awkward one. In this situation, convenience has been served most commonly by using the word 'cash' to mean 'nonfutures'. The practice probably originated in the Chicago grain trade, contemporaneously with the origin of sustained futures trading. Its application involved two shifts of meaning: (1) use of 'cash' to designate, not immediate *payment*, as is usual, but immediate *delivery*; and (2) extension of the altered meaning to cover all terms of delivery except those involved in futures contracts. These changes left the word with no logical merit for the purpose except its brevity. In the cotton trade, the common word for 'nonfutures' is 'spot'. This is inherently more confusing than use of the term 'cash,' because 'spot' continues to be used in the trade also in its specific sense of 'immediate delivery'; but the grain trade has lost such potential relative advantage of clarity as it might have had, by using 'cash' also as equivalent to 'spot' in the sense of 'immediate delivery.'[2] Most seriously misleading is the frequent resort to use of 'actual' to mean 'nonfutures,' as when purchases on terms other than those of futures contracts are distinguished as purchases of the 'actual commodity.' That expression is used to *include* forward purchases other than on futures contracts, even though all forward purchases are alike in the fact that there is no acquisition of the actual commodity at the time of purchase.[3] Like the other expressions used for the same purpose, it is a verbal expedient only vaguely defensible in terms of the normal meaning of the expression. Futures contracts involve transactions in the actual commodity as truly as do any other forward transactions.

As regards failure of the definition to give easily and objectively recognizable criteria for identifying futures trading, it should be noted that there is no practical problem of identification except in cases of primitive futures trading, and in such cases purpose is the only available criterion;[4] otherwise, futures trading has always gone under that name, or the equivalent in another language. The definition should indicate the essential distinguishing nature of futures trading, and that is not done by mere listing of superficial technical characteristics, specified in regulations intended to promote convenience and economy. Reliance on these superficial characteristics for definition encounters also the difficulty that they have varied widely from time to time and from place to place. Consequently, definitions based on such characteristics show an historical trend toward increasing complexity and obscurity as later writers tried to remedy technical shortcomings found in earlier definitions.[5]

HEDGING AS A BASIS FOR FUTURES TRADING

An interesting conflict of evidence has emerged regarding the comparative roles of speculation and hedging in sustaining futures trading. Most of the available information prior to about 1920 encourages the view that futures trading rests primarily on an urge for speculation. Hedging is rarely mentioned except in arguments justifying the continuation of futures trading. One gains the impression that hedging, like a hitchhiker, seized the chance for a ride since speculation presented the opportunity. But as statistics have been accumulated that give appropriate quantitative information on futures markets, year in and year out, hedging begins to look like the driver, and speculation in futures like a companion going where hedging gives it opportunity to go.

The first conspicuous evidence in this direction came in studies of the Grain Futures Administration (predecessor of the present Commodity Exchange Authority) that showed the volume of open (outstanding) futures contracts in each commodity rising and falling each year in rough correspondence with the volume of the commodity in commercial hands and likely to be hedged.[6] Speculators tend to be most heavily committed in futures, not during the growing season of a crop, when prices are most variable, but some time after harvest, when large stocks have moved into commercial storage and been hedged.

As between commodities, the volume of open contracts varies likewise with the amount of the commodity that is hedged. The volume of open contracts in wheat futures in the United States during recent years has averaged about 90 million bushels, while the volume in corn futures has averaged not much over 50 million, though corn has been produced in nearly three times the volume of wheat. The reason is that much less corn than wheat gets into commercial hands (farmers rarely or never hedge the stocks that they hold). Oats, produced in volume less than half that of corn and, like corn, stored mainly on farms, has had an average volume of open futures contracts less than half that of corn.[7] So one may go through the list of commodities in which there is futures trading and find, wherever there is information on the amount of hedging use of futures markets, an unmistakable connection between size of the futures market and the amount of hedging that the market is called on to carry.[8]

Though the amount of speculation on a futures market seems to depend so much on the volume of hedging, there is also a connection in the other direction. As between different exchanges dealing in the same commodity, there is a strong tendency for hedgers to prefer to use the exchange which has the largest volume of speculative trading. We shall examine the reason for this later. As regards commodities, it may be observed that in some the volume of hedging has, at times at least, been restricted by absence of sufficient speculative interest to carry the hedges.[9] In the United States, no futures market for a commodity which is chiefly imported, has flourished like the markets for the more important domestically produced commodities. This may be not entirely because the imported commodities give less occasion for hedging, but partly because there are relatively few people in the United States who have acquired an interest in those commodities sufficient to inspire speculation in them.

When one reviews evidence on the earlier history of futures trading, making allowance for the tendency for sporadic news and comment to concentrate on the unusual, and for exceptional outbursts of speculation to draw special attention, one can find reason to think that a desire for hedging opportunities may have always provided the primary support for futures trading. It seems reasonable to suppose that a primitive form of futures trading in grains was able to survive and develop to maturity in Chicago in the middle of the last century, whereas similar trading tried somewhat earlier in Europe was abandoned, because there was much more occasion for hedging the large stocks of grain that came into commercial hands in the Chicago area than for hedging the much smaller stocks of European markets. It seems quite clear that the first successful futures trading in wheat in Great Britain was based on contracts for Californian wheat because that was the wheat which importers found most need to hedge, on account of the long periods over which importers held ownership while the wheat travelled by sailing vessel around Cape Horn to Britain.[10]

One can imagine existence of futures trading purely on the basis of desire of people to speculate; but apparently futures trading cannot long persist except on the basis of conditions that create speculative risks which somebody must carry, and which some people are led to transfer to others by hedging. The reasons for choosing thus to transfer risks deserve our attention next.

MISAPPREHENSIONS ABOUT HEDGING

It is common to suppose that hedgers exercise no part in determining the price of the commodity in which they deal, and this supposition is substantially valid as regards those who practice hedging uniformly.[11] But most hedgers are engaged in a business that requires them to keep informed on many aspects of the commodity situation, with the result that many hedgers often form quite definite opinions on price prospects. Except in firms that have a strict rule against taking hedgable risks, it is common, therefore, for stocks to be carried unhedged at times, when the responsible individual expects a price advance, and for stocks of the commodity to be hedged at other times. Some individuals and firms hedge stocks only when they are particularly fearful of price decline.

Such discretionary hedging, involving a firm in the practice of both hedging and speculation, seems to be especially prevalent among dealers and processors who handle commodities such as wool and coffee, that have relatively little public speculation in their futures markets.[12] When hedge selling in such a futures market becomes heavy, the price may readily be depressed to a point where a good many dealers and processors are attracted by the possibilities of profit through speculative holding of the commodity. Even among handlers of commodities which attract broad public participation to their futures markets, such as wheat, discretionary hedging is not uncommon.[13] Consequently the existence of futures trading in a commodity and widespread use of futures for hedging do not in fact mean that the responsibilities of price formation are shifted entirely, or even mainly, to people who deal only in the commodity futures.

A major source of mistaken notions of hedging is the conventional practice of illustrating hedging with a hypothetical example in which the price of the future bought or sold as a hedge is supposed to rise or fall by the same amount that the spot price rises or falls. Let us instead consider hedging realistically in terms of some actual prices. The prices to be used will be those for wheat at Kansas City on the first trading day of each month in which futures matured during the crop-year 1951–52.[14]

On the first business day of July 1951, a merchant or processor[15] considering the purchase of the cheapest quality No. 2 Hard Winter wheat (the quality represented by quotations on Kansas City wheat futures) found such spot wheat selling at 3 cents per bushel under the price of the September future. If he bought spot wheat, hedged it in the September future, and carried the wheat until the first business day of September, the results, in cents per bushel, would have been as shown below:

Quotation	*Date and Price*		*Gain or Loss*
	July 2	*Sept. 4*	
Spot No. 2 Hard (low)	229¼	232½	....
September future	232¼	233½	....
Spot premium	−3	−1	+2 (gain)

The profit of 2 cents per bushel is calculated above, in what may seem an awkward way, from the change in spot premium (a negative premium, or discount, on each of these dates). It is awkward, however, only for those to whom it is unfamiliar. The hedger tends to calculate his profits in this way because he would buy the wheat on July 2 primarily for the reason that he could get it at discount of 3 cents per bushel under the price of the September future. In fact, the bargaining which preceded the purchase would normally proceed in terms of discount rather than of price, the price being ascertained by reference to the latest futures price quotation, after sale at a mutually satisfactory discount had been agreed on.[16]

The fact that on September 4, No. 2 Hard Winter wheat sold at a discount under the September future, though it is the grade of wheat currently deliverable on the future, is accounted for by the fact that the spot price applies to wheat 'on track,' requiring additional expenditure to get it into a warehouse.[17] Wheat was then moving into commercial storage on a large scale because of heavy marketing by producers.

On September 4, our grain merchant or processor would probably not have sold the wheat he bought earlier, but instead would have bought more wheat. If he did that, and held until December 1, the results, in cents per bushel, would have appeared as follows:

Quotation	*Date and Price*		*Gain or Loss*
	Sept. 4	*Dec. 1*	
Spot No. 2 Hard (low)	232½	252	....
December future	238¼	252	....
Spot premium	−5¾	0	+5¾ (gain)

In this case the spot price of the cheapest deliverable wheat came, on December 1, to exact equality with the price of the December future, and the gross return for storing the wheat was exactly what might have been expected, on September 4, from the fact that such wheat was then selling at a discount of 5¾ cents under the price of the December future.

In these calculations we have left out of account the possibility that a merchant who bought at a discount of 5¾ cents on September 4 might have got wheat of a little better than minimum No. 2 quality – wheat which might have been sold on September 4 at a discount of, say, 5½ cents, rather than 5¾ cents, if the seller had been willing to look farther for a buyer. And we have ignored the possibility that on December 1 the merchant might have sold at a premium of ½ cent over the December future by virtue of the slightly superior quality of the wheat, and by finding a buyer who did not choose to shop around enough to get the best bargain possible. In other words, we have left out of account sources of normal *merchandising* profits.

On December 1 a merchant or processor may seem to have had no incentive for longer holding of wheat for which he had no immediate need. The spot price then was on a par with the December future, and at a premium of 1 cent over the price of the May future. But let us suppose that he continued to hold, with a hedge in the May future, and see what would have happened if he held until May 1. Though we imagine that the wheat is already in storage, we may make the next calculation as though it concerned a new purchase:

Quotation	*Date and Price*		*Gain or Loss*
	Dec. 1	*May 1*	
Spot No. 2 Hard (low)	252	247¼	....
May future	251	238¼	....
Spot premium	+1	+9	+8 (gain)

This time a merchant would have gained a gross return of 8 cents per bushel from storage. It would have been in part a windfall profit, since he had no advance *assurance* of obtaining it; but he would have gained it on a quite conservative venture. He was well assured of not losing more than 1 cent per bushel (because the spot wheat that he held would surely sell at as high a price as the May future at some time in May), and he could count with virtual certainty on spot wheat going to a substantial premium over the price of the May future at some time between December and May.[18]

As of May 1, there remained no prospect of profit from continued storage of wheat during that crop-year, unless perhaps for a few days more. Before the end of the month, the spot premium, based on the May future, would have to fall from 9 cents to near zero.[19] Moreover, the spot price on May 1 was at a premium of 18 cents over the July future, and that premium should be expected to fall to zero or below by July 1. The outcome, if a merchant in fact held any wheat in storage from May 1 to July 1, was as follows:

Quotation	*Date and Price* *May 1*	*July 1*	*Gain or Loss*
Spot No. 2 Hard (low)	247¼	218½	....
July future	229¼	225	....
Spot premium	+18	−6½	−24½ (loss)

Probably some merchants did store a little wheat from May 1 to July 1, hedged in the July future, and did take the loss per bushel indicated by the above calculation. Grain merchants, like operators of retail stores, must try to keep adequate stocks on their shelves to serve their customers. But a merchant who hedged would have seen clearly on May 1 that any wheat that he might continue to hold until July would involve a loss, as surely, though not so completely, as would Christmas trees held until December 26.

The foregoing examples of hedging tend in one respect to be a little misleading; spot premiums do not always follow so obviously logical a pattern through the course of a crop year as they did in 1951–52. If spot wheat in July, were regularly, in all years, at a moderate discount under the September future, and if spot wheat, in September, were always at a large discount under the December future, and spot wheat in May always at a large premium over the July future, merchants and processors would have less need than they do for futures markets.[20] They would then have no need to watch spot-future price relations in order to judge when to accumulate stocks, and when to draw them low. But our purpose at the moment is merely to see how hedgers use spot-futures price relations as a guide in inventory control, thereby earning a return for holding stocks that must be stored by someone. We may reasonably avoid being led here into discussion of the frequent effects on spot premiums produced by exceptional export demand, by governmental price supports, or by unusual holding disposition on the part of producers.

We should now note three facts concerning hedging. First, contrary to a common impression, hedging of the sort here considered is not properly comparable with insurance. It is a sort of arbitrage. We shall consider later an example of conditions under which hedging may in fact be profitably compared with insurance, but such conditions obtain for only a small proportion of the hedging that is done on futures markets. Most hedging is done in the expectation of a change in spot-future price relations, the change that is reasonably to be expected being often indicated quite clearly by the current spot-future price relation.

Secondly, hedging does not eliminate risks arising from price variability. Risk is less than on stocks held unhedged, but it still exists. When the commodity involved is of quite different quality than that represented by the future, or in a location remote from that to which the futures price relates, the risks assumed by hedgers tend to be much larger than is suggested by the examples given here.

And thirdly, hedging is not necessarily done for the sake of reducing risks. The role of risk-avoidance in most commercial hedging has been greatly overemphasized in economic discussions. Most hedging is done largely, and may be done wholly, because the information on which the merchant or processor acts leads logically to hedging. He buys the spot commodity because the spot price is low *relative to* the futures price and he has reason to expect the spot premium to advance; therefore he buys spot *and* sells the future. Or in the case of a flour miller, he sells flour for forward delivery because he can get a price that is favourable *in relation to* the price of the appropriate wheat future; therefore he sells flour *and* buys wheat futures. (Here the arbitrage, it may be noted, is between two forward prices, that for flour and that for wheat.)[21]

Incidentally, recognition of the fact that hedging may be done purely as a logical consequence of the reasoning on which the hedger acts (reasoning, for example, that the spot price is low relative to the future) rather than from any special desire to minimize risks, helps to explain why many dealers and processors sometimes hedge and sometimes do not. As we have remarked, merchants and processors, even though they hedge, have need to keep informed on conditions that affect the price of the commodity and they may often have opinions on prospective price changes. If a merchant is accumulating stocks at a time when spot premiums are low – his most reliable basis for such action – and if at the same time he is fairly confident of an advance in futures prices as well as in spot premiums, why should he not carry the stocks unhedged, if he can afford to take some extra risk?

Perhaps the main reason that hedging, as commonly practiced on futures markets, has been so widely misunderstood and misrepresented is that economists have tried to deal with it in terms of a concept that seemed to cover all sorts of hedging. This would be desirable if it were feasible, but the general concept of hedging as taking offsetting risks wholly, or even primarily, for the sake of reducing net risk, serves so badly as applied to most hedging on futures markets that we need another concept for that most common sort of hedging. To put it briefly, we may say that hedging in commodity futures involves the *purchase or sale of futures in conjunction with another commitment, usually in the expectation of a favorable change in the relation between spot and futures prices.*

An unfortunate consequence of the prevalent misconception of hedging has been that, while it has correctly credited futures markets with allowing merchants and processors to curtail their risks, it has diverted attention from a service of probably larger economic importance. Merely by supplying simultaneous quotations applying to various subsequent dates, futures trading tends to promote economically desirable control of stocks; and futures markets, through their use for hedging, make the holder of stocks sharply aware of any losses that must be expected from carrying unnecessary stocks in times of relative shortage of supplies, and provide assured[22] returns for storage over periods when there is a surplus to be carried. A merchant or processor with warehouse facilities will undertake storage in response to prospect of a 10-cent per bushel gain from carrying hedged stocks about as readily as he will undertake storage in response to an offer of 10 cents per bushel as a fee for storing government-owned grain. Indeed he may undertake storage for the return promised by hedging more willingly than for the fee, because the stocks that he holds hedged need be carried only as long as he wishes, and can be a source of convenience or of profit in connection with his merchandising or processing business. The argument often made that management of reserve stocks of commodities should be a governmental function rests in large part on ignorance of the effectiveness with which the hedging facilities of futures markets assure private carrying of stocks in about as large a volume as can be justified on purely economic grounds.[23]

The claim sometimes made by able economists[24] that prices of such storable commodities as wheat, corn, and cotton fluctuate excessively because stocks are accumulated at wrong times, and not accumulated when they should be, seems also a consequence, indirectly, of the prevalent misconception of hedging. Mismanagement of stocks by nonhedgers would have to be on a very large scale to produce an over-all tendency toward perverse stockholding in any commodity with a futures market much used for hedging.[25]

Section IV, '*Price Fluctuations*'; *Section* V, '*Costs of Hedging*'; *Section* VI, ' "*Insurance*" *Hedging*'; *and Section* VII, '*Summary*', *are not reprinted here.*

Professor Working has asked us to supplement the foregoing extract from his article by reproducing the revised definition of hedging presented in his article, '*Hedging Reconsidered*', Journal of Farm Economics, *vol.*

xxxv, *1953, pp. 544–61: 'Hedging in futures consists of making a* contract to buy or sell on standard terms, established and supervised by a commodity exchange, as a temporary substitute for an intended later contract to buy or sell on other terms' (*p. 560*).

NOTES

1 This, in two sentences, is the story that can be read from scattered comments in Charles H. Taylor, *History of the Board of Trade of the City of Chicago*, Chicago, 1917. Passages in Vol. I, pp. 146–47, 192, 217, 317 and 332, among others, cover the main developments through 1865, when the Board of Trade at last assumed responsibility for aiding and governing the conduct of futures trading.

H. C. Emery, in *Speculation on the Stock and Produce Exchanges of the United States*, New York, 1896, traces the history of trading that had at least essential characteristics of that done in futures, from institution of the use of warrants by the East India Company in 1733 (p. 35), and says that 'Futures were sold in some kinds of grain in Berlin by 1832, and some years earlier in France and Holland' (footnote, p. 41).

2 This is not to say that anybody in either the cotton or the grain trade *is* confused by these practices any more than initiates are confused by the colloquial uses of 'buck,' 'date,' and 'doll' (all words with the same brevity as 'cash' and 'spot'); but the usage is a bit frustrating, and even misleading, to an inquiring novice.

3 Whether use of the expression has its foundation directly in this characteristic, or in the related fact that *speculators* use futures contracts, as they may any forward contracts, to avoid necessity for *handling* of the actual commodity, is a matter of surmise.

4 The characteristics of convenience and economy being at that stage not well developed.

5 See, for example, the evolution of definitions from H. C. Emery, *op. cit.*, p. 46, through J. G. Smith, *Organized Produce Markets*, London, 1922, p. 44; C. O. Hardy, *Risk and Risk Bearing*, Chicago, 1923, pp. 205–06; J. B. Baer and O. G. Saxon, *Commodity Exchanges and Futures Trading*, New York, 1949, pp. 132–34.

6 See, for example, the summary of much earlier work in G. Wright Hoffman, *Grain Prices and the Futures Market*, U.S. Dept. Agric., Tech. Bull. No. 747, January 1941, pp. 33–38.

7 Data are conveniently available in *Agricultural Statistics* (Washington) for any recent year.

8 Size of a futures market is better judged by volume of open contracts than by volume of trading because of the wide variation between markets in proportion of trading contributed by 'scalping' and by other trading that involves holding a commitment for only a few minutes or hours, with correspondingly small speculative risk and small economic significance.

9 For example, such an inference seems to follow from information in Blair Stewart, *Trading in Wool Top Futures*, U.S. Dept. Agric., Circ. No. 604, August 1941, pp. 16–26.

10 See Holbrook Working and Sidney Hoos, 'Wheat Futures Prices and

Trading at Liverpool since 1886,' *Wheat Studies of the Food Research Institute*, vol. XV, 1938, pp. 125, 142–44. I would now attach less importance than is done there to the uniformity of the quality of the Californian wheat, judging that factor to have been important mainly in the preference for the Californian over the Indian wheat contracts, in which also there was effort for a time to maintain futures trading.

11 Not entirely valid because hedgers are the active agents in determining the *relation* of spot to futures prices, and to that extent they play a major role in formation of the spot price.

12 The case of wool has been documented (*cf.* Blair Stewart, *op. cit.*); the inference that similar situations exist in certain other commodities is based on fairly reliable trade reports.

13 *Cf.* the Federal Trade Commission's *Report on the Grain Trade* (Washington), vol. I, 1920, pp. 213–27; and vol. VII, 1926, pp. 38–57; and Holbrook Working, 'Financial Results of Speculative Holding of Wheat,' *Wheat Studies*, vol. VII, 1931, pp. 417–28.

14 Kansas City is used rather than Chicago because changes in the major wheat-producing areas and in the normal lines of movement of the commodity have left Chicago with a vestigial spot wheat market that no longer affords a good source of spot price quotations.

15 The case of a merchant or processor deserves to be considered rather than that of someone not in such a business, who might buy merely for storage, because merchants and processors gain auxiliary benefits from having stocks on hand that give them a competitive advantage in storing. Their competition for the returns available from storage leaves little opportunity for profitable storing as an independent enterprise.

16 This is the normal procedure in connection with spot sales of wheat at Kansas City and at other markets with active futures trading. The actual bargaining on July 2, however, would have been in terms of premium or discount in relation to the price of the *July* future, the prospective hedger bearing in mind the prevailing discount of the July future under the September.

Since the gain or loss from hedging calculated in such tabulations as that in the text above depends only on the spot premiums, the prices included in the tabulations are no more than interesting collateral information. The spot premium or discount for a specified quality of the commodity rarely changes much during the course of a day or even a week. With regard to the futures prices, however, it is pertinent to note the time of day. Those used here are the closing prices for the day. The spot prices are closing prices of the future currently being used as a basis for spot sales, plus the quoted premium for lowest quality No. 2 Hard Winter Wheat. The source is the Kansas City *Grain Market Review*, which quotes also daily high and low spot prices for the various grades, in which the low quotation for each grade is obtained by adding the premium for lowest quality wheat in that grade to the lowest price of the future for that day.

17 Sometimes the spot price on track in a delivery month falls to a considerable discount under the near future because of lack of warehouse space for economical storage. The spot price on track tends to be at a

discount under the price of a current-month future, which is then also effectively a spot price, when the prevailing direction of movement of the commodity is into storage; it tends to stand at a premium over the future when the prevailing direction of movement is out of storage. Moreover, the spot quotations for the cheapest wheat of deliverable grade may represent wheat of slightly better quality than that which will be delivered on futures contracts. To be graded No. 2, wheat must meet all of several requirements; the wheat delivered on futures contracts may be at or near the minimum in all respects when the cheapest wheat on which spot quotations are available is close to the minimum in only one of the grade requirements.

18 One of the indications of this prospect was the fact that spot wheat had already reached a premium of 1 cent over the May future by December 1. The cause, of which any holder of large wheat stocks would have been well aware, was the holding by growers of some 300 million bushels or more under nonrecourse loans offered by the Commodity Credit Corporation.

19 Not necessarily to zero, because deliveries on futures contracts would consist of wheat in public elevators; in May, wheat on track tends to be worth more than the same quality of wheat in a public elevator because it is already loaded in a freight car and ready to be moved to wherever it is wanted.

20 When spot wheat in May is at a premium over the July future, it is not because the new wheat crop – coming to market in large volume by July – is expected to be large, but because current supplies of old wheat are scarce. (In May 1952 the scarcity applied only to commercially available supplies, being a result of the large holdings of wheat by the Commodity Credit Corporation in connection with its price-support operations.) On the subject of 'inverted' intertemporal price relations in general, see Holbrook Working, 'Theory of the Inverse Carrying Charge in Futures Markets,' *Journal of Farm Economics*, vol. XXX, 1948; 'Professor Vaile and the Theory of Inverse Carrying Charges,' vol. XXXI, 1949; and 'The Theory of Price of Storage,' *American Economic Review*, vol. XXXIX, 1949.

21 Two instructive explanations of hedging written by hedgers themselves, such as are not often found, are: Ellis D. English, 'The Use of the Commodity Exchange by Millers,' *Proceedings, Fifth Annual Symposium*, Chicago Board of Trade, 1952, mimeo., pp. 22–29; Virgil A. Wiese, 'Use of Commodity Exchanges by Local Grain Marketing Organizations,' *ibid*, pp. 108–16.

22 Though subject to some risk, as we have seen.

23 If considerations of national defense warrant the carrying of commercially uneconomic stocks of a commodity, government should of course assume the responsibility and the financial burden of carrying such excess stocks.

24 For example, T. W. Schultz in *Production and Welfare of Agriculture*, New York, 1949, pp. 172–74.

25 The hypothesis of perversity of stockholding tendencies is not supported by any statistics that I know, but is contradicted by them. Of particular

interest is the fact that in the years when one could speak realistically of a world wheat market, the countries in which year-end (June 30) stocks of wheat varied in rational correspondence with world wheat supplies were the countries where hedging was practiced on a substantial scale. In most countries, year-end stocks of wheat varied little, and primarily with size of the previous *domestic* crop. Britain, with a futures market but with only small storage facilities, contributed little to the carrying of world wheat surpluses. Canada contributed more; and the country which most consistently carried large stocks at the end of any year of world wheat surplus, and reduced stocks to a minimum in times of world wheat shortage, was the United States. *Cf.* Holbrook Working, 'The Changing World Wheat Situation,' *Wheat Studies*, vol. VII, 1930, pp.433–52.

3 The Theory of Hedging and Speculation in Commodity Futures

LELAND L. JOHNSON

Although significant contributions have appeared in the literature in recent years, the present day theory of hedging and speculation appears to account inadequately for certain market practices. In particular, the motivation of the trader who undertakes hedging activities, the role that hedging plays in his over-all market operations, and the distinction between a trader who hedges and one who speculates have given rise to difficulties in the literature. My purposes here are (1) to outline briefly the purposes and mechanics of a commodity futures market, (2) to discuss and appraise the theory of hedging and speculation as it exists today, (3) to present a reformulated concept of hedging, and (4) to construct a model that may both assist in clarifying the concepts of hedging and speculation and contribute to a better understanding of certain market phenomena.

THE NATURE OF FUTURES TRADING

Organized commodity futures trading facilitates two kinds of activity – speculation and hedging. When futures trading in a given commodity exists, the speculator generally finds it advantageous to deal in futures contracts rather than either (1) buying a quantity of the commodity at the current 'spot' price and holding it in the hope of a rise in the spot price, (2) selling the commodity short by promising in private negotiations with a buyer to deliver at a specified later date, at a price which he expects to be above the spot price that will prevail at that date. Equally important, if not more so, futures markets are useful for hedging operations. An essential feature of commodity hedging is that the trader synchronizes his activities in two markets. One is generally the 'cash' or 'spot' market (the market for immediate delivery); the other is generally the futures market.

* From *Review of Economic Studies*, vol. XXVII, 1959–60, pp. 139–51. Reprinted by permission.

A future contract, being merely a promise of the seller to deliver within a specified month and a promise of the buyer to take delivery of a *standard* quantity and quality of the commodity at an agreed price is readily adaptable by its homogeneous character to being traded on an exchange. The commodity exchange provides a central location where potential buyers and sellers make bids and offers for contracts covering delivery in various later months. Each delivery month in which trading takes place is referred to as a 'future'. Because of the centralized nature of the market and the rapidity and ease with which sales and purchases can be made, the price of any sale in a given future during the trading day is a near-perfect reflection of supply and demand conditions existing at that instant of time for contracts of that particular future.

In most futures markets, only a small fraction of contracts sold is closed out by delivery of the actual commodity. Because nearly all participants are motivated by the desire to trade on price movements, they liquidate by undertaking offsetting transactions. The buyer (seller) can liquidate his position in the futures market *prior to actual delivery* of the commodity by merely *selling* (buying) on the exchange contracts of the *same* future. The second transaction offsets and cancels the previously existing commitment. For each contract purchased or sold and subsequently liquidated the trader takes a total profit or loss equal to the difference between his buying and selling price multiplied by the number of units of the commodity specified in the contract.

THE THEORY OF HEDGING

Most commodity trading theorists have visualized the hedger as a dealer in the 'actual' commodity who desires 'insurance' against the price risks he faces. For example, if he purchases a unit of the commodity at a given spot price and the price falls (rises) prior to his reselling it, he is exposed to a capital loss (gain), in addition to whatever merchandising profit he receives, by the amount of that price change. According to these theorists he would typically protect his inventory position of x units from the risk of such price fluctuation by simultaneously *selling* a sufficient number of future contracts to cover delivery of x units;[1] when he resells his inventory he would simultaneously liquidate his position in futures by *purchasing* the same number of contracts (of the same future) as before. If the net change in spot price is equal to the net change in the price of his future, i.e., if the price movements are parallel to each other, the gain he enjoys in one market offsets the loss in the other and he would be left with only his 'normal' merchandising profit.[2] Otherwise he would be left with a residual capital gain or loss.

As an illustration, assume a hedge carried in a future from time t_1 to time t_2 (where the future specifies delivery at t_3) against x units of inventory purchased at t_1 and sold at t_2. Let S_1 and S_2 denote the spot price and F_1 and F_2 the price of the future that exist at t_1 and t_2 respectively. The hedger will take a total gain (loss) arising from price movements from t_1 to t_2 equal to the positive (negative) value of $x[(S_2 - S_1) - (F_2 - F_1)]$. The hedge is perfectly effective if $[(S_2 - S_1) - (F_2 - F_1)]$ is equal to 0.

A major role of the speculator in futures, according to the bulk of the literature, is to assume the risks that hedgers desire to transfer from their own shoulders;[3] the futures market is visualized as a convenient mechanism through which price risk can be transferred from one group to another. The hedger is often described as an apparently unsophisticated participant in futures dealings who, in the words of Hawtrey, 'regards the making of price as a whole-time occupation for experts [speculators?], and, in general, will not pit his fragmentary information against the systematic study at the disposal of the professional dealers.'[4] Expanding upon this thesis, J. M. Keynes, in his *A Treatise on Money*, deduced the theory of 'normal backwardation' in which he asserted that hedgers are willing to pay a 'risk premium' to relieve themselves of price risk, while speculators are willing to enter the futures market only if they have the expectation of collecting a premium. Therefore, since hedgers are predominately short in futures and speculators are predominately long, the current future or 'forward' price must fall *below* the future price expected to prevail at any later time by the amount of this risk premium. If the expected future price is equal to the current spot price, the current future price must fall below the current spot price by the amount of the premium. The existence of a discount of a future below the current spot price by an amount equal to the premium is a condition of normal backwardation.[5]

In recent years Holbrook Working has written a series of articles that run counter to the older, 'traditional' concept of the nature of hedging and the function of a futures market. He envisages the hedger as one who does not seek primarily to avoid risk but one who hedges because of an expected return arising from anticipations of favourable *relative* price movements in the spot and futures markets. The trader does not somehow find himself with a given size inventory that has to be hedged against, but he takes positions in *both* markets as a form of 'arbitrage'.

> The rôle of risk-avoidance in most commercial hedging has been greatly over-emphasized in economic discussions. Most hedging is done largely, and may be done wholly, because information on which the merchant or processor acts leads logically to hedging. He buys the spot commodity because the spot price is low *relative* to the futures price and he has reason to expect the spot premium to advance; therefore he buys *spot* and sells the future.[6]

Since the hedger is not motivated primarily by desire to reduce risk it is also misleading, Working asserts, to judge the effectiveness of hedging according to the degree to which futures price and spot price movements are parallel.

> . . . the basic idea that complete effectiveness of hedging depends on parallelism of movement of spot and futures prices is false, and an improper standard by which to test the effectiveness of hedging. The effectiveness of hedging intelligently used with commodity storage, depends on *inequalities* between the movements of spot and futures prices and on reasonable predictability of such inequalities.[7]

AN APPRAISAL

On the basis of personal interviews with representatives of 20 firms in one particular commodity market – the New York coffee trade – I have concluded that the present-day body of theory outlined above does not account adequately for certain market phenomena. On the basis of interviews with several representatives of brokerage firms dealing in a wide range of commodities, there is reason to believe that this situation extends to trading in other commodities as well.

On one hand, it is true that hedgers in the coffee market sometimes at least act on the basis of expected relative price movements between spot and futures and adjust both their stockholdings and their positions in futures somewhat as described by Working. The price of a given future is almost always at a large discount relative to spot at the time trade in it begins a year prior to its delivery period, and this discount tends to diminish as the delivery month approaches. According to our previous terminology, $(S_1 - F_1)$ and $[(S_2 - S_1) - (F_2 - F_1)]$ tend to be positive and negative respectively. Therefore, the trader tends to take a loss, aside from merchandising profit, on his hedged inventory. For this reason most of the traders contacted who claim to hedge at all stated that they often carry very small inventories ('buy hand-to-mouth') and thereby maintain only small positions in futures. At the same time, however, they claim to be motivated to hedge primarily in order to reduce price risk. The importance of the price 'insurance' factor in coffee hedging most clearly manifests itself in the fact that one group of traders, the roasters, who face little price risk in holding inventory almost never hedge, while another group, the importers, who *do* face large price risks make extensive use of the futures market for hedging purposes.[8]

Furthermore, the traders in the survey take cognizance not only of expected relative price movements but of expected *absolute* price movements as well. Generally, if traders expect spot prices to rise they tend to remove hedges and increase their inventory holdings. In some cases they take long positions in both the spot and futures markets as a more obvious speculative venture. On the other hand, if they are bearish they increase their short futures positions in excess of hedging requirements. In other words, hedging activities get mixed in very closely with speculative operations in the accounts of the individual trader.

In general, hedging activities appear to be motivated by the desire to reduce risk, as described in traditional theory, but levels of inventory held appear to be not independent of expected hedging profits, as emphasized by Working. Furthermore, that an individual may hold a mix of hedged and speculative positions in response to his expectations concerning *absolute* price changes is a practice not well explained in either traditional theory or in Working's theory. In the former the tendency, as illustrated by Keynes' 'normal backwardation,' is much more to speak of the hedger and the speculator as if they were entirely separate individuals with entirely different motivations.[9] In the latter, there is no treatment of the conditions under which the trader may speculate in lieu of or in combination with hedging. In fact, the very distinction between hedging and speculation is fuzzy; when the trader takes market positions on the basis of expectations concerning *relative* price changes, he is speculating insofar as he is not betting on a 'sure thing'.

In view of the disparities between theory and these market phenomena one could well ask: 'Precisely what is a hedge? Can a hedge be meaningfully defined in the case in which the trader acts on the basis of absolute price expectations? Can hedging be treated theoretically as an activity conducted simultaneously with speculation?'

A REFORMULATION OF THE THEORY OF HEDGING

First, a reformulated definition and analysis of hedging in commodity futures is in order. Given a position consisting of a number, x_i, of physical units held in market i, a 'hedge' is defined as a position in market j of size x_j^* units such that the 'price risk' of holding x_i and x_j^* from time t_1 to time t_2 is *minimized.* The scope of the term 'market' is restricted in this definition to include trading in a commodity of sufficiently exact specification so that its price may be considered a scalar magnitude.

'Price risk' can be considered a reflection of the variance (or standard deviation) of a subjective probability distribution (or a subjective probability density function) for price change from t_1 to t_2 that the trader holds at time t_1, where *actual* price from t_1 to t_2 is treated as a random variable. The variance of price change, denoted by σ_i^2 in the i market is equal to the *variance of return* or 'price risk' of holding one unit in the i market from t_1 to t_2, since the (absolute) value of actual return attributed to price change from t_1 to t_2 is equal to the (absolute) value of the actual price change itself. The variance of return or the price risk of holding x_i units is equal to $x_i^2 \sigma_i^2$. Likewise, the price risk of holding one unit in the j market can be considered as the variance, denoted by σ_j^2, of a subjective probability distribution of price change in the j market. The variance of return of holding x_j units, when these units are considered alone, is equal to $x_j^2 \sigma_j^2$. Where cov_{ij} denotes the covariance of price change (or covariance of return due to price change) between market i and market j, a *combination* of positions in i and j has a total variance of return $V(R)$ due to price change given by:

$$V(R) = x_i^2 \sigma_i^2 + x_j^2 \sigma_j^2 + 2x_i x_j \text{cov}_{ij} \tag{1}$$

The combination also has an actual return R and an expected return $E(R)$ due to price change given respectively by:

$$R = x_i B_i + x_j B_j \tag{2}$$

and

$$E(R) = x_i u_i + x_j u_j \tag{3}$$

where B_i, B_j denotes the *actual* price changes from t_1 to t_2 in i and j, and u_i and u_j denote the price changes from t_1 to t_2 *expected at* t_1. As such, u_i and u_j are the mean values of the probability distributions of return existing in the i and j markets respectively at time t_1.[10]

Differentiating equation (1) with respect to x_j and setting the derivative equal to 0, we have the value x_j^* minimizing the variance of return for the combination x_i, x_j^*.

$$x_j^* = -\frac{x_i \text{cov}_{ij}}{\sigma_j^2} \tag{4}$$

Substituting the value x_j^* for x_j in equation (1) and letting $V(R)^*$ denote the total variance of return of the combination x_i, x_j^*, we have:

$$V(R)^* = x_i^2 \sigma_i^2 + \frac{x_i^2 \text{cov}_{ij}^2}{\sigma_j^2} - \frac{2x_i^2 \text{cov}_{ij}^2}{\sigma_j^2}$$

or

$$V(R)^* = x_i^2 \left(\sigma_i^2 - \frac{\text{cov}_{ij}^2}{\sigma_j^2}\right)$$

Since the coefficient of correlation, ρ, estimated by the trader is equal to $\frac{\text{cov}_{ij}}{\sigma_i \sigma_j}$, then $V(R)^* = x_i^2 \sigma_i^2(1 - \rho^2)$. Generally speaking the larger the (absolute) value of the coefficient of correlation, the greater the reduction in price risk of holding x_i that can be effected by carrying the hedge x_j^*. If the trader believes at time t_1 that price movements are perfectly correlated between t_1 and t_2, ρ is equal to 1 and over-all price risk is reduced to 0. If he believes that there is no correlation whatever,

$V(R)^*$ is equal to $x_i^2 \sigma_i^2$ – the variance of x_i held alone. The effectiveness e of the hedge is measured by considering the variance of return, $V(R)^*$ associated with the combination x_i, x_j^* in a ratio with the variance $x_i^2 \sigma_j^2$ associated with the position x_i held alone so that

$$e = \left(1 - \frac{V(R)^*}{x_i^2 \sigma_i^2}\right) \text{ or } e = \rho^2$$

Although this reformulated concept resembles the traditional theory insofar as the hedge is considered as a mechanism to reduce price risk, the concept of price risk itself is quite different. In traditional theory price risk is measured by the size of *actual* gain or loss due to price change that the trader incurs. The effectiveness of the hedge is measured by considering the gain or loss due to price changes incurred in an unhedged position relative to that incurred in a hedged position. If price movements in i and j from t_1 to t_2 were equal to each other, any loss in one market would be exactly offset by the gain in the other; price risk would therefore be reduced to zero, and the hedge would be considered perfectly effective. However, in the reformulated framework both price risk and the effectiveness of the hedge are treated quite apart from the effects of *actual* price change. Price risk is something that exists in the mind of the trader at t_1; namely it is the variance of his probability distribution of return due to price change. Hence, it is treated only in subjective terms – not in terms of ex post price changes. The effectiveness of the hedge is likewise considered only in subjective terms – it is measured by the extent to which the trader believes at t_1 that the variance of return of holding x_i is reduced by simultaneously holding x_j^*.

Parallelism of actual price movements would be indicative of a perfectly effective hedge only if the trader believed with certainty at t_1 that any change in one price would be equal to the change in the other; but the condition of actual parallelism itself would be neither a necessary nor a sufficient condition to make possible a perfectly effective hedge. It is not a necessary condition because if the trader believed with certainty that *any* relationship held perfectly between price movements in i and j he could take a perfectly effective hedge. If, for example, he believed with certainty that the price in the j market would fall from t_1 to t_2 by c cents relative to the price in the i market, he could take a long position x_i in combination with short position in j of the same number of units, and be certain of achieving a return equal to $c(x_i)$, and no price risk as such would be involved. In other words, neither the expected return nor the actual return of the combination need be equal to zero to make possible a perfectly effective hedge.

The reformulated theory is similar to the traditional theory in that a 'primary' market is postulated, the primary market visualized here as one in which the trader is some sense 'makes his living'. More specifically, the primary market is defined as one in which the trader (assumed to be normally efficient) is able to obtain a net merchandising profit by carrying positions in that market. As such he can most generally be considered a middleman in the handling of a commodity. References to the middleman role played by the hedger are frequently found in the literature, although the 'primary' market condition is generally not defined explicitly. Here it is essential to postulate the primary market within the definition of hedging because the market in which the risk of a given position is to be minimized *must be specified in advance.* Only if the (subjective) coefficient of correlation were equal to 1 would the x_j* that minimizes the risk of holding x_i be of a value such that the x_i* which would in reverse minimize the risk of holding x_j* be equal to x_i.[11]

A MODEL OF HEDGING AND SPECULATION

With this general concept of hedging in mind we shall consider a model within which a wide range of trading activities may be examined. Given a framework of particular assumptions about the trader and the nature of his world, it will be possible to demonstrate under what conditions various market phenomena arise.

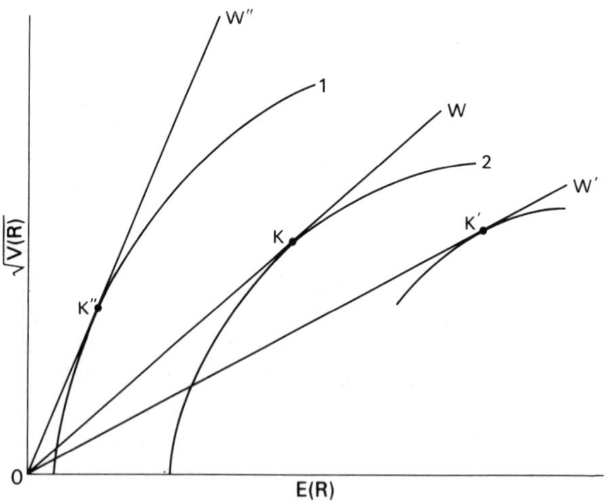

FIGURE 1

As to the nature of the trader himself, he is postulated to have an indifference map illustrated in Figure 1. The total expected net return $E(R)$ generated by all of his market positions together from t_1 to t_2 is plotted on the X-axis. As a direct measure of price risk, the standard deviation $\sqrt{V(R)}$ of return is plotted on the Y-axis. Curves 1 and 2 represent indifference curves among which the trader has ranked all possible combinations of $\sqrt{(VR)}$ and $E(R)$. The shape and positions of the curves indicate that to remain on a given indifference level the incremental ratio of $\sqrt{V(R)}$ to $E(R)$ must fall as he moves to a higher $E(R)$. With a given level of $E(R)$ he moves to a higher (lower) indifference curve as $\sqrt{V(R)}$ decreases (increases). His optimum over-all market position is defined as that position or combination of positions which generates an $E(R)$ and $\sqrt{V(R)}$ such that he attains the highest indifference curve that he is able to attain under given constraints.

I shall assume further that the trader can engage in one or more of the following activities:

(1) He can take a long position in the *spot or i market* at t_1 by purchasing a stock of the commodity at the spot price prevailing at t_1 and reselling it at t_2 at the spot price prevailing at t_2; he receives for this operation, in addition, a net merchandising profit (m) equal to a fixed markup per unit held from t_1 to t_2. This profit is simply a net return for services rendered as a middleman. The institutional environment is assumed to be such that the size of this return is known with certainty. The total risk faced by the trader is confined to 'price risk'. In this case equation (3) must be modified to

$$E(R) = x_i(u_i + m) + x_j u_j \text{ where } x_i > 0. \quad (3a)$$

The spot market is, therefore, regarded as the primary market.

(2) He can take a long position in a *given future of the j market* at t_1 by purchasing contracts of a given future at the price prevailing at t_1 and liquidate them at t_2 at the price prevailing at t_2.

(3) He can take a *short* position in the given future by selling contracts at t_1 and liquidating them at t_2, also at the relevant prevailing prices. In all cases future contracts are assumed to be completely divisible – he can take positions in a future representing any number of units of the commodity he chooses.

The co-ordinate system in Figure 2 illustrates geometrically the market positions he can take at t_1. The number of units *purchased* in the spot or i market is measured along the positive X-axis, the number *sold* in the given future or j market along the negative Y-axis and the number *purchased* in the same future along the positive Y-axis.

Iso-expected return lines of slope $\frac{u_i + m}{u_j}$ appear in Figure 2 to denote combinations of market positions for which total expected return remains constant.[12] Suppose, first, that the trader expects no price changes in either the spot or the future markets, i.e. u_i and u_j are both equal to 0. Vertical iso-expected return curves such as AB and CD

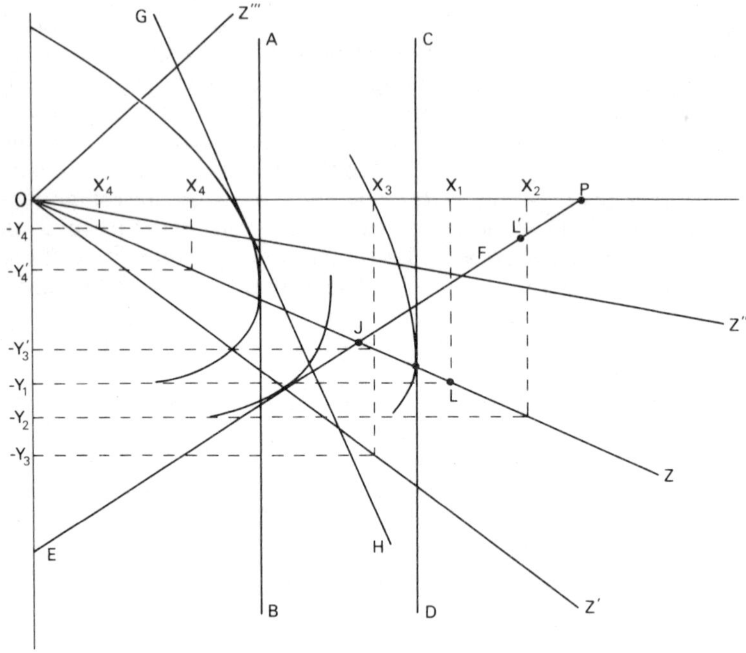

FIGURE 2

in Figure 2 would be appropriate in this case to denote the fact that positive expected return for any combination is generated solely by merchandising profit, *m*, from positions in the spot market on the *X*-axis.

Iso-variance of return ellipses (which are centred at 0) are drawn on the basis of equation (1) to connect combinations for which variance of return remains constant. Because short positions in the spot market are not postulated, only quadrants 1 and 4 of the co-ordinate system are relevant. The locus of tangencies *OZ* indicates the combinations of positions such that for any given level of total expected return $E(R)$, variance (or standard deviation) of return $V(R)$ is minimized. Each such combination of $E(R)$ and standard deviation of return $\sqrt{V(R)}$ is in turn plotted in Figure 1; the opportunity line *OW* which is necessarily linear, connects these points. The trader's optimum combination of $E(R)$ and $\sqrt{V(R)}$ is at point *K* where he attains his highest indifference curve; therefore he would take the market combination in Figure 2, let us say X_1 and $-Y_1$ read from point *L*, which generates this combination of $E(R)$ and $\sqrt{V(R)}$.

According to the earlier definition of hedging, $-Y_1$ represents a hedge against X_1 because this is the short position in the future which minimizes the variance of holding X_1. It can be seen that any combination read from the line OZ would represent a position in spot against which a hedge in the future is held. By substitution in equation (4), the position $-Y_1$ is equal to $-\dfrac{X_1 \text{cov}_{ij}}{\sigma_j^2}$. Therefore, the slope of OZ is equal to $-\dfrac{\text{cov}_{ij}}{\sigma_j^2}$ or to $-\rho\dfrac{\sigma_i}{\sigma_j}$. OZ, then, indicates the appropriate value along the Y-axis that constitutes a hedge against any given value along the X-axis.

The empirical observation that the individual trader may assume market positions representing a mixture of hedging and speculative activity can be analyzed in this model by comparing various alternative market combinations with the one that the trader would take if he engaged in no speculative activity. Letting α_0 denote a position held in either the spot or future market under conditions in which *both* u_i and u_j are equal to 0, and letting α_1 denote the position in the same market when either u_i or u_j is non-zero, I shall define a 'speculative element' of a market position as $\alpha_1 - \alpha_0$. The value of $\alpha_1 - \alpha_0$ will be called a *direct* speculative element if it arises because of an expected non-zero price change in the *same* market to which the value $\alpha_1 - \alpha_0$ refers; it will be called an *indirect* speculative element if it arises because of an expected non-zero price change in the *other* market. Under these definitions the combination X_1, $-Y_1$ read from point L in Figure 2 involves no speculative element since both u_i and u_j are equal to 0. The trader in this situation may be considered a 'pure' hedger because he takes a position in spot on the basis of an expected return composed entirely of merchandising profit and he takes a position in the future only to minimize the price risk of holding his position in spot. Suppose, however, that u_i is positive, and u_j remains equal to 0. The iso-expected return lines would still be vertical and the locus of tangencies would remain along OZ, but AB and AC would indicate higher levels of expected return for given levels of variance than before. A new opportunity line, OW', in Figure 1 indicates that for any given level of $\sqrt{V(R)}$, $E(R)$, is higher than before. The trader's optimum combination of $\sqrt{V(R)}$ and $E(R)$ is at K'; the corresponding market combination is, say, at X_2 and $-Y_2$. Because of an expected spot price rise the trader carries a larger position in spot than if no price rise had been expected. The increase in spot from X_1 to X_2 is a direct speculative element. He maintains a hedge against X_2 by increasing his short position in the future to $-Y_2$. He is motivated to increase his short position only to minimize the risk of holding a now larger position in spot, and not because of any return expected in the future itself; nevertheless, the gap between $-Y_1$ and $-Y_2$ is in some sense a speculative element because it arises in response to an expected price rise although it is one in the other market. Therefore, the change in the future may be termed an *indirect* speculative element. In the case of an expected price *fall* in spot by less than the amount of merchandising profit ($u_i + m > 0$) and an expected constant future price, iso-expected return lines remain vertical and the locus of tangencies remain along OZ. For any $\sqrt{V(R)}$, $E(R)$ is *lower* than in the pure hedge case and a new opportunity line OW'' in Figure 1 is generated. The market combination is calculated from K'' in the same manner as before, and deviations from X_1 and Y_1 are respectively regarded as direct and indirect speculative elements.

If, instead, he expects a price fall in the future and no price change in spot, the iso-expected return lines such as EF would have a positive slope and a new locus of tangencies OZ' would be generated. On the basis of a corresponding opportunity line in Figure 1, the trader would pick a market combination, say X_3, $-Y_3$ indicated in Figure 2. Because of the expected price fall in the future, the trader increases his position in the future beyond that required for a hedge against X_3 by the distance $-Y_3'$ to $-Y_3$. The movement from X_1 to X_3 is an indirect speculative effect; the movement from $-Y_1$ to $-Y_3$ is a direct speculative effect. Or suppose he expects a price *rise* in the future and a constant price in spot. In this case the iso-expected return lines such as GH are negatively sloped, a new locus of tangencies OZ'' is generated, and a market combination, say X_4, $-Y_4$ is taken. In this case the trader would go short in the future, even though he would expect a negative return in the future in so doing, for the sake of reducing the risk of holding X_4 in spot. This situation is illustrative of Keynes' 'normal backwardation' – the trader is willing to pay a risk premium (in the form here of an expected loss in the future) for the sake of reducing the risk of holding a position in another market. However, he would not carry a full hedge against X_4 which would require a position of $-Y_4'$ in the future; due to the effect of the expected price rise in the future the trader carries a hedged position X_4' in spot and leaves $X_4 - X_4'$ unhedged. In this case the hedge is partially withdrawn. The reduction in spot from X_1 to X_4 is an indirect speculative element, the reduction in the short future from $-Y_1$ to $-Y_4$ a direct speculative element. If the expected price rise in the future is of sufficient magnitude, the slope of the iso-expected return curves will move the locus of tangencies, say OZ''' to quadrant 1. In this case the trader would withdraw his hedge completely and go long in the future.

Both expected prices could be allowed to vary simultaneously from 0, but in this case it would be impossible to distinguish in Figure 2 between direct and indirect speculative elements. Market combinations could be derived as before, however, and deviations from X_1 and Y_1 could be considered simply as a mixture of direct and indirect speculative elements.

In general, this model appears to account to some degree for the phenomena mentioned earlier that I have observed in the New York coffee market – traders may well undertake hedging activities but these activities are not independent of expected price changes. A hedge may be lifted, a long position taken in the future, inventories adjusted, all on the basis of price expectations. This model explains how price expectations can affect market positions in a like manner.

HEDGING AND RELATIVE PRICE CHANGES

What about the case of Working, however, in which the trader may have expectations only about *relative* price changes? Suppose it is true at least in some instances that the trader takes position in one market to offset a position in another market because of the expected gain in so doing and not primarily in order to avoid risk. So long as it can be assumed that the trader has an indifference map between *overall* $E(R)$ and $\sqrt{V(R)}$ as illustrated in Figure 1, the concept of hedging as a form of arbitrage fits into the present model as a special case – a case in which the model collapses from a two-market to what is in effect a one-market analysis. Since the trader has no price expectations in the separate markets, he has no subjective probability distribution of return in each of the two markets and, therefore, faces no price risk as defined previously in terms of a variance of return. But since he takes a unit-for-unit hedge, his expectations concerning relative price changes can form the basis of a probability distribution whose mean u_h and variance σ_h^2 measure the expected return and price risk respectively of holding the hedged commodity. Both expected return and variance can be defined only in terms of a unit of hedged commodity consisting of one unit in spot and one unit in a future *taken together and inseparably*. Where X_h denotes the number of units held long in spot and hedged, $E(R)$ is equal to $X_h(u_h + m)$ and $V(R)$ is equal to $X_h^2\ \sigma_h^2$. The hedger, since he is dealing here in a one-to-one ratio in two markets, can be considered to be dealing in one market – the market for the hedged commodity. A non-zero mean and variance of the probability distribution of return have the same significance here as they would for any commodity normally considered in one market. Figure 3 represents a co-ordinate system identical to that in Figure 2. There are no iso-variance or iso-expected return curves, however, since expected return and variance of return are not computed from spot and futures positions taken singly. The only combinations the trader can take fall along OH which necessarily has a slope of -1. Each point along OH has a $E(R)$ and a $\sqrt{V(R)}$ combination which can be plotted in Figure 1, say along OW. The optimum combination at K corresponds to the combination at L in Figure 3. If u_h is equal to 0, the combination at L would represent a 'pure' hedge. If u_h is greater than 0, the trader might take a combination other than L on the basis of a new opportunity line. The difference, measured along the X-axis, between this combination and the one at L

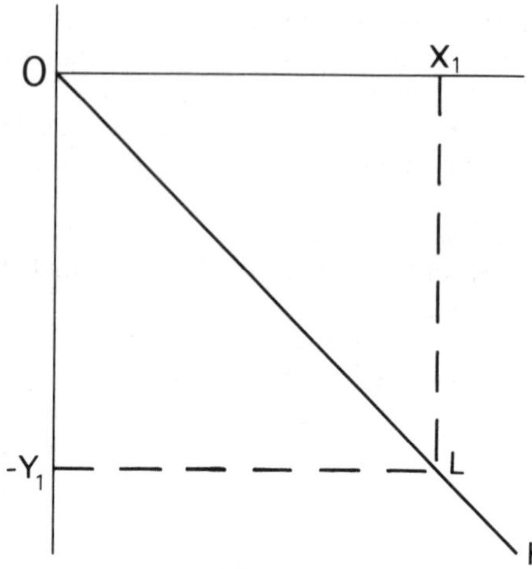

FIGURE 3

is what I would call the direct speculative effect on stocks held and hedged. For a u_h less than 0 the analysis runs symmetrically in reverse as long as $m + u_h > 0$. If $m + u_h \leqslant 0$, the trader would take no position at all. Since there is only one market to consider, no indirect speculative effects can be analyzed.

This one-market model illustrates the reason why the theory of hedging has not been satisfactorily integrated with the general theory of speculation and why the tendency has been to speak of the hedger as one kind of trader and the speculator as another. Since the trader has no expectations of absolute price level movements, $E(R)$ and $V(R)$ can be expressed in quantitative terms only along OH. Although we may speak of the direct speculative effect that may exist in a hedge as deviations from L in Figure 3, there is no way to demonstrate under what conditions the trader would alter his positions in the two markets in other than a one-to-one ratio, or under what conditions he would move to a combination in quadrant 1.

CONCLUDING REMARKS

In conclusion, the major points of this analysis can be summarized as follows: If a trader has expectations regarding only relative price changes, he necessarily takes a unit-for-unit position in the two markets. However, this hedge may contain a speculative element, depending on his reaction to expected non-zero relative price-changes. If he has expectations regarding absolute price changes, his activities can be analyzed on a general iso-variance, iso-expected return co-ordinate system; however, a hedge can be meaningfully defined only in terms of 'given a position in one market,' i.e., one market must be regarded as his primary market. With this definition of hedging, the pure hedge and the deviations from it generated by expected non-zero price changes can be geometrically analyzed. There is no distinction between the hedger and the 'ordinary' speculator insofar as both are motivated by a desire to obtain a for-them optimum combination of $E(R)$ and $V(R)$ as determined by their respective utility functions. The only essential distinction between them is that the hedger has a primary market which in this model gives rise to a merchandising profit. A necessary condition for a full hedge to be taken against the position in the primary market is that u_j be equal to 0. The ordinary speculator could also work within the framework of Figure 2. But unless we postulate the primary market condition (conceptually it could be either the spot or futures market) nothing can be said about a hedging element within his combination of market positions.

This model is expressed under quite simple assumptions. Only the effects of expected price changes and a fixed rate merchandising profit enter into (net) expected return; all business risk is confined to a price risk. No money budget constraints, imputed interest costs or brokerage commissions are postulated.

Analysis is confined to two narrowly defined markets. If a budget constraint were postulated, the principal effect would be that the trader could be pushed off the locus-of-tangency curve in Figure 2 because of a preference for some other combination along the budget line. For example, letting the budget constraint be represented in quadrant 4 by *EF*, and considering vertical iso-expected return curves (u_i and u_j both equal to 0) we can see that he might prefer L' to J[13].

Several markets, both primary and futures markets, could be included in a multidimensional analysis in which the trader selects an optimum combination on the basis of his indifference map again in terms of $E(R)$ and $V(R)$. In this case the hedge would be defined as 'given the combination found in the primary markets, what is the combination in the futures which would minimize overall variance.'

Finally, the 'marginal convenience yield,' a concept which has appeared on occasion in the literature, could be introduced into the model.[14] This yield is a 'convenience' return enjoyed by the trader who holds an inventory. The marginal yield is a declining function of the size of inventory held. The effect of its inclusion here would be to make convex to the origin non-vertical iso-expected return lines.

NOTES

1 This abstracts from the problem of indivisibility which arises from the fact that a contract covers a fixed quantity of the commodity.

2 In a case where he carries a permanent stock he could also carry a 'perpetual' hedge by liquidating his contracts prior to delivery and

simultaneously selling contracts of a later future to maintain the hedge. This procedure, however, does not alter the basic principles of hedging outlined above.

3 See, for example, P. A. Samuelson, *Economics, An Introductory Analysis*, 4th edition, New York, 1958, p. 425.

4 R. G. Hawtrey, 'Mr. Kaldor on the Forward Market,' *Review of Economic Studies*, vol. VII, 1940, p. 203.

5 *A Treatise on Money*, London, 1930, vol. II, chap. XXIX. This theory has been elaborated by J. R. Hicks in *Value and Capital*, 2nd ed., Oxford, 1946, pp. 137–9, and has been extensively treated by N. Kaldor in 'Speculation and Income Stability,' *Review of Economic Studies*, vol. VII, 1939, pp. 1–27. An interesting recent analysis of the financial results of speculation in commodity futures is contained in H. S. Houthakker, 'Can Speculators Forecast Prices?' *Review of Economics and Statistics*, vol. XXXIX, 1957, pp. 141–51.

6 'Futures Trading and Hedging,' *American Economic Review*, vol. XLIII, 1953, p. 325. Italics in the original.

7 'Hedging Reconsidered,' *Journal of Farm Economics*, vol. XXXV, 1953, pp. 547–9. Italics in the original.

8 For a detailed discussion of this point, see L. L. Johnson, 'Price Instability, Hedging and Trade Volume in the Coffee Market,' *Journal of Political Economy*, vol. XLV, 1957, pp. 319–21.

9 L. G. Telser in 'Safety First and Hedging,' *Review of Economic Studies*, vol. XXIII, 1955–56, pp. 1–16, demonstrates the rationality of holding hedged and unhedged positions simultaneously but operates under the highly restrictive assumption that the trader maximizes expected income under the constraint that the probability of the occurrence of a given 'disaster' level of income not exceed a given value. M. J. Brennan in 'Supply of Storage,' *American Economic Review*, vol. XLVIII, 1958, pp. 69–70, mentions briefly the simultaneous holding of both hedged and unhedged stocks on the basis of risk above a 'critical' level being transferred to speculators via hedging.

10 Equations 1, 2, and 3 are based on the general equations involving the actual return, expected return, and variance of return of a linear combination of random variables. Given a number n markets in which actual return B_i in each is a random variable, total return R is a weighted sum of random variables such that $R = \sum_{i=1}^{n} x_i B_i$ where each weight is the size of position x_i held in each market. The expected return $E(R)$ is given by $E(R) = \sum_{i}^{n} x_i u_i$ and the variance of return $V(R)$ is given by $V(R) = \sum_{i=1}^{n} x_i^2 \sigma_i^2 + 2 \sum_{i=1}^{n} \sum_{j>i}^{n} x_i x_j \text{cov}_{ij}$.

11 The value of x_j^* is $\dfrac{x_i^* \text{ cov }_{ij}}{\sigma_j^2}$. By substitution in equation 4 the value of

x_i, denoted here by x_i^* that minimizes the risk of holding x_j^* is given by $\left(\frac{x_i \operatorname{cov}_{ij}^2}{\sigma_i^2 \sigma_j^2}\right)$. x_i^* is equal to x_i only if $\frac{\operatorname{cov}_{ij}^2}{\sigma_i^2 \sigma_j^2}$ is equal to 1.

12 According to equation (3*a*), $E(R) = x_i(u_i + m) + x_j u_j$. Therefore, $x_j = -\frac{x_i (u_i + m) + E(R)}{u_j}$ and $\left.\frac{\partial x_j}{\partial x_i}\right|_{E(R)} = -\frac{u_i + m}{u_j}$.

13 The opportunity line in Figure 1 would be kinked upward at the point corresponding to market combination at *J* in Figure 2, and the upper segment would represent combinations of $E(R)$, $\sqrt{V(R)}$, attainable along the constraint segment *JP*.

14 N. Kaldor, *op. cit.*, and M. J. Brennan, *op. cit.*

4 The Supply of Storage

MICHAEL J. BRENNAN

It is a familiar proposition that the amount of a commodity held in storage is determined by the equality of the marginal cost of storage and the temporal price spread. Why then do we observe stocks being carried from one period to the next when the price expected to prevail in the next period – reflected in the futures price quotation for delivery in that period – is below the current price.

In an attempt to explain 'inverse carrying charges' in futures markets (futures prices below spot prices or prices of deferred futures below that of near futures) the concept of a convenience yield on stocks has been introduced.[1] Stocks of all goods provide a yield or compensation to the holder which must be deducted from storage costs proper in calculating *net* storage costs. In equilibrium the spread between a futures and a spot price is equal to the marginal expenditure on rent for storage space, interest, handling charges, etc., minus the marginal convenience yield of stocks. Since marginal convenience yield is a decreasing function of stocks held, the marginal convenience yield may exceed the marginal expenditure on physical storage when stocks are relatively small; hence the futures price will be below the spot price.

We shall attempt here to generalize this theory in terms of the demand for and the supply of stocks for storage. Our theory purports to provide an explanation of the holding of all stocks, including those for which there is not an active futures market. It will be shown that, on the supply side, in addition to the marginal expenditure on physical storage and the marginal convenience yield another variable, a risk premium, is required to explain the holding of stocks as a function of price spreads. In the empirical part of the study the theory will be applied to stocks of several agricultural commodities. The risk premium for each commodity will be measured residually under specified conditions by deducting from the price spread between two periods the other two components of the marginal cost of storage.

* From *American Economic Review*, vol. XLVIII, 1958, pp. 50–72. (Parts II and III are not reprinted here.) Reprinted by permission.

THEORY OF STORAGE

During any period there will be firms carrying stocks of a commodity from that period into the next. Producers, wholesalers, etc., carry finished inventories from the periods of seasonally high production to the periods of low production. Processors carry stocks of raw materials. Speculators possess title to stocks held in warehouses. These firms may be considered as supplying inventory stocks or, briefly, supplying storage. The supply of storage refers not to the supply of storage *space* but to the supply of *commodities* as inventories. In general, a supplier of storage is anyone who holds title to stocks with a view to their future sale, either in their present or in a modified form.

On the other hand there will be groups who want to have stocks carried for them from one period (in which they do not intend to consume them) to another period (in which they do intend to consume them). These consumers may be regarded as demanding storage. Since production is not stable for all commodities, consumers demand that the storage function be so performed that the flow of commodities for sale will be made relatively stable. We assume that there is no significant time lag between sales out of stocks by suppliers of storage and utilization of the commodity by households, for otherwise we could not distinguish suppliers from demanders of storage. For example, in the case of butter, storage is normally performed by the manufacturer – stocks are carried from the months of seasonally high production to the months of seasonally low production. Sales out of stocks by manufacturers to wholesalers (or retailers) are assumed equivalent to sales to consumers, and the relevant price entering storage decisions is the wholesale price. This is a simple analogy to the derived demand for a commodity: with no time lag between wholesale purchases and household consumption the demand for consumption can be expressed as a function of the wholesale price.

The Demand for Storage

The demand for storage of a commodity can be derived from the demand for its consumption. We assume that consumption during any period depends only upon the price in that period; all other variables affecting consumption are exogenous. Let P_t be the price in period t and let C_t be consumption during t. The demand function in period t can then be written:

$$(1) \qquad P_t = f_t(C_t), \quad \frac{\partial f_t}{\partial C_t} < 0$$

The subscript indicates that demand may shift periodically.

Consumption in any period equals stocks carried into the period plus current production minus stocks carried out of the period. Consequently we may rewrite (1) as:

$$(2) \qquad P_t = f_t(S_{t-1} + X_t - S_t)$$

where S_{t-1} is stocks at the end of period $t - 1$, X_t is production during t and S_t is stocks at the end of t. For convenience it is assumed that current production and subsequent levels of production and stocks are known. To derive the demand for storage of the commodity from period t to period $t + 1$, consider the effect of an increase in carryout from period t, i.e., an increase in end-of-period stocks. Under the specified assumptions, if the price in t rises, less will be consumed. With stocks carried into the period known and current production given, the rise in price in t results in less of the commodity offered for sale in t and more carried out of t. Since futures levels of production and stocks are given, more of the commodity is consumed in period $t + 1$, i.e., price in $t + 1$ will fall. Conversely a reduction in carryout from period t will, under these assumptions, be associated with an increase of P_{t+1} relative to P_t. In general, price in the next period minus price in the current period may be expressed as a decreasing function of stocks carried out of the current period.

Symbolically the demand for storage from period t to period $t + 1$ can be represented as follows:

$$(3) \qquad \begin{aligned} P_{t+1} - P_t &= f_{t+1}(C_{t+1}) - f_t(C_t) \\ &= f_{t+1}(S_t + X_{t+1} - S_{t+1}) - f_t(S_{t-1} + X_t - S_t) \end{aligned}$$

If we differentiate this expression with respect to S_t, we see that the partial derivative is negative. With S_{t-1} known and X_t, X_{t+1} and S_{t+1} exogenously determined, the price spread is a decreasing function of S_t. The price spread may be positive or negative. Figure 1 shows the demand curve for storage.

The assumption that demand may shift periodically is a realistic and, for our purposes, useful one. In general, the demand curve for storage of a commodity from period t to period $t + 1$ will shift upward (*e.g.*, to $D'D'$ in Figure 1) as a result of (1) an increase in production in t, (2) a decrease in production in $t + 1$ or (3) an increase in stocks carried out of $t + 1$. Opposite movements of these exogenous variables will produce a shift downward.

The supply of storage

The supply of storage is forthcoming from those firms holding title to stocks carried from one period to another. In a competitive industry in an uncertain world a firm seeking to maximize net revenue will hold an amount of stocks such that the net marginal cost of storage per unit of time equals the expected change in price per unit of time. We have seen that the net marginal cost of storage need not be positive. The net marginal cost of storage is defined as the marginal outlay on physical storage plus a marginal risk-aversion factor minus the marginal convenience yield on stocks.

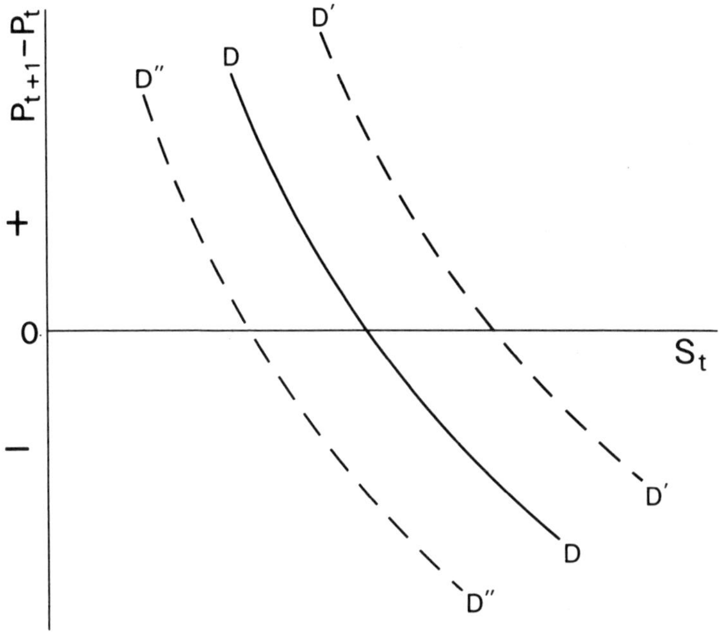

FIGURE 1

The total outlay on physical storage is the sum of rent for storage space, handling or in-and-out charges, interest, insurance, etc. As the quantity of stocks held by a firm increases, the total outlay increases. Although for any single firm this cost may increase at either a constant or an increasing rate, it seems reasonable to suppose that the marginal outlay is approximately constant until total warehouse capacity is almost fully utilized (each firm can store all it wishes without affecting the cost per unit of the commodity stored). Beyond this level marginal outlay will rise at an increasing rate.

Suppliers of storage are mostly engaged in production, processing or merchandising with storage as an adjunct. The costs of storage must be considered as charged against the business operation as a whole. Given day-to-day fluctuations in the market, a producing firm can meet a sudden and 'unexpected' increase in demand by filling orders out of finished inventories or by adjusting its production schedule or by some combination of these. The convenience yield is attributed to the advantage (in terms of less delay and lower costs) of being able to keep regular customers satisfied or of being able to take advantage of a rise in demand and price without resorting to a revision of the production schedule. Similarly, for a processing firm the availability of stocks as raw materials permits variations in production without incurring the trouble, cost and perhaps delays of frequent spot purchases and deliveries. A wholesaler can vary his sales in response to an increased flow of orders only if he has sufficient stocks on hand.

The smaller the level of stocks on hand the greater will be the convenience yield of an additional unit. It is assumed that there is some quantity of stocks so large that the marginal convenience yield is zero. Distinction is sometimes made between 'surplus' stocks which will not be carried to a future period without expectation of a monetary return and 'pipeline' or 'working' stocks. There is an implication that pipeline stocks are relatively small and fixed in quantity. Such a distinction has little functional meaning. Actually working stocks may vary through a considerable range, their upper limit being defined as the level at which the marginal convenience yield is zero.

The third component of the net marginal cost of storage is the marginal risk-aversion factor. We should expect total risk aversion to be an increasing function of stocks. If a comparatively small quantity of stocks is held, the risk involved in undertaking the investment in stocks is also small. An unexpected fall in the price at which stocks must be sold will result in a relatively small loss to the firm holding stocks for later sale. For firms holding a small quantity of stocks as raw materials for use in production, an unexpected fall in the price will involve a relatively small loss. However, given the total capital resources of the firm, the greater the quantity of stocks held, the greater will be the loss to the firm from the same unexpected fall in the future price. There is probably some critical level of stocks at which the loss would seriously endanger the firm's credit position, and as stocks increase up to this point the risk incurred in holding them will steadily increase also – the risk of loss will constitute a part of the cost of storage. The marginal risk-aversion factor may be assumed to be either constant or, more likely, an increasing function of stocks held.

Again let S_t denote the stocks carried out of period t. Let $o_t(S_t)$ be the total outlay on physical storage, $r_t(S_t)$ the total risk-aversion factor and $c_t(S_t)$ the total convenience yield. Then the net total cost of storage $m_t(S_t)$, is defined as:

$$m_t(S_t) = o_t(S_t) + r_t(S_t) - c_t(S_t) \tag{4}$$

o_t and r_t are increasing functions of S_t so that the marginal outlay and marginal risk aversion are either constant or are increasing functions of S_t, *i.e.*, $o_t' > 0$ and $o_t'' \geq 0$; $r_t' > 0$ and $r_t'' \geq 0$. c_t is also an increasing function of S_t, but the marginal convenience yield declines and reaches zero at some large level of stocks, *i.e.*, $c_t' \geq 0$ and $c_t'' \leq 0$. The net marginal cost of storage in period t may be written as:

$$m_t'(S_t) = o_t'(S_t) + r_t'(S_t) - c_t'(S_t) \tag{5}$$

The net marginal cost of storage need not be positive. When stocks are relatively small, c_t' will be large. If c_t' is large enough relative to o_t' plus r_t', the net marginal cost of storage will be negative. Figure 2 depicts graphically the net marginal cost of storage and its three components for a typical firm.

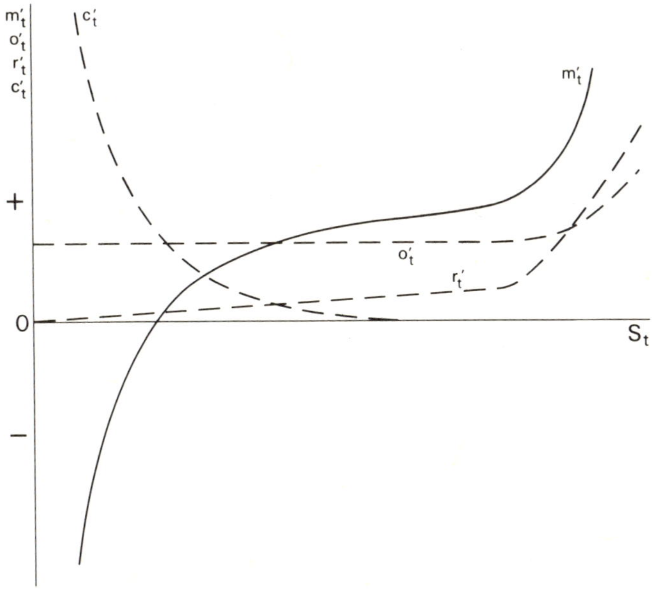

FIGURE 2

Let the expected marginal revenue of stocks carried out of period t be represented by $u_t'(S_t)$. In a competitive industry u_t' equals the expected change in price from period t to a future period, say $t + 1$.[2] Total expected net revenue is equal to:

(6) $$u_t(S_t) - m_t(S_t)$$

The quantity of stocks which maximizes expected net revenue is found by differentiating (6) with respect to S_i and setting the derivative equal to zero. This gives

(7) $$u_t'(S_t) = m_t'(S_t)$$

which expresses the familiar condition that expected net revenue is maximized when expected marginal revenue equals net marginal cost. The conditions on the second derivatives of o_t, r_t and c_t insure that the solution is a maximum.

Under the assumptions of pure competition and no external economies or diseconomies in the storage industry the supply curve of storage is the horizontal sum of all individual net marginal cost functions. Thus the sum of equations like (7), when solved for S_t as a function of u_t', is the supply curve of storage. We denote the supply of storage by

$$u_t' = g_t(S_t) \tag{8}$$

Equilibrium

We can now use the demand for and supply of storage to determine the equilibrium quantity of stocks carried out of t as a function of the price spread. We suppose that prices expected to prevail in future periods are the same for each firm. The equilibrium quantity of stocks is determined by the equality of the demand for stocks and the supply of stocks:

$$u_t' = EP_{t+1} - P_1 \tag{9}$$

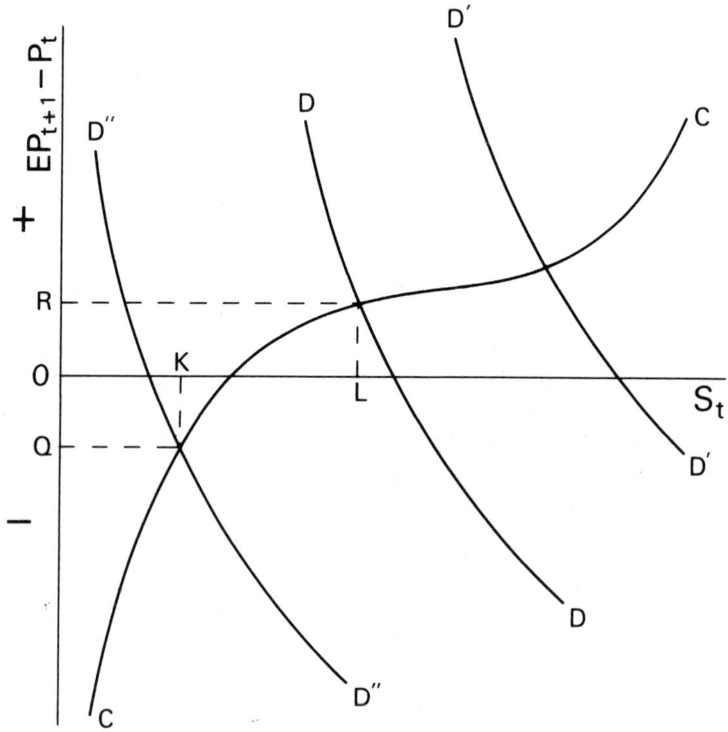

FIGURE 3

where EP_{t+1} is the price expected in period $t + 1$ and P_t is assumed known. Using (3) and (8) this can be written

$$(10) \qquad g_t(S_t) = Ef_{t+1}(S_t + X_{t+1} - S_{t+1}) - f_t(S_{t-1} + X_t - S_t)$$

For a two-period model the equilibrium is illustrated in Figure 3. DD, $D'D'$ and $D''D''$ are demand-for-storage curves; CC is the supply curve of storage. If DD is the demand curve in t, the equilibrium price spread will be OR and the equilibrium quantity of stocks carried out of t will be OL. If production during t or the expected production and/or carryout in $t + 1$ were to change, the demand curve would shift. Take, for example, the case in which production is reduced in period t, production in $t + 1$ is expected to increase or stocks carried out of $t + 1$ are expected to decrease. Then the demand curve will shift downward to $D''D''$ so that the equilibrium expected price spread is negative, OQ, and the equilibrium quantity of stocks is OK.

Part II, 'The Supply Curve of Storage of Selected Agricultural Commodities', is not reprinted here. Estimates of risk premia are presented. Part III, 'Conclusions', is also omitted here.

NOTES

1 N. Kaldor, 'Speculation and Economic Stability,' *Review of Economic Studies*, vol. VII, 1939, pp. 1–27. H. Working, 'The Theory of the Inverse Carrying Charge in Futures Markets,' *Journal of Farm Economics*, vol. XXX, pp. 1–28.

2 For a firm operating under conditions of nonpure competition, u_t' is a decreasing function of stocks held.

Section Two

Price Determination in Storage and Futures Markets

5 Speculation and Economic Stability

N. KALDOR

1. The purpose of the following paper is to examine, in the light of recent doctrines, the effects of speculation on economic stability. Speculation, for the purposes of this paper, may be defined as the purchase (or sale) of goods with a view to re-sale (re-purchase) at a later date, where the motive behind such action is the expectation of a change in the relevant prices relatively to the ruling price and not a gain accruing through their use, or any kind of transformation effected in them or their transfer between different markets. Thus, while merchants and other dealers do make purchases and sales which might be termed 'speculative', their ordinary transactions do not fall within this category. What distinguishes speculative purchases and sales from other kinds of purchases and sales is the expectation of an impending change in the ruling market price as the sole motive of action. Hence 'speculative stocks' of anything may be defined as the difference between the amount actually held and the amount that would be held if, other things being the same, the price of that thing were expected to remain unchanged; and they can be either positive or negative.[1]

2. The traditional theory of speculation viewed the economic function of speculation as the evening out of price-fluctuations due to changes in the conditions of demand or supply. It assumed that speculators are people of better than average foresight who step in as buyers whenever there is a temporary excess of supply over demand, and thereby moderate the price-fall; they step in as sellers, whenever there is a temporary deficiency of supply, and thereby moderate the price-rise. By thus stabilising prices, or at any rate, moderating the range of price-fluctuations, they also automatically act in a way which leads to the transfer of goods from uses where they have a lower utility to uses where they yield a higher utility. (If future conditions of demand and

* From N. Kaldor, *Essays in Economic Stability and Growth*, Gerald Duckworth & Co. Ltd, 1961, pp. 17–31 and by permission of Macmillan Publishing Co. Inc. New York (Copyright 1960 by Nicholas Kaldor). The article originally appeared in *Review of Economic Studies*, vol. VII, 1939–40, pp. 1–27.

supply were generally foreseen, this transfer would no doubt be effected without the agency of speculators. But in a world of perfect foresight nobody could make a speculative gain; speculators would be non-existent. In a world of imperfect foresight, the existence of speculators enables the system to behave with more foresight than the average individual in the system possesses.) Hence speculative gains are very much of the same order as other kinds of entrepreneurial gains; they are earned, similarly to the profits of wholesalers or retailers, as a result of the transference of goods from less important to more important uses.

The possibility that speculative activity might cause the range of price fluctuations to become greater rather than narrower, and that it might lead to the transfer of goods from more to less important uses, was not seriously contemplated in traditional theory. For this would imply that the speculators' foresight, instead of being better than the average, is worse than the average; such speculative activity would be attended by a loss, and not a gain; and such speculators would be speedily eliminated. Only the speculator with better than average foresight can hope to remain permanently in the market. And this implies that the effect of speculative activity must be price-stabilising, and in the above sense, wholly beneficial.

This argument, however, implies a state of affairs where speculative demand or supply amounts only to a small proportion of total demand or supply, so that speculative activity, while it can influence the magnitude of the price-change, cannot at any time change the direction of the price-change. If this condition is not satisfied, the argument breaks down. It still remains true that the speculator, in order to be permanently successful, must possess better than average foresight. But it will be quite sufficient for him to forecast correctly (or more correctly) the degree of foresight of other speculators, rather than the future course of the underlying non-speculative factors in the market.[2] If the proportion of speculative transactions in the total is large, it may become, in fact, more profitable for the individual speculator to concentrate on forecasting the psychology of other speculators, rather than the trend of the non-speculative elements. In such circumstances, even if speculation as a whole is attended by a net loss, rather than a net gain, this will not prove, even in the long-run, self-corrective. For the losses of a floating population of unsuccessful speculators will be sufficient to maintain permanently a small body of successful speculators; and the existence of this body of successful speculators will be a sufficient attraction to secure a permanent supply of this floating population. So long as the speculators differ in their own degree of foresight, and so long as they are numerous, they need not prove successful in forecasting events outside; they can live on each other.

But the traditional theory can also be criticised from another point of view. It ignored the effect of speculation on the general level of activity – or rather, it concentrated its attention on price-stability and assumed (implicitly perhaps, rather than explicitly) that if speculation can be shown to exert a stabilising influence upon price, it will *ipso facto* have a stabilising influence on activity. This, however, will only be true under certain special assumptions regarding monetary management which are certainly not fulfilled in the real world. In the absence of those assumptions, as will be shown below, speculation, in so far as it succeeds in eliminating price fluctuations will, in many cases, generate fluctuations in the level of incomes. Its stabilising influence on price will be accompanied by a destabilising influence on activity. Hence the question of the effect of speculation on price-stability and its effect on the stability of employment ought to be treated, not as part of the same problem, but as separate problems.

In the subsequent sections of this paper we shall deal first with the conditions under which speculation can take place, secondly, with the effect of speculation on price stability, and finally, with the influence of speculation on economic stability in general.

THE PRE-REQUISITES OF SPECULATION

3. Not all economic goods are the objects of speculative activity; in fact the range of things in which speculation, on any significant scale, is possible is rather limited. The two main conditions which must be present in normal circumstances in order that a particular good or asset should be the object of speculation, is the existence of a *perfect, or semi-perfect, market* and *low carrying cost*. For if carrying costs are large, and/or the market is imperfect, and thus the difference between buying price and selling price is large, speculation becomes far too expensive to be undertaken – except perhaps sporadically, or under the stress of violent changes.[3]

The presence of these two conditions presupposes, on the other hand, a number of attributes which only a limited number of goods possess simultaneously. These attributes are: (1) The good must be fully standardised, or capable of full standardisation; (2) It must be an article of general demand; (3) It must be durable; (4) It must be valuable in proportion to bulk.

The first two conditions are indispensable for anything resembling a perfect market to develop in exchange.[4] The last two ensure low carrying cost. For the greater the durability the less is the wastage due to mere passage of time, the greater the value in proportion to bulk the less the cost of storage.

These last two factors make up what might be called carrying costs *proper*. But *net* carrying cost also depends on a third factor: the yield of goods. In normal circumstances, stocks of all goods possess a yield, measured in terms of themselves,[5] and this yield which is a compensation to the holder of stocks, must be deducted from carrying costs proper in calculating net carrying cost.[6] The latter can, therefore, be negative or positive.

From the point of view of yield, it is important to distinguish between two categories of goods: those which are used in production and those which are used up in production. (There is no convenient English equivalent for the German distinction between *Gebrauchsgüter* and *Verbrauchsgüter*, both of which can refer to durable goods.) Stocks of goods of the latter category also have a yield, *qua* stocks, by enabling the producer to lay hands on them the moment they are wanted, and thus saving the cost and trouble of ordering frequent deliveries, or of waiting for deliveries.[7] But the important difference is that with this latter category, the amount of stock which can be thus 'useful' is, in given circumstances, strictly limited; their marginal yield falls sharply with an increase in stock above 'requirements' and may rise very sharply with a reduction of stocks below 'requirements'.[8] When redundant stocks exist, the marginal yield is zero.[9] With the other category of goods, items of fixed capital, the yield declines much more slowly with an increase in stock, and it is normally always positive. Hence as we defined 'speculative stocks' as the *excess* of stocks over normal requirements (i.e. that part of stocks which is only held in the expectation of a price-rise and would not be held otherwise) we may say that with working-capital-goods (*Verbrauchsgüter*) carrying costs are likely to be positive, when speculative stocks are positive, and negative when they are negative; with fixed-capital-goods (*Gebrauchsgüter*), carrying costs are normally negative, irrespective of whether 'speculative stocks' are positive or negative.

It would follow from this that fixed-capital-goods like machines or buildings, whose carrying cost is negative and invariant with respect to the size of speculative stocks, ought to be much better objects of speculation than raw materials, whose carrying costs are so variable. The reason why they are not, is because the condition of high standardisation, necessary for a perfect market, is not satisfied, and hence the gap between buying price and selling price is large. It is not that machines, etc., by being used, become 'second-hand', and thereby lose value, since the depreciation due to use is already allowed for in calculating their net yield. The reason is that all second-hand machines are to some extent de-standardised; it is very difficult to conceive a perfect market in such objects.[10,11] The same lack of standardisation accounts for the comparative absence of speculation in land and buildings.

This explains, I think, why in the real world there are only two classes of assets which satisfy the conditions necessary for large-scale speculation. The first consists of certain raw materials, dealt in at organised produce exchanges. The second consists of standardised future claims or titles to property, i.e. bonds and shares. It is also obvious that the suitability of the second class for speculative purposes is much greater than that of the first. Bonds and shares are perfect objects for speculation; they possess all the necessary attributes to a maximum degree. They are perfectly standardised (one particular share of a company is just as good as any other); perfectly durable (if the paper they are written on goes bad it can be easily replaced); their value is very high in proportion to bulk (storage cost is zero or a nominal amount); and in addition they (normally) have a yield, which is invariant (in the short period at any rate) with respect to the size of speculative commitments. Hence their net carrying cost can never be positive, and in the majority of cases, is negative.

4.[12] If expectations were quite certain, speculative activity would so adjust the current price that the difference between expected price and current price would be equal to the sum of interest cost and carrying cost. For if the difference is greater than this, it would pay speculators to enlarge their commitments; in the converse case, to reduce them. The interest rate relevant in calculating the interest cost is always the short term rate of interest, since speculation is essentially a short period commitment.[13] The carrying cost, as mentioned above, is equal to the sum of storage cost and 'primary depreciation',[14] minus the yield.

If expectations are uncertain, the difference between expected price and current price must cover, in addition, a certain risk premium, which will be the greater (1) the greater the dispersion of expectations from the mean (the less the standard probability); (2) the greater the size of commitments. Given the degree of uncertainty, marginal risk premium is an increasing function of the size of speculative stocks.

It will be useful to re-state the relationship between expected price and current price in algebraical form. We denote marginal interest cost by i, the marginal risk premium by r, the marginal yield by q, the marginal carrying cost proper by c (so that carrying cost $= c - q$); and the current price and expected price by CP and EP respectively. The following relationship must then be satisfied:

$$EP - CP = i + c - q + r$$

For certain problems in the theory of speculation, the concept of the 'representative expectation' is perfectly legitimate; it enables us, as do other similar constructions, to simplify the problem without materially affecting the result. From the point of view of the theory of the forward market, however, it may not be legitimate; for the determination of the futures price, and in particular, the relation of the futures price to the expected price, will not be the same in the case where everybody's expectations are the same as in the case where the 'representative expectation' is an average of divergent individual expectations. It will be convenient therefore to divide the analysis into two stages: in the first stage, to assume that all individuals have the *same* expectations at any one time, and to deal afterwards with the consequences of differences in individual expectations.

In both cases, individuals participating in the forward market can perform three different functions: 'hedging', 'speculation' and 'arbitrage'. 'Hedgers' are those who have certain commitments independent of any transactions in the forward market, either because they hold stocks of the commodity, or are committed to produce the commodity, or are committed to produce, in the future, something else for which the commodity is required as a raw material; and who enter the forward market in order to reduce the risks arising out of these commitments. 'Speculators', in general, have no commitments[15] apart from those entered into in connection with forward transactions; they assume risks by entering the market. Both hedgers and speculators can be, in particular circumstances, buyers or sellers of 'futures',[16] but in both cases, it is the speculators who assume the risks and the hedgers who get rid of them.

The possibility of arbitrage, i.e. buying spot and selling futures simultaneously and holding the stock until the date of delivery, arises when the relationship between the futures price and the current price ensures a riskless profit. An arbitrage operation differs from an ordinary hedging operation only in that the ordinary hedger enters the futures market in order to reduce a risk arising out of a commitment which occurs independently of the existence of the forward market; whereas the arbitrageur assumes risks which he would not have assumed if the facilities of the forward market did not enable him to pass them on, on advantageous terms. Hence, any ordinary holder of stocks of a commodity becomes an 'arbitrageur' in so far as the existence of the futures market tempts him not only to hedge the stocks he would ordinarily hold, but to enlarge his stocks in relation to turnover owing to the advantageous terms on which they can be 'hedged'.

The possibility of arbitrage sets an upper limit to the futures price in relation to the spot price. While there is no limit, apart from expectations, to backwardation, i.e. to the extent to which the futures price may fall short of the current price, there is a limit to contango, in that the futures price cannot exceed the current price by more than the cost of arbitrage, i.e. by more than the sum of interest plus carrying costs. Since, as explained above, ordinary holders of stock automatically become arbitrageurs whenever the relation between the futures price and the spot price tempts them to do so, the carrying cost consists of the costs of storage and wastage *minus the yield*, so that the net cost of arbitrage is $i + c - q$.[17] Denoting the futures price by FP, we have

$$FP - CP = i + c - q$$

and since, in all cases

$$EP - CP = i + c - q + r$$

it follows that

$$FP = EP - r$$

Thus, arbitrage prevents the futures price from rising above $EP - r$, while speculation (see below) prevents it from falling below this amount. This conclusion is quite general,[18] and it is consistent with both contango and backwardation, i.e. with the futures price being either above or below the current price. When the yield is one of convenience, the marginal yield (q) varies inversely with the size of stocks in relation to turnover. When speculative stocks are zero, the expected price equals the current price (the stocks of ordinary holders are 'normal'), and therefore $-(c - q) = i + r$, i.e. the negative of carrying cost must be equal to the sum of interest cost and risk premium. Since i and r are always positive, the carrying cost must be negative – the yield must exceed the sum of storage cost and primary depreciation by the required amount. In this case, $FP = CP - r$, and the futures price falls short of the current price by the amount Mr. Keynes called 'normal backwardation'.[19]

If stocks are sufficiently large in relation to turnover, q declines to zero, though it cannot become negative. It follows that, given an expectation of a rise in price, the upper limit to contango is $i + c$. In this case $FP - CP = i + c$, but as $q = 0$, $EP - CP = i + c + r$; FP again equals $EP - r$. This upper limit to contango is likely to appear at times when the market is unduly depressed by the prevalence of excessive stocks in relation to current consumption; and when, as a result of this, the spot price has fallen to such low levels that there is a definite expectation in the market that the price will recover in the future, with the gradual absorption of excessive stocks. This is another way of saying that when the stocks carried are excessive in relation to turnover (so that q is zero), the current price must be below the expected price, since only the expectation of a rise in price can induce the market to carry the outstanding volume of stocks.

On the other hand, when stocks are scarce, the marginal yield is large so that abnormal backwardation must appear, i.e. $q > i + c + r$. In this case, the high marginal convenience yield ensures that the spot price rises to abnormally high levels and, as a result, the market expects a fall in price in the future as stocks are restored to more normal levels. Just as it is impossible for the market to expect a rise in prices in the (foreseeable) future when stocks are scarce in relation to current consumption (since the spot price will have to rise sufficiently to eliminate any such expectation), so in the absence of an expectation of a change in price (i.e. when stocks are normal and the underlying factors are considered stable) there must always be backwardation.[20]

We have seen that arbitrage prevents the futures price from rising above $EP - r$. It remains to be shown that speculation prevents the futures price from falling below *EP* — *r*. Hedgers, in principle, could be either sellers or buyers of futures, though normally, hedging will be predominantly on the selling side.[21] Since transactions between hedgers who are sellers and hedgers who are buyers cancel out, it is the net sale of futures by hedgers (i.e. the excess of hedging on the selling side) which requires to be taken up by speculators. The hedgers will *sell* futures if the futures price is *equal to or higher than EP* — *r*; whilst speculators will *buy* futures if the futures price is *equal to or lower than EP* — *r* (where *r* is the individual marginal risk premium in both cases).[22] If everybody's expectations are the same, futures transactions between hedgers and speculators can only arise owing to differences in the marginal risk premium, i.e. in the marginal willingness to bear risks among the different individuals in the two groups, and would proceed until these differences are eliminated. Since the marginal risk premium varies, not only with individual psychological propensities to bear risks, but also with the size of commitments, i.e. with the amount of the possible loss relatively to the individual's total assets, we need not assume any variation in psychological propensities in order to account for such differences. When hedgers are predominantly sellers of futures, the buying of futures by speculators therefore prevents the futures price from falling below *EP* — *r*, whilst arbitrage, as we have seen, prevents it from rising above this level.

The above theory of 'normal backwardation' (according to which the futures price must be below the spot price when stocks in relation to turnover are normal, while contango can only develop in times of excess stocks and abnormally low spot prices) is subject however to an important qualification when we allow for the fact that the expectations of different individuals comprising the market are not uniform.[23] Transactions will now take place not only between hedgers and hedgers, between hedgers and speculators, and hedgers and arbitrageurs, but also between speculators and speculators; and transactions of the latter type may swamp all others. We now have to divide speculators into two groups: bulls and bears. Bull speculators will be *buyers of futures*, and their demand price is *EP* — *r* (where both *EP* and *r* are subjective terms and refer to the mean value of the individual speculator's expectation, and his individual risk premium, respectively); bear speculators will be *sellers of futures* and their supply price is *EP* + *r*.

It should be clear at once that if by 'expected price' we mean not the expectations either of bulls or of bears, but some kind of average expectation for the market as a whole, the price which will tend to get established as the outcome of transactions between bulls and bears is neither *EP* + *r*, nor *EP* — *r*, but something in between the two. We cannot say that the futures price will *correspond* to this average 'expected price'; this would only be true if the marginal risk premia of different speculators were equal; and when the expectations themselves are different, there is no reason to assume that the marginal risk premia will be the same. But it is clear that the opposite risks assumed by bulls and bears will tend to cancel each other out – leaving the futures price if not equal to, at any rate fairly near, the 'expected' price.[24] In a market where bulls predominate, the futures price will tend to exceed the 'expected' price and vice versa, when bears predominate. Hedging on the selling side and arbitrage will act in the same fashion as a strengthening of bearish sentiment, while hedging on the buying side will act in the same fashion as a strengthening of bullish sentiment.

Thus, in addition to the factors mentioned above, the determination of the futures price will also depend, in the real world, on *divergence of opinion*; this factor will be all the more important the greater the degree of divergence and the more equally bulls and bears are divided. In markets where this divergence is important, and where transactions between speculators dominate over hedging transactions, we cannot say that the futures price will either be above, or below, the expected price, but simply that it will reflect the 'expected' price; always subject, of course, to the provision that it cannot exceed the current price by more than the cost of arbitrage.

5. The elasticity of speculative stocks may be defined as the proportionate change in the amount of speculative stocks held as a result of a given percentage change in the *ratio* of the expected price to the current price.[25] This elasticity will obviously depend on the variations in the terms i, c and r, which are associated with a change in speculative stocks, in other words on the elasticity of marginal interest cost, marginal carrying cost, and the marginal risk premium, with respect to a change in speculative commitments.

Of these three factors the marginal interest cost, as we have seen, may be subject to discontinuous variation if the 'marginal speculator' in a particular market turns from a lender of money into a borrower, or vice versa, but apart from this its elasticity is likely to be fairly high, if not infinite.[26] The marginal risk premium is normally rising, and its elasticity probably differs greatly between different markets. The more numerous are speculators in a particular market, and the more steady the price on the basis of past experience[27] the higher this elasticity is likely to be. Finally, the marginal carrying cost, as we have seen, can be assumed to be constant in the case of securities, while it will rise sharply (at any rate over a certain range) in the case of raw materials and primary products. Hence, taking all factors together, the elasticity of speculative stocks is likely to be much higher in the case of long-term securities than in the case of raw materials.

The higher the elasticity of speculative stocks, the greater the dependence of the current price on the expected price. In the limiting case when this elasticity is infinite, the current price may be said to be entirely determined by the expected price; changes in the conditions of non-speculative demand or supply can then have no direct influence on the current price at all (since speculative stocks will immediately be so adjusted as to leave the price unchanged); any change in the current price must be the result of a change in price-expectations.[28]

In the opposite limiting case, when the elasticity of speculative stocks is zero, changes in the expected price have no influence upon the current price; the latter is entirely determined by the non-speculative factors.

Part II, 'Speculation and Price Stability', is not reprinted here. It deals with the effect of speculation on price stability.

NOTES

1 The expectations of different individuals composing the market are normally different, of course. But it is permissible to speak of a single expectation for the market as a whole, since *cet. par.* there is always a definite amount of any good that would be held, at any particular expectation, if all individuals' expectations were the same.

2 Cf. Keynes, *General Theory*, chapter 12 on 'Long Term Expectations'. 'We have reached the third degree [in the share markets] where we devote our intelligences to anticipating what average opinion expects average opinion to be.' (p. 156.)

3 In conditions of hyper-inflation – as in Germany in 1923 – the range of goods in which speculation takes place is, of course, very much extended.

4 In particular the degree of standardisation required is very high. For the difference between the simultaneous buying price and selling price can only be small when there is a large and steady volume of transactions, in the same article, per unit of time, so that it pays individuals to undertake purchases and sales through the agency of an organised market. It is necessary for this that the commodity in question should have but few attributes of quality (that it should be simple) so that a specification of standard qualities ('grades') can be drawn up without difficulty. In the organised exchanges of the world this standardisation is carried so far that buyers rarely see the article they are actually buying – contracts are made between buyers and sellers with reference to standard grades and places of delivery. It is also necessary that the amount bought by the representative individual in a single transaction should represent considerable value. Nobody would go to the trouble of buying, say, cigarettes, through the agency of a central market, even if this would imply some saving.

5 By defining yield as that return which goods obtain when measured in terms of themselves, we exclude here any return due to appreciation of value (in terms of some standard) whether expected or unexpected.

6 Our definition of net carrying cost is, therefore, the negative of Mr. Keynes' 'own-rate of own-interest' in chapter 17 of the *General Theory* – except that no allowance is made here for the factor termed 'liquidity premium'. Our reason for deducting the yield from the carrying cost, and not the other way round, is because (as will be clear below) from the point of view of speculation, net carrying cost is the significant concept rather than the own-rate of interest.

7 There is, of course, in addition, the stock of goods in the course of production (goods in process) which depends on the length of the production process, but with this we are not here concerned (since they are not standardised).

8 This, as we shall see below, is equally true of stocks of money, as of other commodities.

9 Mr. Keynes, in the *Treatise on Money*, uses the term 'working capital' for stocks which have a positive yield, and 'liquid capital' for those which have a zero yield. (vol. II, p. 130.)

10 I.e. the seller of a second-hand machine must not only allow for a reduction of value due to depreciation, but also an extra loss due to the fact that he is selling the machine and not buying it.

11 Mr. Keynes, in certain parts of the *General Theory*, appears to use the term 'liquidity' in a sense which comes very close to our concept of 'perfect marketability'; i.e. goods which can be sold at any time for the same price, or nearly the same price, at which they can be bought. Yet it is obvious that the attribute of goods is not the same thing as what Mr. Keynes really wants to mean by 'liquidity'. Certain gilt-edged securities can be bought on the Stock Exchange at a price which is only a small fraction higher than the price at which they can be sold; on this definition, therefore, they should have to be regarded as highly liquid assets. In fact it is very difficult to find a satisfactory definition of what constitutes 'liquidity' – a difficulty, I think, which is inherent in the concept itself. As will be argued below, what appears to be the result of a preference for 'liquidity' may be explained as the consequence of certain speculative activities in which 'liquidity preference' in any positive sense, plays a very small part.

12 [This section is a revised amalgam of § 4 as published in the original version of the article, *Review of Economic Studies*, 1939–40, pp. 5–7, and of my contribution to the Symposium, 'A Note on the Theory of the Forward Market', *Review of Economic Studies*, 1939–40. pp. 196–201.]

13 If there is a difference between the speculators' borrowing rate and their lending rate, one or the other will be relevant, according as the marginal unit of commitment is made with borrowed funds or not. Hence when speculators reduce their commitments, interest costs may fall, and this has (even if the market rate is unchanged) a similar effect as a fall in carrying cost (rise in yield).

14 The term 'primary depreciation' is Mr. Hawtrey's (*Capital and Employment*, p. 272), and is used to denote that part of depreciation which inevitably arises through the mere passage of time.

15 Ordinary stockholders and producers of the commodity may of course also indulge in speculation, in so far as they carry extra stocks in the expectation of a rise in price.

16 I use the term 'futures' here as equivalent to a forward purchase or sale; in other words, I assume that the commodity dealt in is completely standardised – as in the case of the foreign exchange market – and hence there is no difference in the obligations assumed in a spot contract or a futures contract. If there are differences then as Mr. Dow has shown, they can be introduced as an additional element causing some further

deviation in the futures price from the spot price. Cf. J. C. R. Dow, 'A Theoretical Account of Futures Markets', *Review of Economic Studies*, 1939–40, pp. 185–95.

17 We must bear in mind however that the marginal convenience yield of stocks varies (in some cases fairly rapidly) with changes in the size of stocks in relation to turnover, so that even a moderate enlargement of stocks for arbitrage purposes might be sufficient to reduce q to zero.

18 [In the original article and again in the Symposium, *Review of Economic Studies*, 1939–40, I held that where the yield was one of convenience, arbitrageurs may not obtain it (since the convenience yield accrues only to those who hold stocks as part of their normal course of business), so that the upper limit to contango is $i + c$ even in cases where q is positive, and $FP = EP - r + q$. I ignored, however, the fact that when the futures price exceeds the current price by more than $i + c - q$, it will pay ordinary holders to enlarge their stocks and hedge by selling futures at the same time.]

19 J. M. Keynes, *Treatise on Money*, vol. II, pp. 142–4.

20 The reason why this is not the case in the forward transactions of the Stock Exchange is due to the convention that the yield is credited to the forward buyer (from the date of the contract) and not to the forward seller who actually holds the stock. Hence the forward price is equal to the current price plus interest cost and there is contango (since in this case $c = 0$, $FP = EP - r + q = CP + i$). Backwardation can only arise on the Stock Exchange if a fall in price is expected, and this expected fall, on account of a shortage of stock for immediate delivery which is known to be purely temporary, cannot be adequately reflected in the current price (e.g. in the case of trans-Atlantic stocks, when arbitrageurs run out of stock and have to wait for fresh supplies to be sent across the Atlantic). It is always a sign, therefore, of the current price not being in equilibrium in relation to the expected price.

21 This is because the risk normally hedged against is the risk of a fall in the prices of the commodities actually carried by the manufacturer or trader, i.e. the risk of an inventory loss. The opposite risk of a future rise in the prices of the materials which the manufacturer uses, with its attendant possibility of a lower profit on fabrication (or at least the sacrifice of the inventory profit he would have made if he had bought earlier) is not normally compensated by buying futures, simply because manufacturers are less afraid of making losses on account of rising raw material prices than on account of falling prices (since in times of rising raw material prices the increase in cost can normally be passed on to the buyer). A failure to make a profit on account of the failure to make an investment is not considered as contributing the same kind of 'risk' as that of a loss on the capital actually invested. In exceptional cases, however, e.g. where the manufacturer works on long-term contracts, and does not expect to be able to pass on the higher prices of materials by raising his selling price, or where the futures price is abnormally low in relation to the spot price (due to temporary shortages of stock), manufacturers may well allow their stocks to be run down below normal levels,

and compensate for the risks arising therefrom by becoming buyers in the futures market.

22 If hedgers are buyers of futures on balance, they will buy futures if *FP* is equal to or lower than $EP + r$; whilst the speculators will sell futures if *FP* is equal to or higher than $EP + r$. However, with uniform expectations, this will not establish the futures price at $EP + r$ on account of the fact that it will be the arbitrageurs and not the speculators who provide the supply of futures to match the excess hedging on the buying side. Arbitrage, as we have seen, will always bring the futures price to $CP + i + c - q$ which, on the assumption of unanimous expectations, equals $EP - r$. Speculation on the selling side can only appear as a result of differences in expectations.

23 [I am indebted to Mr. R. G. Hawtrey's criticism of the original version of this paper for the conclusions that follow.]

24 The more favourable relationship between the futures price and the expected price resulting from this will mean however that the market will carry larger stocks than it would have carried otherwise. For, as we have seen, when expectations are uniform and the expected price is the same as the current price, the futures price will necessarily be *below* the current price. In a market where the bullish sentiment expecting a rise in price and the bearish sentiment expecting a fall are equally strong, the futures price may well establish itself in the neighbourhood of the current price, as being the only price capable of bringing speculative supply and demand into equilibrium. In that case, however, ordinary traders will enlarge their stocks in connection with arbitrage operations until the marginal convenience yield falls sufficiently to eliminate the profitability of such operations. This action by arbitrageurs may not depress the futures price significantly, when the speculative demand and supply is large in relation to the non-speculative demand for holding stocks.

25 [In the original version this elasticity was defined with reference to the percentage change in the *difference* $EP - CP$. It was pointed out by E. Rothbarth in 1942 and recently by Mr. Streeten that to be consistent with the formula on p. 33, the elasticity should be defined in terms of the *ratio* of the two prices. The latter definition is correct in cases where the items $(i + c + r - q)$ are proportional to *CP*, whilst the former definition is appropriate when $(i + c + r - q)$ is fixed in money terms and hence varies, as a percentage, with a change in *CP*. The correct formula corresponding to the former definition is that given by Streeten in equation (3*a*). (*Review of Economic Studies*, 1958, p. 67.)]

26 In certain markets the lending rate only is normally relevant, and not the borrowing rate. In this case the elasticity of interest cost can be taken as infinite.

27 In other words, the elasticity of the marginal risk premium is likely to vary inversely with the amount of the risk premium. When the risk premium is low, its elasticity is also likely to be high.

28 This does not imply, of course, that the current price must be *equal* to the expected price, this would only be the case if in addition, the sum of $i + c - q + r$ were zero. Nor does it imply that changes in the non-speculative factors can have no influence upon price at all, for changes in these factors may influence price-expectations.

6 The Simultaneous Determination of Spot and Futures Prices

JEROME L. STEIN

This paper develops a simple geometric technique for the simultaneous determination of spot and futures prices in commodity markets; and it explains the allocation between hedged and unhedged holdings of stocks. On the basis of this analysis, it is possible to determine whether changes in spot and futures prices have occurred as a result of (a) changes in the excess supply of current production, or (b) changes in price expectations.

The possessor of stocks has two alternatives. He may contract to sell a given physical entity at a stated price, or he may hold stocks for sale at a later date at an uncertain price. If the first alternative is chosen, he may sell either *spot* or *forward.* A forward sale involves delivery at a later date; any storage that the seller is performing is merely a service to his customer.

If the second alternative is chosen, he may hold his stocks either hedged (by selling a *futures* contract) or unhedged; but this form of stockholding involves an uncertain expected return and a probability of a capital loss. Consequently, the owner of stocks will allocate his stocks between hedged and unhedged holdings to maximize his expected utility.

This paper is concerned with both alternatives: the spot sale and the holding of stocks for sale at a later date. Part I develops a theory of holding stocks. It is shown how the possessor of a given quantity of stocks allocates his holdings between hedged and unhedged stocks. Thereby, the supply of hedged and unhedged storage is derived.

Part II discusses the spot and futures markets. Two curves are developed to determine simultaneously the spot and futures prices. One curve gives the pair of spot and futures prices which equilibrate the supply and demand for storage. The other curve gives the pair of spot

* From *American Economic Review*, vol. LI, 1961, pp. 1012–25. (Parts II and III are not reprinted here.) Reprinted by permission.

and futures prices which equilibrate the supply and demand for futures contracts. Equilibrium exists where the two curves intersect.

Part III indicates how these prices are affected by (1) variations in the supply and demand for current production, and (2) changes in the prices expected to prevail at a later date.

Throughout this paper, pure competition is assumed to prevail.

THE DECISION TO HOLD HEDGED AND UNHEDGED STOCKS UNDER PURE COMPETITION

Unhedged holding of stocks

The expected gain from holding unhedged stocks (u) is equal to the spot price expected to prevail at a later date (p^*) minus the current spot price (p) minus the marginal net carrying costs (m). There are two components of the marginal net carrying costs: the marginal costs of storage and the marginal convenience yield, the latter a negative element in carrying cost. The concept of the marginal convenience yield has been developed by Brennan [1, pp. 53–56] and Telser [4, pp. 235–37]. Since the convenience yield is a measure of the advantage (to the producer, processor, or wholesaler) of having stocks readily available, it depends upon the total quantity of stocks carried – hedged and unhedged. Since the marginal convenience yield is negatively related to the total quantity of stocks carried, the marginal net carrying costs rise with the total quantity of stocks held [1] [4].

The variable p^* is a stochastic variable. There is a probability that a capital loss will be made on the holdings of unhedged stocks: i.e., that $p^* - p - m$ will be negative.

The holding of hedged stocks

When stocks are hedged, the owner incurs a liability to offset his holding of assets (stocks). His liability is the sale of a futures contract, for the delivery of one of several grades of a commodity sometime within the period of the futures contract. The owner of hedged stocks does not intend to deliver a physical commodity in fulfillment of his futures contract, but intends to repurchase a futures contract at the time that he sells his inventory of stocks [2, Ch. 12–14] [3, p. 153] [6]. The expected gain from holding hedged stocks is equal to the expected gain from holding unhedged stocks minus the expected loss involved in the sale and purchase of a futures contract. At worst, the holder of hedged stocks can deliver one of several grades of a physical commodity in fulfillment of the futures contract, at a premium or a discount to the contract price [2, pp. 33–34].

Let q be the current price of a futures contract and q^* be the price of the futures contract expected at a later date. Then, the expected gain from holding hedged stocks is h,

$$h = (p^* - p) - (q^* - q) - m \tag{1}$$

The firm buys stock at p and sells a futures contract for q. The marginal net carrying costs are m. The firm expects to sell the stock at p^* and repurchase its futures contract for q^*. In the event that it costs more to repurchase the futures contract than can be received from the sale of the unit of stock, it is cheaper to make delivery on the futures contract than to repurchase it, provided that the futures contract permits the delivery of the commodity which is held in storage. In this way, hedging may bound the possible losses that can be suffered in connection with holding stocks. The expected gain from holding *hedged* stock, h, can be written:

$$h = u - (q^* - q) \geqq q - p - m \tag{2}$$

The term $q - p - m$ is the cost of delivering the basic grade on the futures contract.

There are two stochastic variables involved in h: p^*, the expected commodity price, and q^*, the expected price of the futures contract. Inventory losses can be made on hedged inventory, despite the fact that the loss is bounded at $q - p - m$.

The optimum combination of hedged and unhedged stocks

An owner of stocks, for sale at an uncertain price, is assumed to allocate his holdings between hedged and unhedged stocks so as to maximize his expected utility. The method of optimizing developed here is based upon James Tobin's theory of liquidity preference [5, pp. 71–77].

As the proportion of unhedged stock varies between zero and 100 per cent, the expected return per unit of stock varies from h to u. Risk is inherent in each form of stockholding, where risk is defined as the situation whereby the owner may fail to receive his expected return. Many different measures of risk are possible. Tobin [5, p. 72] used the standard deviation of the expected return as his measure of risk. Since he assumed that the probability density functions are symmetrical, a high standard deviation or variance means a high probability of both negative and positive deviations from the mean. Other reasonable measures of risk, which emphasize the disutility aspects of uncertainty, are the probability of loss or the expected value of the loss. These two measures of risk do not presuppose symmetrical density functions. For expositional convenience I shall use the variance of the expected return as a measure of risk, with the assumption that the density functions are symmetrical.

An owner of a unit of unhedged stock has a risk equal to the variance of u. Given p and m, the variance of u is equal to the variance of p^*. The possessor of a unit of hedged stock has a risk equal to the variance of h. Given p, m and q, this is equal to: var p^* + var q^* − 2 cov p^*q^*. As the proportion of unhedged stocks varies from zero to 100 per cent, the risk varies from var p^* + var q^* − 2 cov p^*q^* to var p^*.

An opportunity locus for expected return and risk, facing the owner of 100 units of stock, is given by line HU in Figure 1. At point H all of

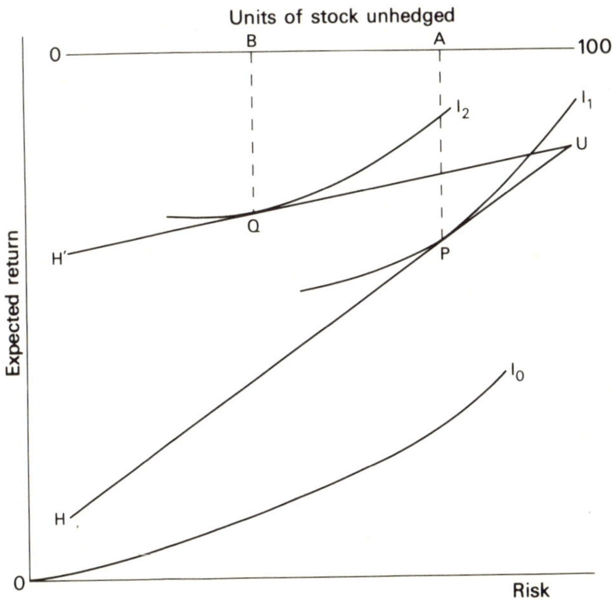

FIGURE 1

the stocks are hedged, giving an expected return of h and a risk of var h. At point U all of the stocks are unhedged, giving an expected return of u, and a risk of var u. As the ratio of unhedged to total stocks rises (see the scale at the top of Figure 1), the combination of expected return and risk is given by opportunity locus HU. In this diagram it is assumed that unhedged stocks are both riskier and carry a higher expected return than hedged stocks, thereby making line HU positively sloped. There is no reason why line HU could not be negatively sloped. In such a case (as will be apparent from the argument below) no unhedged stocks would be carried. Points H and U are based upon given price expectations and risks. As price expectations change, points H and U will move accordingly.

The indifference curve between expected return and risk will be convex – rising at an increasing rate – if the individual has a declining marginal utility of income and a total utility function which can be approximated by a quadratic. The proof of this proposition is given by Tobin [5, pp. 76–77].[1] A family of such indifference curves is given in Figure 1. Given the risk – a point on the abscissa – a higher expected return implies a higher expected utility of income; the utility expected from the ownership of 100 units of stock rises as we rise vertically in Figure 1. Curve I_2 is preferred to curve I_1 because expected utility is greater along curve I_2 than along curve I_1.

Point P represents the optimum combination of hedged and unhedged stock, given opportunity locus HU and the indifference map, since expected utility from 100 units of stock is maximized at this point. The individual will hold OA units unhedged and $100 - OA$ units hedged.

Suppose that the price of a futures contract rises, other things remaining unchanged; then the expected return from hedged stock rises to H'; but the expected return (and risk) on unhedged stock does not change. The new opportunity locus is $H'U$.

The new equilibrium combination of hedged and unhedged stock is given by point Q. As the slope of the transformation line, or opportunity locus, is decreased there is a substitution effect. The ratio of unhedged to total stock will be decreased as the hedging of stock becomes relatively more attractive. Tending to offset this substitution effect is an income effect. The higher expected utility, made possible by the rise in the price of a futures contract, may affect the individual's aversion to risk. In so far as he is more willing to take an additional unit of risk per increment of expected return, when his expected utility is increased, the income effect will induce him to increase the ratio of unhedged to total stock. The crucial question is which effect will dominate? Will the greater attractiveness of holding hedged stock be offset by a greater willingness to assume risk? The substitution effect will be dominant, so that the ratio of unhedged stocks will be decreased as hedging becomes more profitable, given the utility function described above and the occurrence of tangency solutions. *Mutatis mutandis*, the proof of this proposition is found in Tobin [5, p. 79].

The demand for stocks or the supply of storage

The total quantity of stocks demanded by owners of stocks (i.e., the supply of storage) is assumed to be an increasing function of the maximum expected utility derived from holding stocks. Initially, the maximum expected utility from holding 100 units of stock was given by I_1. When the expected return from holding hedged stocks is increased, the maximum expected utility from holding 100 units of stock is given by I_2, which is preferred to I_1. As the expected utility from stockholding is increased, the total quantity of stocks demanded (i.e., storage supplied) will also increase.

Storage will only be supplied if the maximum expected utility from storage exceeds the utility derived from a spot sale. Consider an indifference curve I_0 (in Figure 1) passing through a point 0 (= 0, 0) with an expected return of 0 and a risk of zero. This curve will be convex, under the assumptions made above. No stocks will be held for later sale at an uncertain price unless the opportunity locus is tangent to an indifference curve which is preferred to I_0. In the event of a corner solution, stocks will be held only if the highest attainable indifference curve is preferred to I_0.

A rise in the maximum expected utility will also occur if the opportunity locus *HU*, fixed at *H*, rotates in a counterclockwise direction. For example, suppose that p^* and q^* rose by equal amounts; then, all other things remaining the same, the expected return from unhedged storage rises relative to the expected return from hedged storage—risk remaining constant. The ratio of unhedged to the total stocks will rise; and there will be an increase in the total quantity of stocks demanded. Both income and substitution effects operate in the same direction in this case.

The demand for stocks (i.e., the supply of storage) then depends upon points *H* and *U*. Given the risks (var *h*, var *u*), the demand for stocks rises with (1) $p^* - p - m$, and with (2) $(p^* - q^*) + (q - p) - m$. The first term is the expected return derived from holding unhedged stock; the second term is the expected return derived from holding hedged stock. The demand for stocks in the market (S_D) is given by equation (3):[2]

(3) $S_D = U(p^* - p - m) + H[(p^* - q^*) + b - m]; \quad U' > 0, H' > 0,$
where $b = q - p$, the spread.

U is the market demand for unhedged stock and *H* is the market demand for hedged stock. That is, *U* is the supply of unhedged storage and *H* is the supply of hedged storage.

The duality of long and short hedging

There are people, such as millers, who have contracted to sell a certain number of units forward at a fixed price. A miller contracts to sell x units of flour for p dollars, to be delivered in (say) 90 days. His stock of flour is $-x$ units, just as the stock of the individual in Figure 1 was +100 units. The miller does not know the exact price at which he will be able to purchase his wheat. His gross profit will be $p - p^*$, where p^* is the price at which he expects to purchase the wheat. A miller can hedge by purchasing a wheat futures contract at price q, at the time that the flour is sold forward. His expected return is $(p - q) + (q^* - p^*)$, where q^* is the price at which he expects to sell the wheat futures contract.

The miller, i.e., the potential long hedger, holds a negative quantity of stock. Moreover, the expected return from his hedged or unhedged position is the negative of the short hedger discussed in the sections above (excluding the marginal net carrying costs).

On the basis of the analysis described in Figure 1, the potential long hedger (e.g., miller) can determine (1) how much of his short position should be covered by the purchase of a wheat futures contract and (2) how many units of flour he should sell short. The first problem is solved by hedging that proportion which will maximize his expected utility – exactly as described above. The second problem is solved by varying his short sales on the basis of the maximum expected utility that he can derive from a short position, where he hedges the proportion called for in the answer to the first problem. The position of the long hedger is the negative of the position of the short hedger, and the same method of analysis is applicable in both cases.

Part II, 'Market Equilibrium', and Part III, 'Comparative Statics', are not reprinted here. Their scope is indicated in the author's introduction.

NOTES

1 Tobin also considers individuals with constant and rising marginal utility of incomes, i.e., individuals with indifference curves which do not rise at increasing rates. I shall restrict the present analysis to individuals with declining marginal utility schedules.

2 The process of aggregation is difficult in so far as expectations of individuals differ. Let p^* and q^* refer to the 'average' expectations, appropriately weighed, of those who are in the business of supplying storage. See Telser [4, pp. 239–40] on this point.

REFERENCES

[1] M. J. Brennan, 'The Supply of Storage,' *American Economic Review*, vol. 48, 1958.
[2] Gerald Gold, *Modern Commodity Futures Trading*. New York 1959.
[3] H. S. Houthakker, 'The Scope and Limits of Futures Trading,' *The Allocation of Economic Resources*, Moses Abramovitz *et al.* Stanford 1959, pp. 134–59.
[4] L. G. Telser, 'Futures Trading and the Storage of Cotton and Wheat,' *Journal of Political Economy*, vol. 66, 1958.
[5] James Tobin, 'Liquidity Preference as Behavior Toward Risk,' *Review of Economic Studies*, vol. 25, 1958.
[6] Holbrook Working, 'Futures Trading and Hedging,' *American Economic Review*, vol. 43, 1953.

7 Inter-Temporal Price Relationships with Forward Markets: A Method of Analysis

M. H. PESTON and B. S. YAMEY

In this paper we present a method of approach to the analysis of inter-temporal price relationships in markets with forward dealings. The method involves, first, a five-fold classification of types of behaviour, and second, the application of traditional supply and demand analysis. It is used here to elucidate a simplified problem. The relevance of the classification of types of behaviour extends, we believe, beyond the narrow confines of the particular problem, whereas the method of analysis as applied to the problem may, we should like to think, serve as a basis for a more comprehensive analytical treatment of price formation in markets with forward dealings.

I

The specific problem to be examined is the allocation of a given supply of a commodity between consumption in the present period and 'storage' (or carry-over) to the next period. The markets in which trading takes place are assumed to be perfectly competitive. There are arrangements for the purchase and sale of forward contracts calling for delivery of the commodity in the next period. It is assumed that the market expectations of all traders are given, and the problem is to set out the influences determining the equilibrium compatible with these expectations. It is not assumed that all operators have the same expectations about the price of the commodity in the next period, or that any operator necessarily expresses his expectations in the form of a single most likely forward price, or acts as if he does so.[1] (We expressly exclude the problem of the revision of expectations,

* From *Economica*, vol. XXVII, 1960, pp. 355–67. (The last three sections and the appendix are not reprinted here.) Reprinted by permission.

though we are aware of its importance for the more comprehensive analysis of price formation.)

Five categories of operator are distinguished in the analysis; for purposes of comparative static analysis this classification appears to be exhaustive.[2] The first three categories are:

(a) *Hedgers*, who carry stocks of the commodity in varying amounts according to circumstances and shed market risks by selling forward contracts for the quantities of the stocks they intend to carry over to the next period.[3]

(b) *Merchants*, who carry stocks of the commodity in varying amounts according to circumstances, but do not hedge any part of their stocks by the sale of forward contracts.

(c) *Speculators*, who buy forward contracts in varying amounts according to circumstances, but do not carry stocks of the commodity.[4]

These three categories may be regarded as categories of operator, each with a simple pattern of behaviour. Hedgers are concerned only with the difference between the two prices, present price and forward price, and do not form expectations about price movements (or ignore them if they do). Merchants do not respond to changes in the price of forward contracts and act on the basis of their expectations of the prices to be realised on the eventual sale of their stocks. Speculators do not respond to changes in the present price of the commodity and act on the basis of the forward price in the light of their price expectations.

To round out the analysis it is necessary to introduce two 'hybrid' categories of operator:

(d) *Mixed traders* (i.e. hedger-merchants), who carry stocks hedged and unhedged in varying amounts and proportions according to circumstances.

(e) *Mixed speculators* (i.e. merchant-speculators), who do not hedge, but carry unhedged stocks and buy forward contracts in varying amounts and proportions according to circumstances.[5]

Both categories of 'mixed' operator take into consideration the present price of the commodity and the price of forward contracts in relation to their own expectations. The two hybrid categories take advantage of the possibilities of substitution, respectively, between hedged stock-holding and unhedged stock-holding, and between investment in commodity stocks and investment in forward contracts. It will be seen that the possibilities of substitution have interesting consequences.

The markets for 'storage' and for forward contracts have to be distinguished. 'Storage' is supplied by those who plan to hold stocks of the commodity to the end of the present period; it is demanded by those who plan to remain or to become holders of stocks at the end of the present period. The market for storage determines the extent of the carry-over, which consists of the hedged stocks carried by hedgers and mixed traders and the unhedged stocks carried by mixed traders, merchants and mixed speculators. The demand comes from mixed speculators and speculators in respect of their holdings of forward contracts, and from merchants and mixed traders in respect of their holdings of unhedged stocks. (It will be noticed that the carrying of unhedged stocks involves an equivalent supply of and demand for storage.) In the market for forward contracts, the supply comes from hedgers and mixed traders in their hedging operations, and the demand from speculators and mixed speculators.

Lastly, there is the market for present consumption, where that part of the stocks of the commodity which is not to be stored is sold to users for consumption in the present period. It is assumed that consumers do not carry stocks. The demand in the market for present consumption, moreover, is taken to be independent of the supply and demand for storage or forward contracts.

II

We begin the analysis by considering a situation in which there are only hedgers, merchants and speculators.

Consider the position of the hedger. His alternative to carrying over his stock of the commodity (with hedging sales of forward contracts) is to sell it in the present period. For any given present price, the higher the forward price the greater the attraction of carrying stock forward. *Ex definitione*, the hedger is not subject to market risk, and knows the outcome of his stock-holding in advance as he makes sales of forward contracts equivalent to the stocks held by him. The certain outcome of his stock-holding will be the more favourable (or the less unfavourable) the higher is the forward price at which the hedge is placed (i.e. at which the forward contract is sold) relative to the present price (representing the initial cost of the investment). It follows that the supply of hedged storage is an increasing function of contango (i.e. the excess of forward price over present price) and hence that *for any present price* the supply of storage (and hence also of forward contracts) is an increasing function of forward price.[6]

The supply of storage by hedgers (as a function of forward price) varies inversely with present price; this is so because with a higher present price the contango associated with any given forward price is smaller, and hence the quantity supplied is smaller.

Consider next the merchant, who carries stocks but neither hedges (i.e. sells forward contracts) nor buys forward contracts. He carries stocks for trading reasons (convenience yield) and/or in the expectation of an increase in price. Given his market expectations, the holding of stocks by a merchant for a given present price is unaffected by forward price or contango; his demand for storage (and hence also his supply of storage) has zero elasticity with respect to forward price. But the higher the present price, the more expensive it is in terms of forgone opportunities to hold stocks; therefore, his holding of stocks varies inversely with present price.

The speculators provide the demand for forward contracts. Given his expectations, a speculator will expect to make a greater profit the lower the forward price, so that the quantity of forward contracts demanded is greater with a lower than with a higher forward price. As it has been assumed that the speculators' demand for forward contracts is unaffected by the present price of the commodity, the demand for forward contracts can be specified simply as a decreasing function of forward price.

The simple model may now be studied in its entirety by incorporating the demand for present consumption. This is a decreasing function of present price, and is not influenced by the price in the forward market.[7] The static equilibrium conditions may then be introduced: that the total stock of the commodity traded in the period must be allocated between present consumption and storage, and that present and forward prices must be found equating demand and supply in the market for present consumption and in the forward market, respectively.[8]

III

Figure 1 represents a market consisting of hedgers, merchants and speculators, and incorporates the assumptions specified in section II and the conclusions derived from the discussion in that section. The amount of the commodity to be allocated between the present and the next periods is *OH*. *UU* is the demand for present consumption, quantity being measured from right to left on the absicissa and present price on the right-hand ordinate. All other quantities are measured from left to right on the abscissa. S_1S_1 is the supply of storage, and of forward contracts, by hedgers, quantities being related to forward prices (measured on the left-hand ordinate) for a given present price P_1; S_2S_2 is the corresponding supply curve, to the left of S_1S_1, for a higher present price, P_2. R_1R_1 is both the supply curve and the demand curve for storage (related to forward prices) of merchants for the given present price P_1; and R_2R_2 to the left of R_1R_1 corresponds to the higher present price, P_2. *WW* represents the demand for forward contracts (and thus for storage) by speculators, its location being, by assumption, unaffected by the level of present price.[9]

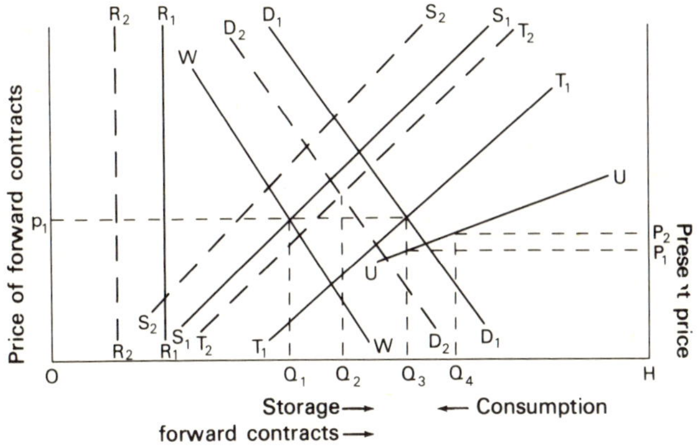

FIGURE 1

The D and T curves are total curves, representing, respectively, the demand for storage (by speculators and merchants) and the supply of storage (by hedgers and merchants); the subscripts relate the curves to the two present prices, P_1 and P_2.

It will be seen that the two markets are in equilibrium with present price P_1, and price of forward contracts p_1. At these prices HQ_3 goes into present consumption, and OQ_3 (equals $OH - HQ_3$), is stored, thus accounting for the total amount OH to be allocated. Of the amount OQ_3 which is carried over, OQ_1 is supplied by hedgers (and hedged by sales of an equivalent volume of forward contracts to speculators), and the balance Q_1Q_3 (equal to the distance of R_1R_1 from the left-hand ordinate) by merchants (representing the quantity of storage simultaneously demanded and also supplied by them).

Two features need to be noted. First, consider the same situation as in Fig. 1 (including the same expectations) except that there is a greater demand for present consumption, i.e. the UU curve is to the left of the present UU curve. It can be shown that, in equilibrium, the quantity going into current consumption will be greater than in the previous situation and the present price will be higher; that the quantities in storage, both hedged and unhedged, will be smaller;[10] and that, though the price of forward contracts will be higher, the difference between this price and the higher present price will be smaller (i.e. contango will be smaller).[11] Second, the equilibrium for the conditions represented in Fig. 1 is stable. Assume that the present price is displaced to P_2. At this price HQ_4 goes into present consumption. But at the same present price, P_2, the quantity going into storage is OQ_2. This leaves Q_2Q_4 unallocated, that is, there will be an excess supply in the market for current consumption. Thus, assuming that there is no revision of expectations causing a change in the position or slope of some of the curves, there will be a tendency for the present price to be forced back to P_1, at which both markets are in equilibrium.

It will be shown now that the introduction of the two hybrid classes of operator, adding greater realism to the model, in the sense of relaxing limitations on the freedom of action of participants in the market, removes the possibility of arriving unambiguously at the 'commonsense' conclusions which are implicit in the simpler model.

The remaining sections of the paper, not reprinted here, provide the demonstration referred to in the preceding paragraph. The appendix provides an algebraic exposition of the discussion in the paper.

NOTES

1 Alternative assumptions have been made by some economists dealing with other, sometimes related, problems in the field of forward trading. Our objective here is not to be critical of their methods of approach, but to present an alternative technique which is not committed to any specific theory of behaviour under uncertainty, but is sufficient for the construction of the relevant economic models.

2 For the analysis of dynamic change, further categories may be necessary to allow for possible patterns of change in modes of behaviour with changes in market conditions as well as for possible patterns in the revision of expectations.

3 Throughout this paper the terms 'hedgers', 'speculators', etc. are used in the special meanings given to them here.

4 Speculators may, of course, be sellers or buyers of forward contracts. For convenience, however, they are treated here as buyers only, i.e. we deal with their net trading position which is taken to be that of buyers. Again, traders in a commodity market can carry negative stocks by entering into commitments to supply at a future date; and they can hedge their risks by buying forward contracts. For convenience, negative stockholding and hedge-buying of forward contracts are ignored here. These simplifications do not vitiate the analysis.

5 It will be seen that there cannot be a hybrid 'hedger-speculator', for at any time his net position must be that of a mixed trader; likewise there cannot be a 'hedger-merchant-speculator'. Note also that the hedger and the merchant are the two limiting cases of the mixed trader, while the merchant and the speculator are the two limiting cases of the mixed speculator.

6 The shape of the supply curve of storage (or its slope with respect to forward price) is determined by the marginal *net* carrying costs of different levels of stocks. These are the costs of storage at the margin minus the marginal convenience yield, convenience yield being defined as the value of having stocks readily available. It is assumed that the marginal convenience yield varies inversely with the quantity of stock held, whereas the marginal cost of holding stock varies directly with the quantity of stock held; and thus that the net carrying cost at the margin

also varies directly with the quantity of stock held. The supply curve of storage is upward sloping, and for large volumes of stocks its elasticity may tend to approach zero.

On the basis of this formulation it is possible that some storage by hedgers will be forthcoming when contango is negative (i.e. when there is backwardation). This will occur if at some levels of storage the value of the convenience yield exceeds the cost of storage so that the net carrying costs are negative.

7 In practice present consumption may be influenced by both the present and forward prices. A manufacturer may be able to postpone production (and hence consumption of his raw materials) to take advantage of lower forward prices. However, there are likely to be strict limits to the postponability of consumption of raw materials by manufacturers. The main effect of marked backwardation in the raw material market is likely to be a curtailment of manufacturers' raw material stocks rather than a reduction in the rate of production in their factories. In our model, however, stocks are carried only by various categories of operator, so that this main effect is looked after. (It would be possible, in Fig. 1, to have a set of present demand curves, one for each forward price, but this refinement would not add materially to the usefulness of the analysis.)

8 It is obvious that while three conditions are specified here, only two are independent. Static equilibrium requires merely that any two of these conditions are satisfied.

9 All the figures in this paper are drawn on the basis of linear relationships between the variables. While non-linearity may be more realistic, it will not affect the comparative static conclusions to be drawn, while the discussion of the stability of the equilibrium may be interpreted as relevant only in the neighbourhood of the comparative static equilibrium points.

10 These two conclusions follow from the leftward shift of both the S and R curves with a higher present price, and from the lack of responsiveness of the W curve to changes in the present price. The *proportion* of the carry-over which is hedged may be either greater or smaller, depending upon the relative shifts of the S and R curves with the higher present price.

11 This last conclusion follows from the condition that the supply of hedged storage is an increasing function of contango, and the finding that a smaller quantity of hedged stocks will be held.

Section Three

Speculation and Returns to Speculators

8 The Search for a Risk Premium

ROGER W. GRAY

In very recent years the search for a risk premium in the price statistics of organized commodity-futures markets has been renewed. In the statistics produced on futures markets some outstanding economists have recognized unsurpassed possibilities for empirical analysis of prices. Valuable special compilations and new survey data have been added to the already excellent regularly published information, in pursuit of estimates of the risk premium, or in more general investigations which have included estimates of the risk premium. The substantive and methodological contributions that this search has yielded mark it a clear success, but this is not because ores laden with risk premium have been discovered – indeed, the tailings from these diggings may prove richer than the findings, and in unsuspected ores.

The evidence to be displayed in this article has been mostly obtained in the process of poking around in mine shafts sunk by others, sifting the tailings from their operations, and re-examining their findings. Their contribution to my efforts is implicit in this process, but there is particular reason to stress the conflict of evidence and interpretation that occurs. Few economists are familiar with the uses and operations of commodity futures markets, and the economic literature on the topic, being rather sparse, may be presumed to have attracted little careful study. The reader thus deserves to be made aware of conflict and to receive assistance in resolving it. For these reasons I point to what appear to me to be flaws in the assumptions, procedures, or interpretations of some of the recent work in this area, but only where it seems to me to aid in the presentation of new evidence and after pointing out that there were good reasons for the search being conducted as it was.

I

It would be difficult to think of a more appropriate hypothesis for the econometrician to test than the one that a commodity futures market

* From *Journal of Political Economy*, vol. LXIX, 1961, pp. 250–60. (The addendum is not reprinted here.) Reprinted by permission of the University of Chicago Press.

produces a risk premium. The hypothesis is thrice blessed. The most famous economist of our time, who was also a successful financier, stated a theory of 'normal backwardation' which envisages a general tendency for futures prices to rise as the mechanism whereby hedgers, as holders of short positions, reward speculators, as holders of long positions, for assuming the risk of price change.[1] Business users of futures markets commonly adduce risk reduction as their prime or sole motive. Moreover, futures markets originated under circumstances that leave little doubt regarding the emphasis that was placed upon shifting the risk of price decline to those willing to assume it. The vast amount of data that has been accumulated in recent years makes it all the more reasonable that the hypothesis should have been examined. Yet, without intending iconoclasm, I wonder whether the focus upon the risk premium in these recent probings has not been unfortunate, diverting attention from results of possible value and leading explorers to misconstrue what they have found or to construe what they have not found.

The search for a risk premium has been conducted in a theoretical framework that has a close analogy in the insurance principle. The owner of inventory, if he should wish to avoid any risk of changes in its value, might sell a futures contract against which that inventory is deliverable. He could expect to pay for the protection from price risk so obtained, much as one must expect to pay for fire insurance, and this payment might well be called a 'risk premium.' The mechanism by which the premium is paid is a price change in the futures contract. So any general downward bias in futures prices, which would produce hedging costs and speculative profits in a market where the hedging was predominantly selling, or short hedging, is termed a risk premium.

The major premise in the theory is that risk aversion is the leitmotiv of hedging. Granting this, any general hedging costs (other than brokerage commissions) may be considered a risk premium. If risk aversion is not the leitmotiv of hedging – and Working has presented persuasive evidence to this effect[2] – then a price bias, if any is found in searching for a risk premium, needs to be explained in other terms.

II

One recent writer who has not laid claim to the discovery of a risk premium in the futures markets he investigated is Telser.[3] He draws what seems to me to be the correct major conclusion: that prices in the New York cotton- and Chicago wheat-futures markets displayed no trend over the twenty-three- and twenty-four-year periods studied.[4]

My reasons for referring to this article, other than to commend it to the reader's attention, concern a problem that Telser only touches upon; hence, my comments are not to be construed as a criticism of his results. The risk-premium postulate must, of course, be symmetrical, long hedgers paying a premium to short speculators. To conclude, as

Telser correctly does, that some futures prices displayed no trend is *not* tantamount to a conclusion that hedging costs tend to be zero even in markets where the typical excess of short over long hedging prevails. What if, for example, futures prices rose during a time of year when short hedging greatly exceeded long hedging and declined during a time of year when long hedging somewhat exceeded short hedging? General hedging costs might well occur in a market with no general trend in future prices, whether or not their occurrence should be interpreted as the transfer of a risk premium.

Telser's conclusions are thus subject to the criticism that he has measured only the price bias and has not estimated hedging costs directly. Houthakker, on the other hand, has measured the hedging costs (with Telser's assistance).[5] Telser criticizes Houthakker's evidence, but his concern with the price bias leads him to miss the more important defects in that evidence, thereby depriving his own conclusions of their full weight.

Telser says of Houthakker's evidence: 'It is not conclusive because transactions costs are not deducted from the speculators' income, only nine years are studied . . . , and the method of estimating gains and losses neglects changes in commitments and prices within each month."[6] There are two additional criticisms which I deem more important than any of these. Houthakker uses open contract data from several markets and prices from only one market for most of his analysis. This discrepancy is of little importance in corn, of real importance in cotton, and so important in wheat as to render his computations meaningless. The open interest in wheat at Minneapolis and Kansas City consists of hedging contracts in much larger part than does that at Chicago; and the price movements are also sufficiently different to support a sizable spreading trade between each of the two lesser markets and Chicago. The Minneapolis futures contract is for hard spring wheat, the Kansas City contract for hard winter wheat, and the Chicago contract, while it permits delivery of either of these, tends to reflect soft-wheat values most closely and consistently. During the past ten winters, including 1958–59, the average change in spread between Minneapolis and Chicago, for May futures, December 15–May 15, has been larger than the average price change in the Minneapolis May future. Flour mills that have accumulated wheat at Buffalo before the close of lake shipping, having often had to choose between these two markets for their hedge in the event this wheat is not fully sold into flour, are well aware of changing spread relations. Yet the effect of Houthakker's procedure is to take Chicago price movements as an indication of the profits or losses on Minneapolis hedges.

In cotton the disparity in trading composition between New York and New Orleans is almost equally great, New York being the predominantly hedging and New Orleans the predominantly speculative market.

Because the contract grades in cotton do not differ so much between markets as in the case of wheat, price movements are more nearly parallel, and the criticism less strong. Nevertheless, Houthakker's implicit assumption of identical price movements (or identical trading composition) is of negligible importance only in the case of corn, where approximately 99 per cent of the open contracts were held at Chicago.

A second criticism of Houthakker's interpretation is of particular importance to the estimates that he derives for corn. He says that 'corn prices declined on balance during each of the two subperiods.'[7] Since his computations show large hedgers making profits and other traders incurring losses during the first subperiod (1937–40), these comments are confined to the second, and longer, subperiod (1946–52). On October 1, 1946 (the first day of this subperiod), the spot price of the contract grade of corn reported by the Chicago Board of Trade was 186 cents per bushel, and the range for the March and May futures was $130\frac{1}{8}$–$132\frac{1}{4}$ cents. On September 30, 1952, the last day of the subperiod, the spot price was $173\frac{1}{4}$–$174\frac{1}{2}$ cents, and the various futures prices ranged from $167\frac{7}{8}$–$175\frac{3}{8}$ cents. The spot price had declined; but, more important to the consideration of bias, the futures price gained approximately 52 cents on the spot price over the six-year period. When the futures price rises relative to the spot price, as happened here, a strong presumption of bias is raised. Suspicion is immediately cast on the presumption in this instance, however, when it is recognized that the gain came about through elimination of inverse carrying charges that prevailed for about two months at the beginning of the period and which were the largest in history. That these would be eliminated or sharply reduced within a matter of weeks (with harvest of the new crop) was a virtual certainty; the consequences for the results obtained by Houthakker are interesting. If the second subperiod is made to begin on December 9, 1946, instead of October 1, the net results obtained by Houthakker would undergo negligible change; *but the results would now appear to be attributable almost entirely to rising corn prices*. From October 1, 1946, to September 30, 1952, spot prices *declined* by about 12 cents; from December 9, 1946, to September 30, 1952, spot prices *rose* by about 40 cents; yet the few weeks intervening between the two initial dates would have seen less than $150,000 change hands between large speculators and large hedgers in Houthakker's computations, whereas he estimated that large hedgers lost $6.6 million and large speculators gained $11.7 million in the entire period.[8] Far from being based upon a nine-year record, which Telser criticized as being too brief, Houthakker's allegation of the existence of general bias comes to rest on the historically unique events covering a little more than two months. While Houthakker's method involves a further refinement than Telser's in that it attempts to measure hedging costs directly, Houthakker's conclusions must be rejected on account of faulty application of the method, whereas Telser's major conclusion, construed in terms of bias only, can be accepted.

Another recent article, by Brennan, exhibits evidence of a risk premium which is superficially quite impressive.[9] Brennan employs an ingenious procedure which reveals a risk premium as a residual after expected prices, storage costs, and convenience yields have apparently been accounted for. He generates his 'expected prices' out of past prices and past errors. But Brennan makes what appears to me to be a fatal error when he finally verifies his finding of the risk premium by substituting futures prices for expected prices. The same 'risk premium' is revealed after the substitution as before, which, contrary to Brennan's reasoning, should *not* be the case, because the risk premium must be the *difference* between futures prices and expected prices.

In concluding this brief review, I reiterate the hope that my rejection of some conclusions, and my criticism of the presentation of some which I accept, may serve some constructive purposes. It should provide a background for my interpretation of some evidence presented in the next section, for indeed this work provides the background against which I sought the evidence. It may also show the complexity of a seemingly simple subject, perhaps partially absolving me of errors that may be found in my analysis, and suggesting that a great deal remains to be done in this area.

III

In this section it will be shown, by employing a different measurement technique than has been heretofore employed, that no significant downward bias can be found in corn-futures prices over an extended period of time. Then, using the same measurement technique, it will be shown that although no *downward* bias was found, a bias relevant to hedging costs and speculative profits *was* found. If futures prices tend to rise as the contract approaches maturity, routine buying of futures will, in general, yield profits. The routine buying program which has been assumed here consists in buying each future on the first trading day in the delivery month of the preceding future and selling it on the first trading day of its own delivery month. (If we call a future in its own delivery month the 'expiring' future, the program consists in buying the near future and selling the expiring future seriatim.) Thus, for example, the program in a given calendar year for wheat would consist in buying the May future on the first trading day in March; switching to the July future (that is, selling the May and buying the July) on the first trading day in May; switching to the September future on the first trading day in July, to the December future on the first trading day in September, and to the March future on the first trading day in December. An advantage of using this program in testing for bias is that each future is carried until the day its price quotation is effectively a 'spot' quotation, so that the futures and spot prices are carried in the same series, while at the same time the future is sold before its price may have been influenced by the consideration that it is now a spot price as well, that is, before carrying charges or any delivery-month squeezes are reflected in the futures price. Care has been taken to initiate and terminate these hypothetical trading programs at approximately the same price level, so that any profits are clearly attributable to bias. The price at which the first future in a series is purchased is close to that at which the last is sold in all cases; moreover, the carrying charge (that is, the difference between the prices of the near future and the expiring future) on the initial date is close to that on the terminal date. Since costs of transactions are ignored, there is no reason for not buying every future instead of buying further ahead of delivery and holding longer. For all these paper 'transactions' of past years the closing price of the future on the trading date has been used where available, the middle of the daily range where closing prices were not provided.

The results of such a trading program are shown first for corn futures for four selected periods, in the terms of the *t*-ratio, which is employed to test the hypothesis that the mean profit does not exceed zero.[10]

1. For an interwar series of seventy-seven successive trades[11], initial purchase of July corn on May 1, 1921, at 61 cents, when the May future was at 63 cents, and final sale of July corn on July 1, 1940, at 60½ cents, when the September future was at 59 cents. The *t*-ratio is .364, and the null hypothesis is accepted.

2. For a postwar series of sixty successive trades, initial purchase of March corn on January 1, 1947, at 130 cents when the January future was at 131½ cents and final sale of May corn on May 1, 1959, at 125⅜ cents when the July future was at 125⅜ cents. The *t*-ratio is .770, and the null hypothesis is accepted.

No 'downward' bias was evident in corn futures in either of these two periods. Failure to find a *downward* bias does not imply that *no* bias could be found, however; and there was in fact a pronounced bias, having particular relevance to the question of hedging costs, manifest in a somewhat different trading system. If, instead of recurrent buying, the trading program had consisted of what may be called 'buying discounts and selling premiums,' the profits over each of the periods would have been significant.

By 'buying discounts' is meant that the future is *purchased* (on the same trading dates as in the previous program) when it is priced *below* the preceding (expiring) future.[12] By 'selling premiums' is meant that the future is *sold* when it is priced *above* the preceding (expiring) future. For illustration, on March 1 the May future is purchased if it is priced below the March future, but sold if it is priced above the March future; whereas in the previous program the May future was purchased on March 1 irrespective of prices. The results of the program of buying

TABLE 1

Comparison of results of two buying programs (t-*ratios*)

No. of Trades	*Recurrent Buying*	*Buying Discounts: Selling Premiums*
77 (interwar period)	.364	2.125
60 (postwar period)	.770	3.020
137 (both periods combined)	.816	3.647

discounts and selling premiums in Chicago corn futures are compared in Table 1 with the results of the recurrent buying program already described. Even more conclusive evidence of this bias is obtained by considering the seventy-eight premium (sell) and fifty-nine discount (buy) situations separately. The *t*-ratio for the former is 2.677 and for the latter 3.047, each significant at the 1 per cent level. *The interpretation of this bias in relation to hedging costs is that these must have been significantly negative in the Chicago corn futures market over this period, for the premium relationships occur when short hedging is heavy and the discount relations when it is light.*

The interpretation of the foregoing evidence in relation to *speculation* must be: first, that no evidence of a tendency to profit from a consistently long position is revealed and, second, that indirect evidence of a tendency for speculators to lose money is revealed. Lest this evidence be construed as a mere revision of the rule by which it is easy to make a profit in commodity futures, however, a contrast between corn and wheat futures at Chicago may be noted. Whereas maintaining a long position in either market led to no significant profits in the post-war period, it is possible to devise, in retrospect, simple rules which would have led to large profits. The interesting catch in this instance is that the high road to fortune in the wheat market ran in the *opposite* direction from that in the corn market. In the corn market, as just noted, buying the discounts and selling the premiums would have been a good trading rule. If one moderate adjustment is made in this trading rule, it can be shown that *selling* the discounts and *buying* the premiums would have been profitable in wheat while the reverse was profitable in corn.[13] In order to show this contrast, the trading periods for corn and wheat are chosen so as to coincide almost exactly and at the same time require no adjustment for price change. The period beginning on December 1, 1949, is ideal for this purpose in that wheat prices returned to virtually their initial level after forty-one successive trades (March 1, 1958), as did corn prices after forty-two successive trades (May 1, 1958). The comparative *t*-ratios for recurrent buying over these periods were .116 for wheat and .234 for corn, neither significant. For *buying discounts* and *selling premiums* in corn the *t*-ratio was 3.274. For *selling discounts* and *buying premiums* in wheat the *t*-ratio was 2.419. It is not an easy matter to interpret such a contrast, much less to forecast it.

IV

But there are markets in which speculators who followed the dictum, 'Maintain a long position,' in the postwar period would today be very rich. It remains to present and interpret some evidence of this.

To the extent that discount situations, as first defined above, prevail over premium situations, buying leads to profits; that is, if the sum of all the discounts exceeds the sum of all the premiums, after adjustment for price change, net profits from recurrent buying equal this difference. The point in introducing this tautology is to suggest where to look for markets that display a significant downward bias over some extended period – one looks naturally to the so-called 'discount markets,' of which there are several, on which quotations on distant futures are fairly persistently lower than are quotations on near futures.

Anyone who has maintained a long position in coffee futures at New York, bran futures at Kansas City, or wheat futures at Minneapolis during the postwar period, has enjoyed hadsome profits.[14] Such facts are not secrets in the commodity trade. The world's largest brokerage firm has published a pamphlet, recommending such a trading system in coffee futures, which was distributed to all of their commodity clients and many others.[15] In 1952, the commodity economist for the same firm published an article in the coffee trade journal outlining the same trading system.[16] One of the leading brokerage firms has for some time urged its clients to buy Minneapolis wheat futures in general and, in particular, to shift their buying of wheat futures from Chicago to Minneapolis.

The same trading routine (recurrent buying) as was used for corn futures in the previous illustration has been applied to these three markets, and the comparative *t*-ratios for the postwar period are shown in Table 2.

The initial and terminal dates for these postwar programs were selected so as to minimize the net price change over the trading span. Thus, for example, the coffee program was assumed to have been initiated after the major price rise of 1949, and the wheat program after the major decline of 1948.

How should the significant bias in the three markets be interpreted? In particular, should the interpretation be that there was a *risk premium* in coffee, bran, shorts, and Minneapolis wheat in the postwar period, but not in corn or in Chicago wheat? One of the difficulties with this interpretation is already apparent: risk presumably has its objective referent in price variability, and yet Minneapolis wheat prices were not

TABLE 2

*t-Ratios computed to test the hypothesis that the mean profit from maintaining a long position does not differ from zero**

Commodity and Market	Dates of First Purchase and Last Sale	Price at Beginning and Ending Dates: Expiring Future	Price at Beginning and Ending Dates: Next Future	No. of Trades	Average Profit per Trade	t-Ratio
Corn, Chicago Board of Trade	Dec. 1, 1949–	$128\frac{3}{4}$	$130\frac{1}{2}$			
	May 1, 1958	$126\frac{1}{4}$	$125\frac{1}{4}$	42	−0.35	0.234
Wheat, Chicago Board of Trade	Dec. 1, 1949–	$218\frac{1}{2}$	$218\frac{1}{2}$			
	Mar. 1, 1958	$220\frac{3}{4}$	$217\frac{7}{8}$	41	−0.22	0.116
Wheat, Minneapolis Grain Exchange	May 1, 1949–	$216\frac{1}{2}$	$202\frac{1}{2}$			
	July, 1, 1959	$205\frac{1}{8}$	$207\frac{1}{8}$	41	3.35	2.279
Brazilian coffee, New York Coffee	May 1, 1950–	45.10	43.20			
and Sugar Exchange	Dec. 1, 1958	42.00	37.90	43	1.73	1.788
Bran, Kansas City Board of Trade	July 1, 1947–	58.50	51.50			
	May 1, 1952	53.00	49.00	24	2.35	1.886
Bran, Kansas City Board of Trade	July 1, 1953–	40.75	43.75			
	Dec. 1, 1956	41.75	43.88	17	−1.14	1.827
Shorts, Kansas City Board of Trade	July 15, 1947–	70.00	60.00			
	Sept. 1, 1952	62.25	60.90	26	2.63	2.398
Shorts, Kansas City Board of Trade	May 1, 1953–	55.45	50.75			
	May 1, 1956	48.00	†	15	−1.54	2.429

* Grain prices in cents per bushel; coffee in cents per pound; bran and shorts in dollars per ton.

† No quotation.

Source: R. W. Gray, 'The Characteristic Bias in Some Thin Futures Markets,' *Food Research Institute Studies*, I (November 1960), 298, Table 1.

more variable than Chicago wheat prices. What is reflected here is clearly the different behavior of two markets, not different levels of risk. It begs the question to say that these markets operate differently and therefore arrive at different estimates of the risk premium. In suggesting some explanations for the market behavior illustrated here, the chief purpose will be to indicate the likelihood that *different* explanations are required for different markets. Insufficient evidence is provided here to substantiate any one of these as a singular explanation.

In the case of coffee futures the most likely general explanation parallels that offered by B. S. Yamey for the behavior of the Liverpool cotton market.[17] The coffee trade in the United States has viewed Brazil as a weak seller and has consequently resisted forward commitments at prevailing price levels, in either spot or futures markets. Importers, however, cannot shorten the period of their forward commitments, which covers essentially the time required for shipment. Because the banks that finance them require it, moreover, they cannot afford not to hedge. They have attempted at least three general paths out of the dilemma in which the bias places them: (1) They hedge in the New York green-coffee market, which is a forward-delivery spot market. (2) They employ the 'underdraw' transaction in Brazil. In this transaction the importers purchase a better grade of coffee than is registered and pay for the lower grade registered. (Brazilian traders are willing to participate because the quota system chafes them.) If the underdraw is as large as the bias, the importer has escaped the bias. (3) They hedge in distant futures, hoping to buy back the hedge before the discount on that future has been reduced by approaching delivery. The implications of these adjustments will not be pursued here, nor will other reactions in the market. A futures marked is a dynamic institution in which readjustments are continuous and in which each adjustment made by one group of users presents profit opportunities to others. This paper cannot appropriately develop the evidence and implications of this fact for particular markets, some of which are to be developed in forthcoming publications of the Food Research Institute.

In the case of the Minneapolis wheat-futures market one possible explanation is that the absence of provision for protein differentials in the futures contract accounts for the bias. When the open interest in a particular (remote) future is small, transactions are undertaken on the (then) realistic assumption that wheat low in protein content will be delivered against the contract. There is at a given time, or out of a given crop, however, only a limited amount of low-protein wheat; and the open interest may approach and surpass this quantity, with the result that the futures contract comes to represent a commercially higher quality of wheat over the course of its life.

A similar explanation runs in terms of storage space. Contracts purchased when storage space is available are underpriced relative to their value in a situation which may subsequently develop, in which storage space tightens up and the owner of a futures contract stands to obtain higher prices, not for wheat alone, but for wheat *in store*.

There is some evidence to support each of these explanations, and there are additional hypotheses that seem to ring true. I make no attempt here to explain the situation, as I am continuing to investigate it, but suggest merely that 'risk premium' is almost certainly not an adequate explanation and probably not a very helpful partial explanation.

The bias in the Kansas City bran and shorts futures markets (now defunct) is, from the standpoint of a risk premium, perhaps the most illuminating of those illustrated here. For the first part of the postwar period these markets displayed a significant downward bias which, during the last part of the period, wreaked a fearful vengeance upon any who tried to profit from it; for they then displayed a significant *upward* bias! Should it be said that there was a risk premium which became a risk discount? Or that risk first impinged upon those who were therefore prompted to *sell* futures contracts and later came to impinge upon those who were therefore prompted to *buy* futures contracts? The first suggestion is absurd and the second is question-begging. The general question which it begs is: Who are the buyers and who are the sellers of futures contracts, and what are their purposes?[18]

CONCLUSION

This paper has presented some findings of bias or of hedging costs that differ from one futures market to another and suggested some new points of departure for analysis of commodity futures prices. At the same time the inadequacy of the risk premium as a focal concept is revealed by adding to the existing evidence on the reasons for hedging, wherein risk aversion plays but a small part, evidence that analyses broadly premised upon hedging motivated by risk aversion have failed.

The Addendum is not reprinted here. It contains a commentary on a controversy between L. G. Telser and P. H. Cootner on the presence or absence of a risk premium in certain markets.

NOTES

1 J. M. Keynes, *A Treatise on Money*, vol. II, London, 1930, pp. 142–47.

2 Holbrook Working, 'Hedging Reconsidered,' *Journal of Farm Economics*, vol. XXXV, 1953, p. 561.

3 L. G. Telser, 'Futures Trading and the Storage of Cotton and Wheat,' *Journal of Political Economy*, vol. LXVI, 1958, pp. 233–55.

4 I also agree with his other major empirical conclusion – that the seasonal pattern of stocks determines the spreads between futures of successive maturities in these commodities over the periods considered; but his conclusion regarding trends in futures prices is the relevant one here.

5 H. S. Houthakker, 'Can Speculators Forecast Prices?' *Review of Economics and Statistics*, vol. XXXIX, 1957, pp. 143–52; and his 'The Scope and Limits of Futures Trading,' pp. 133–59 in Moses Abramovitz *et al.*, *The Allocation of Economic Resources*, Stanford, Calif., 1959.

6 Telser, *op. cit.*, p. 243.

7 'Can Speculators Forecast Prices?' *op. cit.*, p. 144.

8 *Ibid.*, p. 145.

9 M. J. Brennan, 'Supply of Storage,' *American Economic Review*, vol. XLVIII, 1958, pp. 50–72.

10 The .05 value of t may be taken as the level at which the null hypothesis is rejected. For $n = 30$, this value is 1.697. For the two-tailed test, which might seem more appropriate after seeing some results shown in this paper, the value is 2.042.

11 During this period there were only four trades per year, as the March future was not traded.

12 In applying this rule, a zero difference was counted as a discount.

13 The adjustment which is required is to redefine discounts to include small premiums. Thus, a premium is defined as a premium of 3 cents or more per bushel and a discount as any other relation between spot and future prices. This definition divides the trades into an equal number of buy and sell signals for both corn and wheat in the period considered.

14 By 'handsome' is meant profits in excess of 200 per cent annually after commissions.

15 Merrill Lynch, Pierce, Fenner and Beane (now Smith), 'Coffee.'

16 E. A. Beveridge, 'Using the Coffee Futures Market,' *Coffee and Tea Industries*, November 1952, pp. 1–8.

17 B. S. Yamey, 'Cotton Futures Trading in Liverpool,' *Three Banks Review*, March 1959, pp. 21–38.

18 Again, pursuit of this question for these markets would go beyond the scope of this paper. Some analysis of them has been undertaken, however, which will appear at a later date in publications of the Food Research Institute.

9 Normal Backwardation, Forecasting, and the Returns to Commodity Futures Traders

CHARLES S. ROCKWELL

INTRODUCTION AND SUMMARY

Two theories are advanced to explain the returns of speculators in commodity futures markets. One, the 'theory of normal backwardation,' views speculative returns as directly linked to the bearing of risk; the other, which we shall call the 'forecasting theory,' considers returns to be determined by the ability of speculators to forecast prices accurately. Although competitive, these theories are not mutually exclusive. This paper presents evidence on the extent to which each of these competing explanations may have been operative in United States commodity futures markets from 1947 to 1965.

The approach used here is similar to that employed by Professor Houthakker in his article 'Can Speculators Forecast Prices?' [3]. That is, the commitments of reporting speculators, hedgers, spreaders and non-reporting traders are obtained from Commodity Exchange Authority (CEA) data and are then multiplied by an appropriate price measure to obtain an estimate of that group's futures market return. The principal difference between this study and that of Professor Houthakker is the much broader coverage obtained here. While Houthakker had available approximately 324 monthly observations on three markets (cotton,[1] wheat, and corn) from 1937 to 1940 and 1946 to 1952, we make use of over 7,900 semimonthly observations covering 25 markets for the 18 years since 1947. This broader coverage makes possible much more conclusive inferences about the mechanism which determines the returns to speculators and the futures costs of hedging.

* Reprinted from *Food Research Institute Studies*, supplement to vol. VII, 1967, pp.107–30, with the permission of the publishers, Stanford University Food Research Institute © 1967 by the Board of Trustees of the Leland Stanford Junior University.

The quantitative arguments of this study use only the values of the variables and their first moments. The fact that the sign of the aggregate profit estimates presented in this paper is often critically dependent upon the results of a particular year and market is consistent with the existing evidence that futures prices may be of the stable Paretian type and consequently have infinite variances. Therefore, neither estimates of variances nor significance tests are made. This is not unduly restrictive since the most important findings of the paper are concerned with the sign of variables, and in the fortunate cases where the wrong sign is encountered no measure of dispersion is required. In the less fortunate cases, the persuasiveness of the conclusions concerning the flow of profits must rest upon casual inspections of the consistency over markets and through time of the dollar value of the profit flow and upon the economic significance of these profits as measured by the rate of return on traders' holdings (average annual profits divided by the value of the outstanding contracts which the trader holds). Although it is possible to make significance tests without using second moments, limitations of funds and time prohibited this. Therefore the quantitative breadth of this study is gained at the cost of some statistical sharpness.

The first section of the paper defines the theory of normal backwardation and examines the different assumptions which are made concerning the forecasting ability of speculators. In its simplest form, the theory assumes that speculators: (1) are net long; (2) require positive profits; and (3) are unable to forecast prices. These assumptions may be satisfied if futures prices rise on the average during the lives of each contract, and this is the chief prediction of the theory. If speculators are assumed to be unable to forecast prices, it is appropriate to consider all of their profits to be a reward for risk-bearing and none to be a reward for forecasting. Consequently, advocates of this version of the theory contend that the profit flow between hedgers and speculators is analogous to the flow of insurance premiums between insured and insurer. Speculators, like insurers, are guaranteed an actuarial expectation of gain simply by being long. The amount of their gain depends only upon the size of their position (the amount of risk they bear) and not upon their forecasting ability.

However, because of the third assumption (that speculators are unable to forecast prices) it is possible to construct counter examples showing that the three assumptions are neither necessary nor sufficient to warrant the conclusion of rising prices.[2] More recent formulations of the theory of normal backwardation avoid these counter examples by dropping the third assumption and instead assume that speculators are able to forecast prices. They also contain a corollary that if speculators are net short prices must fall. These improvements in the theory, however, make the interpretation of speculators' profits ambiguous. Since profits depend upon forecasting ability as well as upon the quantity of risk borne, the insurance premium analogy is no longer adequate in itself. Determination of the proportion in which profits divide between a risk premium and a forecasting reward is the principal objective of this paper.

The second section of the paper briefly describes the data and estimation techniques used and presents the estimated profit flows both in terms of dollar values and rates of return. To facilitate reading, the text does not contain data classified by individual markets. Instead, three different market aggregations are used: (1) an 'All Markets' total representing aggregation over all 25 markets; (2) a 'Large Markets' total which includes only wheat at Chicago, cotton at New York and soybeans; and (3) a 'Small Markets' total which excludes the three markets mentioned above. The reason for excluding these three markets is shown graphically on the abscissa of Chart 1A [*not shown*]. Wheat at Chicago, cotton at New York and soybeans have such large average values of open interest that these markets can be meaningfully differentiated from all others. A complete set of tables for individual markets may be obtained from the author.

Inspection of the dollar value of profits and the rates of return before commissions indicates that the flow of profits in the three large markets is quite different from that in the 22 small markets. However, in both aggregations, large speculators make substantial and consistent profits. In the large markets small traders make positive but inconsequential profits so that the losses of hedgers become the profits of large speculators. In the small markets, however, it is hedgers who make positive but inconsequential gains with the result that the profits of large speculators come from the pockets of small speculators. It is a general characteristic of the results for all 25 markets that they are determined by what happens in the three large markets. Consequently, the overall 6 per cent profit rate of large speculators is financed by a modest 2 per cent rate of loss by hedgers. It should be noted that the true rate of return on investment for speculators differs grossly from the rate measured here due to the existence of very small (5 or 10 per cent) margin requirements. Finally, the rates of return on the long open interest tend to be symmetrically distributed around zero for the 22 smaller markets, whereas the rates of return in the three markets with the largest average value of the open interest are positive, and quite substantial.

Having measured the profit flow, we next attempt to determine the proportion of this flow which can be attributed to normal backwardation. This is done by defining normal backwardation as the returns which would accrue to a naïve speculator who is long when hedgers are net short and short when hedgers are net long. The magnitude of his positions is assumed to be proportional to the size of the open interest. An inspection of the naïve traders' returns yields two conclusions: first, the corollary to the theory of normal backwardation which states that prices should fall when speculators are net short is false – prices rise consistently under these conditions causing losses to short speculators; second, the rate of gain which accrues to the naïve speculator when he is net long is so small relative to the dispersion of that rate for different markets that we conclude there is no significant tendency toward normal backwardation in the markets investigated here. The dispersion of the rates of return by market for the naïve trader is plotted in Chart 2, page 163.

This failure to find any consistent evidence of normal backwardation implies the acceptance of the extreme alternative hypothesis that all important profit flows are to be explained in terms of forecasting ability. That is, the proportion of profits attributable to normal backwardation is zero. However, it is possible to define two levels of forecasting skill: first, an elementary ability which is called Basic Forecasting Skill; and second, a more sophisticated ability which is called Special Forecasting Skill. Basic Skill measures the ability of a group to be long in markets where prices rise over the total period of observation and short in markets where prices fall over the total period of observation. Special Skill, therefore, measures a trader's ability to forecast price movements whose duration is shorter than the total period of observation. An examination of the results of this division of profit confirms the conclusion that it is the degree of forecasting ability which controls the flow of profits. We find that hedgers have negative values for both Basic and Special Forecasting Skills; small traders have a positive value for Basic Skill but an equally large negative value for Special Skill; and large speculators have positive values for both measures (1.3 and 4.8 per cent rates of return respectively). Thus large speculators, the only trading group to earn consistent and economically significant profits, acquire three-quarters of these profits because of their ability to forecast short-term price trends and only one-fourth because of their ability to forecast long-term price trends.

In summary, the evidence presented here indicates that it is forecasting ability and not the bearing of risk that determines the profits of speculators. While the theory of normal backwardation may be valid for particular markets under special conditions, it is not adequate as a general explanation of the flow of profits in commodity markets.

The fact that the gross profits of small traders are zero implies that they consistently make substantial net losses after commissions. Since this group is predominantly composed of small speculators, and since this group holds 46 per cent of the value of all contracts, the principal assumptions of the theory of normal backwardation are not met. Small speculators do not require an ex post history of profits in order to continue trading. There are at least three possible explanations of this. Small speculators are either risk seekers (and are consequently willing to lose money for the privilege of speculating); comprise a stable population of risk averters who are unable to forecast prices, but do not realize this;

or finally, constitute a changing population of risk averters, in which the successful forecasters rise to become large speculators while the unsuccessful forecasters withdraw from the market and are replaced with new blood.[3] Unfortunately, we are unable to ascertain the relative validity of these hypotheses.

The implication of these findings with respect to the price effects of speculation may now be stated. The existence of a subset of speculators who are able to forecast price changes causes futures prices on the average to be an unbiased estimate of the ultimate spot price. In a modified form, however, this conclusion readmits a question which the theory of normal backwardation was thought to answer: why are large speculators consistently net long, even when we consider sets of markets where there is clearly no tendency for prices to rise?[4] Since large speculators own only a small fraction of all commitments, it is quite possible for them to be either net short or net long quite independently of the sign of net hedging commitments. The answer to this may be that even the more sophisticated speculators have an irrational preference for the long side. However, it may well be equally true that the distribution of price changes is asymmetric so that skewness and moments other than the mean influence the decisions of speculators to be net long.

That futures prices, on the average, are unbiased estimates of ultimate spot prices need not imply that this result holds either for all markets or for all time periods within a market. As an example of the former, coffee futures prices (a market not covered by this study) have exhibited a strong upward tendency in the postwar period that is quite consistent with the theory of normal backwardation. As an example of the latter, this study shows that if hedgers are net long, futures prices tend to rise. Similar examples of temporary price bias conditional upon special conditions of time and market structure may be found in the papers presented by Telser and Cootner at this Symposium.[5] Perhaps the principal value of this paper is that it puts into better perspective these, as well as other studies, which demonstrate the existence of price bias. The results presented here suggest that this evidence of bias is critically dependent both upon the markets which are selected and upon the special structural characteristics which determine any conditional price forecasts. In contrast, the overall generalization from the data investigated here is that the futures price is an unbiased estimate of the ultimate spot price.

THE ROLE OF FORECASTING IN THE THEORY OF NORMAL BACKWARDATION

The theory of normal backwardation predicts that under certain assumptions it is necessary on the average for the price of futures contracts to rise. Two of the assumptions of the theory as originally stated by Keynes [5, pp. 784–86] are that speculators be net long and be risk averters (that is, they require a positive history of profits if they are to continue trading). Under these circumstances, a rising trend in prices is the mechanism that rewards long speculators for the risks they bear.

To Keynes, the possibility that speculators may be better forecasters than hedgers is a 'dubious proposition' [5, p. 785]. This contention appears to be reversed in later formulations of the theory of normal backwardation by Hicks [2, p. 138] and Houthakker [4, p. 23]. Since forecasting ability, or its absence, is a central theme in this paper, and since Keynes' position as stated in the *Manchester Guardian Commercial* is not very well known, as extensive quote from that source may be helpful [5, p. 785].

> In most writings on this subject, great stress is laid on the service performed by the professional speculator in bringing about a harmony between short-period and long-period demand and supply, through his action in stimulating or retarding in *good time* the one or the other. This may be the case. But it presumes that the speculator is better informed on the average than the producers and consumers themselves. Which, speaking generally, is rather a dubious proposition. The most important function of the speculator in the great organized 'Futures' markets is, I think, somewhat different. He is not so much a prophet (though it may be a belief in his own gifts of prophecy that tempts him into the business), as a risk-bearer . . . without paying the slightest attention to the prospects of the commodity he deals in or giving a thought to it, he may, one decade with another, earn substantial remuneration *merely* by running risks and allowing the results of one season to average with those of others: just as an insurance company makes profits. . . .

In Keynes' version of the theory, it is the speculators' inability to forecast accurately that makes them dependent upon the incidental, and probably unanticipated, rising price level to provide a positive history of profits. The assumption that speculators are unable to forecast prices makes it unambiguous to interpret whatever profits they receive as a risk premium paid to them by hedgers and not as a reward for forecasting. The postulation of 'no forecasting' ability, however, raises problems concerning the prediction that prices must rise. If the level of the net short position of hedgers is subject to variations, it is possible for speculators to have a positive history of profits without prices rising on the average: for example, prices rise one unit in period one and fall one unit in period two, and speculators are net long two units in period one but only one unit in period two.[6] This, of course, implies that speculators do not correctly forecast the price fall in period two, which is quite consistent with the assumed absence of forecasting ability. The converse may also be shown: that is, a rise in prices need not result in profits for long speculators. Thus, the assumptions of the theory of normal backwardation are neither necessary nor sufficient for the prediction that prices rise.

The principal modification of the theory of normal backwardation made by Hicks and Houthakker is to assume that speculators are able to forecast prices. This distinction may be seen by contrasting the position of Keynes as stated above with that of Hicks in *Value and Capital* [2, p. 138].

> Futures prices are therefore nearly always made partly by *speculators*, . . . whose action tends to raise the futures price to a more *reasonable level* (last italics mine) . . . But it is of the essence of speculation, as opposed to hedging, that the speculator puts himself into a more risky position as a result of his forward trading . . . . He will therefore only be willing to go on buying futures so long as the futures price remains definitely below the spot price he expects . . . . The difference between these two prices . . . is called by Keynes 'normal backwardation.'

It seems clear that while both Keynes and Hicks share the same prediction they do not agree upon the underlying model.

One consequence of granting speculators even a modest amount of predictive ability is that it frees the backwardation hypothesis from counter examples (such as the one stated above) that involve speculators being net long during periods when prices fall in a 'predictable' manner.[7] Thus, the assumptions of the Hicks-Houthakker version of the theory necessarily imply that prices must rise on the average. However, this improvement in the logic of the theory is gained at a cost: the returns of speculators may no longer be viewed unambiguously as a reward for bearing risk. Rather they represent a mixed payment for forecasting and risk bearing, the proportions of the mixture being determinable only by empirical investigation. The view held by Keynes that the returns of speculators may be interpreted as an insurance premium, will be valid only if the forecasting component of profits is relatively small.

The empirical procedure originally planned for this study was first to measure a normal backwardation component of profits and then define the difference between this amount and the actual returns as the forecasting component. Either component may be negative in value, but a negative backwardation component causes the selection of a distinctly different path of investigation from that caused by a negative forecasting component. For example, a negative value for forecasting profits, which is more than offset by a positive value for backwardation profits, would be quite consistent with the Keynesian version of the theory; negative forecasting ability is an admissible phenomenon. However, if backwardation profits are nonpositive, it necessitates the rejection of the theory and, hence, requires a different framework of analysis. In practice, we conclude that the backwardation component is zero and, therefore, adopt the position that forecasting ability is the only important determinant of profits. Although the last section of this paper divides profits into two components representing different degrees of forecasting skill, neither of these components is a measure of the profits attributable to normal backwardation. However, the significance of this division depends upon our first being able both to define an empirically meaningful measure of normal backwardation and show that its value is non-positive.

It is convenient to discuss at this point two problems which arise in defining an empirical estimate of normal backwardation. The first problem arises when hedgers are net long rather than net short. The Keynes and Hicks formulations clearly assume hedgers to be net short. These authors, however, were concerned with the futures markets for international industrial commodities during the 1920's and 1930's when it may well be true that hedgers were consistently net short. On the other hand, the 25 markets covered by this study are predominantly for agricultural commodities, and it will be shown that hedgers are net long for substantial periods of time. It is difficult to see and reason why the theory of normal backwardation in either its Keynesian or Hicks-Houthakker formulation should not be broadened to predict a price fall whenever hedgers are net long. This modification is suggested by both Houthakker [4, p. 22] and Cootner [1, p. 400].

The second problem concerns which weights should be used in aggregating over individual contracts and, a fortiori, commodities. There are at least three possibilities: (1) each contract may be given a weight of one; (2) each contract may be given a weight equal to the average value of the open interest in that contract (taken over all time periods during which that contract trades); and (3) each contract may be weighted by the actual open interest existing on that date. The first alternative, unity weights, gives undue importance to inactive contracts and commodities and need not be considered. The choice between alternatives two and three is more difficult. Numerous arguments can be made for either side. The most important consideration, however, would seem to be protection against misleading results caused by changing market structure. For example, although cotton at New York has the second largest average open interest value of any commodity, trading on this market is almost nonexistent by the end of the period. To weight the price performance of these last years with the large open interest that prevailed earlier could cause the same spurious results as applying a weight of one to all contracts and all time periods. Therefore, this study measures normal backwardation as the sum of the return on the total long open interest when hedgers are net short and of the return on the total short open interest when hedgers are net long.

If this measure is to be used, what is its relation to the existing theories of normal backwardation? Normal backwardation describes the profits of marginal speculators who possess no forecasting ability. This is true whether we deal with Keynesian or Hicks-Houthakker versions. We may therefore conceive of normal backwardation as the return earned by a hypothetical speculator who follows a naïve strategy of being constantly long when hedgers are net short and constantly short when hedgers are net long. The naïve strategy used here requires that the hypothetical trader adjusts the size of his positions to maintain them as a constant proportion of the total open interest. In practice, the author's earlier work shows that the results of this strategy do not differ significantly from the results obtained when the trader is assumed to have positions of a fixed size [8, p. 114].

A section 'Returns to Futures Traders', pp. 114–25, *which includes six tables and one chart, is not reprinted here, except for the two concluding paragraphs.*

The results presented in this section may be summarized by two conclusions. First, reporting speculators make significant profits on their long and their short positions. Their net profits are significant both from the point of view of consistency from year to year and market to market, and from the point of view of the magnitude of the rate of return. This cannot be said for small traders, whose returns are essentially zero and are negative if transaction costs are considered. The net costs of hedging are negative, but not large, and the important losses are concentrated in one market, soybeans.

Second, excluding the three largest markets, the rates of return on the total open interest are symmetrically distributed around zero. For the three large markets, however, there is a tendency toward positive returns on the total long open interest. In these large markets there is a 6 per cent average return on the total open interest.

DETERMINANTS OF THE RETURNS TO FUTURES TRADERS

The role of normal backwardation

If normal backwardation is defined as the returns which a naïve speculator earns by keeping his commitments long, in proportion to the total open interest when hedgers are net short, and short, in proportion to the total open interest when hedgers are net long, then the rate of return on the total long open interest, presented above, is closely related to the rate of normal backwardation. However, it is necessary to multiply profits in a given market by minus one for each period that hedgers are net long in that market.

TABLE 7

Comparison of Total Returns and Returns when Hedgers are net short and net long

Item	*Large Markets*	*Small Markets*	*All Markets*
Percentage of periods hedgers net long	25.2	13.5	15.4
Dollar profits on long positions (*Million dollars*)			
Total	751.4	1.5	752.9
When hedgers net short	619.5	−25.6	593.9
When hedgers net long	132.0	27.0	159.0
Profits due to normal backwardation	487.5	−52.6	434.9
Percentage return on long positions			
When hedgers net short	6.1	− 0.4	3.7
When hedgers net long	6.3	4.0	5.7
Rate of normal backwardation	4.0	− 0.8	2.3

Table 7 presents a comparison of profits on the long open interest, for all periods with profits on the long open interest when hedgers are net long. As explained previously, profits which accrue while hedgers are net long are subtracted from total profits to obtain the measure of profits used in computing the rate of normal backwardation (or more exactly, twice the profit for periods hedgers are net long must be subtracted from the profit for all periods). The theory of normal backwardation predicts that the subtrahend will be negative so that profits after the subtraction will be larger than they were before. Line four of Table 7, 'Dollar profits on long positions when hedgers net long,' shows with great force that the theory of normal backwardation is not supported by the data. The profits for both large and small markets are positive, not negative. Given that hedgers are net long only 15 per cent of the time, the magnitude of the profits is sizable. Indeed, not only is the sign of profits inconsistent with the theory of normal backwardation, but also the rates of return for all three aggregations are greater when hedgers are net long than when they are net short! Thus, an adjustment for the sign of net hedging results in a reduction in the rate of normal backwardation for Large, Small and All Markets to 4.0, −0.8, and 2.3 per cent respectively.[8]

Although we must reject the prediction that prices fall when hedgers are net long, it is still possible that the theory of normal backwardation is supported when we aggregate over all time periods. Since hedgers are net long only 15 per cent of the time, the successful performance of the theory of the remaining 85 per cent could easily lead to a correct overall prediction. Chart 2 plots the rate of normal backwardation against the average value of the open interest for each market. The scatter is similar to Chart 1 except that the mean for All Markets is reduced from 4.0 to 2.3 per cent, and a negative skew is introduced. Although the mean is still positive, both its small magnitude and the fact that normal backwardation is negative for 11 out of 25 markets must lead to the conclusion that a tendency toward normal backwardation is neither a consistent nor an important general characteristic of futures markets. In fact, only one of the 14 markets with positive measures of normal backwardation (shorts at 10.1) has a return in the 10 per cent or more range postulated by Keynes [6, p. 143]. In contrast, there are six markets with negative returns of an absolute magnitude greater than 10 per cent.

CHART 2

Rate of normal backwardation compared with average value of open interest, for specified markets

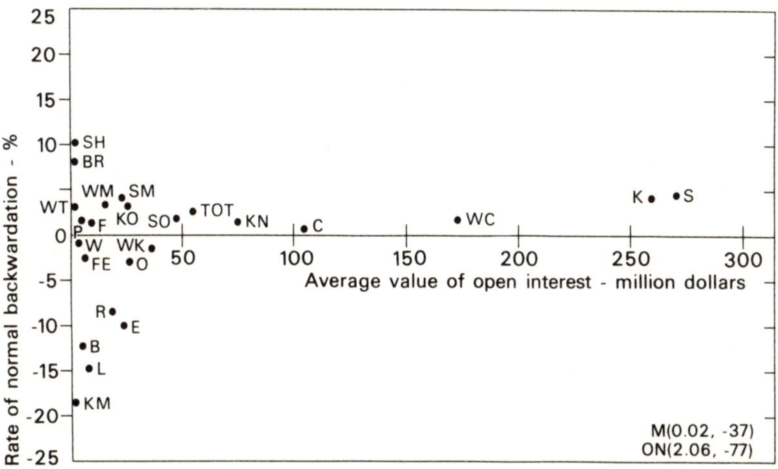

Market symbols:

WC—Wheat, Chicago	K—Cotton, New York	WT—Wool tops
WK—Wheat, Kansas City	KN—Cotton, New Orleans	W—Grease wool
WM—Wheat, Minneapolis	KM—Cotton meal	BR—Bran
C—Corn	KO—Cotton oil	SH—Shorts
O—Oats	L—Lard	M—Middlings
R—Rye	F—Flax	ON—Onions
S—Soybeans	E—Eggs, shell	B—Butter
SM—Soybean meal	FE—Eggs, frozen	TOT—All market total
SO—Soybean oil	P—Potatoes	

The conclusion of this section is that: normal backwardation is not characteristic of the 22 smaller markets either when hedgers are net long or net short; and it is characteristic of the three larger markets only when hedgers are net short. The theory clearly does not have general applicability for all futures markets and it is questionable whether an analysis of variance performed over the 25 markets would indicate a single market with a positive return significantly greater than zero.

The role of basic and special forecasting skills

In this section the rates of return of net trading groups are partitioned into two components: one, a reward defined as Basic Forecasting Skill; and the other, a residual component defined as Special Forecasting Skill.

The decomposition is performed in the following manner. Let V_m^L and V_m^S be the total value of a trading group's long and short commitments, in a single market m, aggregated over all time periods, and let R_m be the rate of return on the long open interest in that market. Then, any net trading group's rate of profit attributable to Basic Forecasting Skill is given by

$$R_m^B = \frac{R_m(V_m^L - V_m^S)}{V_m^L + V_m^S}$$

Denoting the group's actual rate of return by R_m^A, we then obtain the measure of Special Forecasting Skill as a residual of $R_m^F = R_m^A - R_m^B$.

Aggregation over any set of markets is accomplished by computing

$$R^B = \frac{\Sigma_m\, R_m(V^L - V^S)}{\Sigma_m\,(V_m^L + V_m^S)} \text{ and } R^F = R^A - R^B$$

The measure R_m^B will be positive when R_m is positive and the group is net long on the average ($V_m^L - V_m^S > 0$), or when R_m is negative and the group is net short on the average ($V_m^L - V_m^S < 0$). Thus, this measure of Basic Skill is different from that proposed by Professor Houthakker [3, pp. 148–49]. He measures the presence of Basic Skill in terms of the intercept coefficient of a regression of the quantity of commitments upon the change in price. If the intercept is positive, that is, if the expected value of a group's commitments is positive when price change is zero, then a trading group is said to exhibit positive Basic Skill. This, of course, is only proper if the theory of normal backwardation is correct in that prices do rise on the average. However, the conclusion reached in this paper is that there is no important tendency for prices to rise, and, consequently, such a definition of Basic Skill is misleading. The measure used here defines Basic Skill as the ability to be net long on the average in markets where prices rise on the average, and to be net short on the average in markets where prices fall on the average. This measures the long run ability of a trading group to stay on the profitable side of the market. Special Forecasting Skill, defined as a residual, measures the success with which a trading group varies its position, from year to year and period to period, to profit from short run price trends (that is, from price trends whose duration is shorter than the total period of observation).

We may conclude this discussion of definitions by noting that both Houthakker's measure of Basic Skill and the one employed here seek to measure the extent to which traders' returns can be adequately described by a simple naïve strategy of being constantly on one side of a market. The remaining profits may then be interpreted as reflecting the traders' ability to forecast shorter price trends, and this is defined as Special Forecasting Skill. The definitions of Basic Skill differ because this study finds that normal backwardation is not a general characteristic of futures markets: therefore, it is more useful to use the actual trend in prices in defining the naïve trading strategy than to use the hypothetical returns that are predicted by a theory of normal backwardation, a theory which is not consistent with the data.

Table 8 shows that small traders exhibit a consistent negative value

TABLE 8

Division of rate of return according to basic and special forecasting skills by net trading groups
(Per cent)

Trading and skill groups	*Large Markets*	*Small Markets*	*All Markets*
Small traders net			
R^F	– .1	–1.2	– .4
R^B	.7	.0	.4
R^A	.6	–1.2	– .0
Large speculators net			
R^F	5.0	3.9	4.8
R^B	2.2	.7	1.3
R^A	7.2	4.6	6.1
Hedgers net			
R^F	– .9	.8	– .6
R^B	–2.1	– .7	–1.0
R^A	–3.0	.1	–1.7

for Special Forecasting Skill, R^F. This measure is negative for both the Large and Small Markets aggregates and for 18 out of the 25 individual markets. While the absolute negative magnitude of R^F appears small, this is partially due to the fact that the positions of this group are almost balanced and consequently the denominator term $V_m^L + V_m^S$ is large. The only important profits for small traders occur in the three large markets where rising prices reward them for being net long so that Basic Skill R^B, is positive.[9]

For large speculators, the situation is quite different. They have positive values of R^B and R^F for all three market aggregates. Nearly four-fifths (79 per cent) of their total profits, however, are due to Special Skill and only one-fifth to Basic Skill. The conclusion must be that the substantial profits of large speculators are not an automatic return for simply being on the correct side of the market, but instead a reward for forecasting. This is confirmed on an individual market basis where the R^F variable for reporting speculators is positive for 22 out of the 24 markets.

The profit dichotomy for hedgers is not of great interest due to their offsetting commitments in the cash market. However, the positive value of .8 for R^F in Small Markets is consistent with our observation [*not included*] that hedgers are able to adjust the balance of their positions in response to major price movements in order to reduce their losses.[10]

NOTES

1 The data on cotton cover the full period from 1937 to 1952.

2 These counter-examples involve fluctuating commitment levels for speculators. See p. 158.

3 This explanation is stressed by Lester Telser [7, p. 407].

4 Large speculators' long positions account for 11 per cent of the value of the total open interest while their short positions account for only 5 per cent.

5 L. G. Telser, 'The Supply of Speculative Services in Wheat, Corn and Soybeans', *Food Research Institute Studies*, vol. VII, 1967, Supplement, pp. 131–76; P. H. Cootner, 'Speculation and Hedging', *op. cit.*, pp. 65–105.

6 A version of this argument is used by Cootner to support a 'hedging pressure' theory of price movement [1, p. 400].

7 For example, 'hedging pressure' theories, where the direction of price change is directly related to the magnitude of short hedges, imply a lack of foresight by speculators who take positions early in the season that are inconsistent with the assumption of forecasting ability.

8 The sign of net hedging used in all of the above computations is the signs of the difference of the average size of hedgers' long positions less the average size of their short positions for each period and market. That is, $\frac{Q_2^L + Q_1^L}{2} - \frac{Q_2^S + Q_1^S}{2}$. This is consistent with the general definition of

profits as $\Delta P \left(\frac{Q_2 + Q_1}{2}\right)$. However, to test the sensitivity of our conclusions against alternative definitions of what constitutes 'when hedgers are net short,' we also computed dollar profits according to whether hedgers are net long or short at the beginning of the period. That is, according to the sign of $Q_1^L - Q_1^S$, the results are that the total long open interest profits are 488 million dollars when hedgers are net short, and 284.9 million dollars when hedgers are net long. Consequently the profits attributable to normal backwardation are 203.1 million dollars. The results are sensitive, but even more unfavorable to the theory of normal backwardation.

9 This return occurs in the manner predicted by the theory of normal backwardation; but the variable R^B cannot properly be construed as the rate of normal backwardation since it contains long position profits earned while hedgers are net long.

10 The sum of a group's long and short commitments is used as divisor in Table 8 to obtain the rate of return on net positions. This makes cross-group comparisons of R^B and cross-group comparisons of R^F misleading because of differences in the short to long ratio among groups. Calculations based on the rate of return to the 'marginal' traders in each group (using the denominator $/V_m^L - V_m^S/$) yield the following percentage results for all markets:

Trading group	R^A	R^B	R^F
Small traders, net	− .1	2.1	− 2.2
Large speculators, net	12.9	2.8	10.1
Hedgers, net	− 4.2	−2.6	− 1.6

REFERENCES

[1] Paul Cootner, 'Returns to Speculators: Telser versus Keynes,' *The Journal of Political Economy*, August 1960.

[2] J. R. Hicks, *Value and Capital* (2nd ed., Oxford, 1953).

[3] H. S. Houthakker, 'Can Speculators Forecast Prices?' *The Review of Economics and Statistics*, May 1957.

[4] ———, 'Restatement of the Theory of Normal Backwardation,' *Cowles Foundation Discussion Paper*, No. 44, December 18, 1957.

[5] J. M. Keynes, 'Some Aspects of Commodity Markets,' *Manchester Guardian Commercial: European Reconstruction Series*, Section 13, March 29, 1923.

[6] ———, *A Treatise on Money*, Vol. II (New York, 1930).

[7] Lester Telser, 'Returns to Speculators: Telser versus Keynes: Reply, *The Journal of Political Economy*, August 1960.

[8] C. S. Rockwell, *Profits, Normal Backwardation and Forecasting in Commodity Futures* (unpublished Ph.D. dissertation, University of California, Berkeley, 1964).

10 Trading on the Sydney Wool Futures Market: A Test of a Theory of Speculation at the Level of the Individual

B. A. GOSS

The aim of this paper is twofold. Models of futures trading developed recently do not, in my view, deal adequately with certain aspects of individual equilibrium. For example, J. L. Stein's theory does not determine explicitly the quantity of stocks held by the individual; the Peston and Yamey model does not deal with individual equilibrium at all; and that of Leland Johnson does not analyse the market position of an individual who is risk-loving.[1] The purpose of Section I is to present a theory which determines the quantity of futures contracts held by an individual trader, whether he is risk-averting or risk-loving, using a method alternative to the indifference curve analysis.[2]

Economists have long expressed a desire for factual information on the nature of expectations formed by speculative traders, the factors underlying the formation of expectations, and the way in which a trader's market position responds to a change in expectations. Section II analyses data obtained on these questions in a futures-trading context. It is an attempt to test empirically the theory referred to above. It will be seen, first, that the theory predicts well for individual traders in the sample whose $R(x)$ functions slope downward and, secondly, that the proportion of predictions correct (of response to hypothetical changes in price, expectations, etc.), for the sample as a whole, is statistically very significant.

I

The main assumptions of the model are as follows:

1. The individual's price expectations take the form of a subjective probability distribution $f(E)$, which is given.

* From *Australian Economic Papers*, vol. 11, 1972, pp. 187–202. Reprinted by permission.

2. The risk $R(x)$, that the individual is willing to take that he is wrong in his market action is some function of the size of his commitments x.[3] It is assumed that $R(x)$ can be specified in the range $0 \leqslant R(x) \leqslant 1$.
3. That there is some level of probability that his action is wrong (*i.e.*, some level of futures price) at which he changes from buying to selling (or from selling to buying) futures.
4. That the individual determines his market position by equating (a) the probability that the price change will be against him and (b) the risk that he is willing to take that the price change will be against him.

In addition, some simplifying assumptions will be made:

1. The function $f(E)$ is symmetrical with mean μ and lies in the range E_1E_2. (In Figure 1 (i), $G(E)$ and $G_1(E)$ are the descending and ascending cumulative probability functions respectively of $f(E)$.)

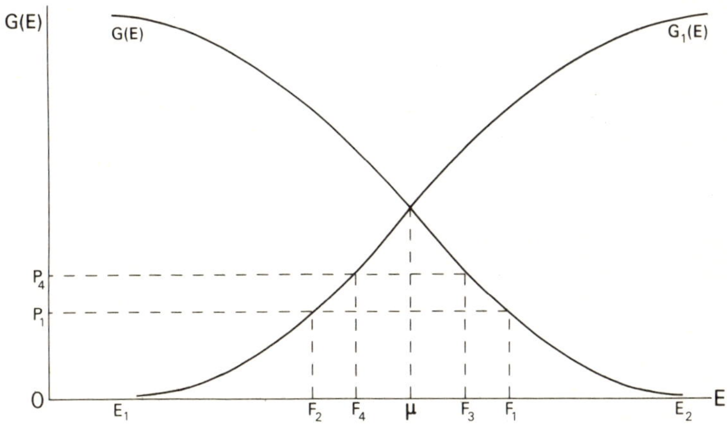

FIGURE 1 (i)

2. The individual will not take a market position for which the subjective probability of an adverse price change is greater than 0.5: that is $R(x)$ exists only in the range $0 \leqslant R(x) \leqslant 0.5$. (See Figure 1 (ii).) If the current futures price $F < \mu$ he will buy futures; if $F > \mu$ he will sell futures.
3. That the function $R(x)$ is linear and the individual has the same $R(x)$ function whether he is buying or selling futures.
4. That we are concerned with two points of time only: t_0 and t_1. The expected price E means the expected spot price and is the same as the expected price of a futures contract maturing at t_1. The price of such a future at t_1 will be the spot price at t_1.[4] The individual is

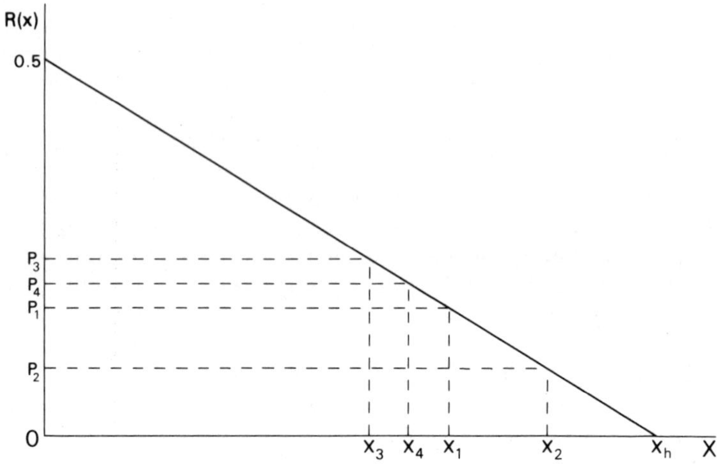

FIGURE 1 (ii)

assumed to close out a futures contract by reversal of the transaction at maturity.

5. The individual's capital is limited so that he can neither buy nor sell more than Ox_h futures contracts.[5] (See Figure 2.)

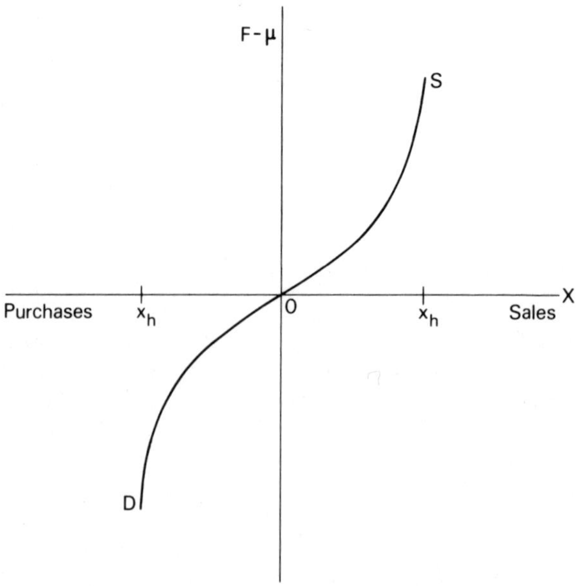

FIGURE 2

The questions are then, first, what quantity of futures contracts the individual will buy or sell for a given futures price and, secondly, what the nature is of the individual's demand and supply functions for futures.

If the current futures price were F_1, which is greater than μ (Figure 1 (i)), the individual would sell futures. With a futures price F_1, the subjective probability that the price will rise is p_1, *i.e.*, the risk of being wrong is p_1. (The risk of being wrong for a seller is given by the descending cumulative probability function $G(E)$). For a risk p_1, with $\partial R(x)/\partial x < 0$, the individual will sell Ox_1 futures contracts (Figure 1 (ii)). The point with co-ordinates (F_1,x_1) is therefore a point on the individual's supply curve.

If the individual had sold Ox_2 futures contracts, he would not be in equilibrium. With commitments of Ox_2, he is willing to take a risk of p_2. With a futures price F_1, however, he estimates the risk of loss as p_1, which exceeds the risk he is willing to take with commitments of that size. He is therefore induced to reduce his market commitments to Ox_1, where the risk he is willing to take coincides with the risk which he estimates to be involved in the current price situation. Similarly, the individual would not be in equilibrium if he had sold only Ox_3 futures contracts. With commitments of Ox_3, he is willing to take a risk of p_3, which is greater than that involved in the current price situation. He is therefore induced to expand his commitments to Ox_1, where the risk he is willing to take is equal to p_1.

Similarly, if the futures price were F_4, which is less than μ, the individual would buy futures. For a futures price F_4, the subjective probability that the price will fall is p_4; *i.e.*, the risk of being wrong is p_4 (the risk of being wrong for a buyer is given by the ascending cumulative probability function $G_1(E)$). For such a risk the individual is willing to buy Ox_4 futures contracts. The point with co-ordinates (F_4,x_4) is therefore a point on the individual's demand curve.

What, then, is the nature of the individual's supply and demand functions for futures contracts? In Figure 2 the vertical axis shows the current futures price minus the price at which the individual changes from buying to selling futures, *i.e.*, $F - \mu$. On the horizontal axis sales of futures contracts are shown; purchases are shown as negative sales. On the stated assumptions the supply curve lies in the first quadrant only and the demand curve lies in the third quadrant only.

In Figure 1 (i), as the current futures price rises from μ to E_2, the probability of being wrong falls at a diminishing rate with respect to price. With a linear $R(x)$ function, sales rise at constant rate with respect to reductions in risk. Therefore sales rise at a diminishing rate with respect to increases in price. The supply curve slopes upward to the right and is concave up. Similarly, as the current futures price falls from μ to E_1, the probability of being wrong falls at a diminishing rate with respect to decreases in price. With a linear $R(x)$ function, purchases rise at a constant rate with respect to falls in risk. Therefore purchases rise at a diminishing rate with respect to falls in price. The demand curve slopes downward to the left and is concave down. Both demand and supply curves exist only up to the ordinate at Ox_h, the limit set by the capital constraint.

On the stated assumptions the supply curve is a mirror image of the $G(E)$ curve below the value $G(E) = 0.5$, with axes rotated through π radians and contracts instead of probability on the horizontal axis. Similarly, the demand curve is a mirror image of the $G_1(E)$ curve below $G_1(E) = 0.5$, with axes inverted and contracts replacing probability.

This method may be used to derive demand and supply functions for, first, an individual whose $R(x)$ function is constant; secondly, one who is risk-loving in the sense that his $R(x)$ function slopes upward; thirdly, a trader who is inoperative for a particular price range because he requires the difference between the current futures price and μ to cover a risk premium; fourthly, an individual who changes from buying to selling futures at a price other than μ; and finally, one who is risk-loving in the sense that he buys futures when $F > \mu$ and sells futures when $F < \mu$. The first three of these cases will be discussed here.

$R(x)$ function constant

Suppose that the individual's $R(x)$ function is constant at $R(x) = p_1$ (Figure 1 (ii)), and that he has the same $R(x)$ function whether he is buying or selling futures. If $R(x) > p_1$, no futures contracts will be bought or sold by this individual. If, however, $R(x) \leqslant p_1$, the individual will buy or sell futures up to the limit x_h. Hence his supply curve is perfectly elastic at a futures price of F_1 and his demand curve is perfectly elastic at a futures price of F_2.

Case of a risk-loving individual

Consider the case of an individual for whom the previous assumptions apply, except that he is risk-loving in the sense that the risk he is willing to take is an increasing function of commitments in the range $0 \leqslant R(x) \leqslant 0.5$. What is the nature of his demand and supply functions for futures contracts?

As the futures price rises from μ to E_2 (Figure 1 (i)), the probability of an adverse price change for a seller falls at a diminishing rate with respect to price. With an upward sloping linear $R(x)$ function, sales fall at a constant rate for decreases in risk. Therefore sales fall at a diminishing rate for increases in price. The supply curve slopes down to the right and is convex down. In this case, the individual is partially risk-loving: he acts so that the odds are in his favour, but he increases his commitments as risk increases.

Risk premium required
It may be that the individual is inoperative for $F_4 < F < F_3$ because he requires the difference between the current futures price and μ to be sufficient to cover a risk premium. In this case, the individual's linear downward-sloping $R(x)$ function would be in the range $0 \leqslant R(x) \leqslant p_4$. Hence his supply curve would be upward sloping, would begin at ($x = 0$, $F = F_3$) and would terminate at ($x = x_h$, $F = E_2$). Similarly, his downward sloping demand curve would begin at ($x = 0$, $F = F_4$) and would terminate at ($x = x_h$, $F = E_1$).

If the individual's willingness to take risk is constant at $R(x) = p_4$, so that he is inoperative for $F_4 < F < F_3$, this is consistent with the interpretation that he requires the difference between F and μ to be sufficient to cover a risk premium.

The method may also be used to analyse changes in, first, the individual's mean expectation; secondly, the dispersion of the distribution $f(E)$; thirdly, the individual's willingness to bear risk; fourthly, the skewness of the distribution $f(E)$; fifthly, the price at which the individual changes from buying to selling futures; and, finally, the individual's available capital. The first three cases only will be discussed here.

Increase in mean expectation
Suppose that the individual's mean expectation of the spot price increases from μ to μ_1, *cet. par.* Using the above assumptions, this means that at any given futures price there is a greater risk of loss for a seller, and in the case of a risk-averting individual less contracts will be supplied. There is, therefore, a decrease in supply. On the demand side, at any given futures price, there is a lower risk of loss and hence more contracts are demanded. There is, therefore, an increase in demand.

In the case of a risk-loving individual (discussed above), an increase in mean expectation will obviously lead to an increase in supply and a decrease in demand. The results of a decrease in mean expectation, *cet. par.*, will be the opposite of those above.

Increase in variance
Suppose that there is an increase in the variance of the individual's distribution of expected prices, $f(E)$. The range of expectations is also assumed to increase. At any given futures price greater than μ there is an increase in seller's risk, and for a risk averting individual a decrease in supply. Similarly, at any futures price less than μ there is an increase in buyer's risk, and hence a decrease in demand.

For an individual who is risk-loving is the sense discussed above, an increase in variance will clearly lead to an increase in both supply of and demand for futures contracts.

Increased willingness to bear risk

Suppose that there is an increase in the individual's willingness to bear risk at any given level of commitments, although he does not act so as to have the odds against him and sells only for a futures price greater than μ. The result is that at any given futures price (above μ) there is an increase in supply of futures, and the maximum quantity of futures Ox_h is supplied at a lower price than before. Similarly, at any given futures price (below μ) there is an increase in demand, and the maximum quantity of futures Ox_h is demanded at a higher price.

For an individual who is risk-loving in the sense discussed above, an increased willingness to bear risk brought about by pivoting the $R(x)$ function upward on the point ($x = 0$, $R(x) = 0$) will obviously lead to a decrease in supply and to a decrease in demand.

II

Do individual traders behave as the theory predicts? The following questions are left open by the theory outlined in Section I:

1. Do traders form price expectations, and if so, of which prices?
2. What is the nature of price expectations formed by traders? In particular, do they attempt to form subjective probability distributions of expected prices, or do they attempt to estimate any of the parameters of such a distribution?
3. What is the attitude of traders to risk? First, are they prepared to take a position only if they believe that the subjective 'odds' are on their side? Secondly, what is the relationship between the risk which the trader is willing to take and the size of his investment in the market?
4. If traders do form price expectations and do have attitudes to risk, do they behave as the theory predicts? First, how does the individual trader alter his market position if the futures price changes, *cet. par.*? That is, what is the nature of his demand and supply functions for futures contracts? Secondly, do his expectations and his willingness to bear risk ever change and, if so, why? Thirdly, what effect does a change in these parameters, *cet. par.*, have upon the individual's market position?
5. What factors limit the size of the individual's market position? In particular, is the amount of capital or funds available a limiting factor?

An attempt was made to obtain this information by factual investigation. The market to which this study refers is the Sydney Greasy Wool Futures Exchange, which conducts transactions in standardized contracts for greasy wool referring to dates up to 18 months in advance. The market is primarily a hedging market, but most traders under-hedge or over-hedge and some take purely speculative positions. To obtain the information required a questionnaire was prepared and the questions were asked by personal interview. One of the basic tasks in preparing the questionnaire was to express the questions in non-technical language, while at the same time retaining sufficient precision to obtain the information required. Before discussing the replies to this questionnaire, however, some explanation of the method is required.

Selection of respondents

The respondents were selected from the lists of Floor Members and Associate Members of the Exchange, as there is no complete list of traders on the Exchange. The sample size is 25. Of the 11 Floor Members at the time the study was commenced, six agreed to be interviewed; the remaining respondents selected were those Associate Members who were frequent users of the Exchange and who were accessible.

A classification of respondents by type of business is given below.[6]

Group	Type of Business	Number
1	Floor Member	6
2	Wool broker or broker-merchant	10
3	Textile manufacturer or manufacturer-merchant	7
4	Speculator	2
		25

All respondents were interviewed during the period January to August, 1970: 15 of the respondents were located in Sydney, four in Melbourne and six in Adelaide.

Use of interview method

The interview method was used because the other three methods of obtaining information – use of documents, observation and mail questionnaire – were either not possible or not desirable. First, the information required for this study was not documented. Secondly, observation of futures market transactions clearly would not yield the information required.

The interview method was preferred to that of mail questionnaire for several reasons. First, it was not certain that the questions were sufficiently simple, clear and unambiguous to be included in a mail questionnaire. The opportunity to clarify questions, which is present in an interview, is not present in a mail questionnaire. Secondly, it was expected that answers would be short and shallow if mail questionnaires were used.[7] In the interviews, respondents answered thoroughly and at length and gave additional information which would otherwise have been lost.

Thirdly, it was important to clarify ambiguous answers. This would have required expensive follow-up work if mail questionnaires had been used. Fourthly, the respondents were all experienced futures traders. There was no certainty that these persons, rather than less experienced members of their firms, would have filled out mail questionnaires.

Types of question asked

One of the limitations to obtaining information by questionnaire is that the answers may be inaccurate, especially if the questions are hypothetical, emotional, personal or contain a prestige element.

Some of the questions asked in this study are factual, some are motivational and some are hypothetical. It is usually objected to hypothetical questions that people are not good at predicting their own behaviour; their answers to hypothetical questions, it is said, may be a mixture of intention and wishful thinking.[8] In the answers obtained in this study however, one would expect the wishful thinking element to be low. One would expect the respondents to be facing some of the situations hypothesized daily (*e.g.*, a change in the futures price) and some very frequently although not daily (*e.g.*, change in price expectations). On the other hand, some hypothetical situations may be encountered only occasionally (*e.g.*, a change in willingness to take risk or in available capital). For the changes hypothesized, respondents were asked explicitly whether the relevant factors ever changed in their cases. Therefore, one would expect the answers to hypothetical questions in this study to be based on generalizations from past experience, rather than on wishful thinking.

The validity of answers to questionnaires is also said to be suspect if the questions are of an emotional, personal or prestige nature. The questions in this questionnaire are clearly not emotional, nor do they relate to the personal life of the respondent. One question is private and has a prestige element: 'Does the amount of capital you have available limit the extent of your dealing in the market?' It may be argued that to answer 'yes' to this question is an admission of financial weakness. Twelve respondents, however, did give affirmative answers to this question, and, of the thirteen who answered 'no', four were large public companies, and five were Floor Members or wool brokers whose answers were based on the experience of clients. The question 'Do you deal up to the maximum point allowed by this (capital) limit?' also contains a prestige element: an affirmative answer may be regarded as a sign of indiscretion. On the other hand, it would be rather restrictive for subsequent dealings if a firm had all available capital tied up in current futures transactions.

Finally, the questions were generally asked as open questions, rather than in pre-coded form. The reason for this is that generally there is no established range of answers. In other cases, although the categories of answer are obvious, the open form was more desirable because frequently respondents offered additional information in such cases, which would probably have been lost if a pre-coded set of answers had been used.

III

There are six hypotheses to be tested for each individual respondent. By an hypothesis is meant the change in the individual's market position, as predicted by the theory, in response to a change in price, in price expectations or in willingness to take risk, *cet. par*. The hypotheses relate to, first, the shape of the individual's supply and demand functions for futures contracts in relation to price; secondly, the response of these functions with respect to a change in price expectations, and thirdly, the response of these functions to a change in willingness to take risk.

It is clear from the previous analysis that for an individual who is risk-averting in the sense of having $\frac{\partial R(x)}{\partial x} < 0$, then the predictions are as follows:

1. $\frac{\partial S}{\partial F} > 0$ 3. $\frac{\partial S}{\partial \mu} < 0$ 5. $\frac{\partial S}{\partial R(x)} > 0$

2. $\frac{\partial D}{\partial F} < 0$ 4. $\frac{\partial D}{\partial \mu} > 0$ 6. $\frac{\partial D}{\partial R(x)} > 0$

where S is the quantity of futures sold by the individual; D is the quantity of futures bought by the individual; and F is the current futures price. In the case of an individual for whom $\frac{\partial R(x)}{\partial x} = 0$, the predictions are as follows:

1. $\frac{\partial S}{\partial F} = 0$ 3. $\frac{\partial S}{\partial \mu} = 0$ 5. $\frac{\partial S}{\partial R(x)} = 0$

2. $\frac{\partial D}{\partial F} = 0$ 4. $\frac{\partial D}{\partial \mu} = 0$ 6. $\frac{\partial D}{\partial R(x)} = 0$

The predictions for an individual who is risk-loving in the sense of having $\frac{\partial R(x)}{\partial x} > 0$ are of opposite sign to those for an individual who is a risk-averter.

Each respondent was asked, first, whether he estimated the price he thought most likely and, secondly, how his willingness to take risk varied in response to the size of his market commitment. It was then assumed that the individual behaved, first, as if he estimated a probability distribution of expected spot prices, and, secondly, as if he determined his market position by equating the subjective estimate of the risk of loss at the current futures price with $R(x)$, his willingness to take risk. The respondent was then asked, in a set of independent questions, how he would adjust his market position in response to a change in price expectations and willingness to take risk. These answers were then compared with the set of predictions for that individual.

The questionnaire used, together with a numerical summary of replies, is given in Appendix I. The sections of the questionnaire correspond to the questions left open by the theory, listed at the beginning of Section II. The results of the interviews will be discussed under three separate headings: first, a summary of the information obtained; secondly, an analysis by type of prediction; and thirdly, an analysis by individual.

Information obtained

It is clear that most traders form expectations about the spot price, the futures price and the price spread. Fourteen respondents always form expectations about all three price variables, although four traders form their expectations in terms of the spot price only, while one trader forms expectations in terms of the price spread only.

More than one quarter of the traders interviewed estimated the percentage chance of a price change. (In the London Metal Exchange study only three of sixteen respondents claimed that they made such an estimate).

Most traders estimate the most likely price, but less than half claimed that they estimate a margin of error. For those who gave affirmative answers to Question 4 (a), the margins varied from approximately one per cent to five per cent of the most likely price, although one trader makes a ten per cent estimate for the whole season and one expresses the margin of error in the flexibility of the timing of his transactions. (In the L.M.E. study eleven of sixteen respondents claimed to estimate margins of error, ranging from one per cent to 16 per cent of the most likely price for copper.) In addition, several traders estimate the range within which they expect the futures price to lie for periods up to eighteen months in advance; this range varies from three cents to twenty cents, but is typically equal to ten cents.

More than half of the respondents estimated the point at which there is a 50-50 chance of the price going either way, although this was usually only when the current price was at this point.

No trader was risk-loving in the sense of being willing to take a larger risk of loss the greater his market commitment. The majority of respondents were risk-averting in the sense of having decreasing $R(x)$ functions: approximately three-quarters were generally risk-averting in the sense that they were not prepared to take a risk of loss in excess of a 50-per-cent chance, and some required a substantial risk premium.

Three traders replied that they did not take the risk of loss into account in determining their futures market positions, because they took positions which were essentially pure hedges.

Approximately half of the respondents claimed that a capital constraint existed, and more than half of those who gave affirmative answers to Part V, Question 1, claimed to deal up to this limit.

All traders but one said that they revised their price expectations, and their principal reasons are given in Appendix I. The trader who said he did not revise his price expectations, because such a revision was not relevant to his pure hedging position, had also replied in answer to Section II that he did not take the risk of loss into account in determining his market position. He did however, claim to form expectations of the three price variables.

More than half of the respondents claimed to revise their willingness to take risk, and their main reasons were the level of market price, their state of psychology, and past profit and loss record. An accumulation of profits in the recent past, some traders claimed, made them more adventurous in their attitude toward risk, and vice versa. This last factor indicates some inter-dependence between the individual's distribution of expected prices in relation to the current price and his $R(x)$ function.

Approximately half of the respondents claimed that capital available for their dealings was subject to change, although three of these traders said that such a change would have no effect on the extent of their transactions.

Analysis by type of prediction

The traders' replies to the questions relating to price and parameter changes were compared with the predictions made in the way described above. The proportion of correct predictions for each price and parameter change, together with an indication of the statistical significance of the proportion, is given in Appendix II. In all cases, the proportions of predictions correct are significant at the half-per-cent level of significance,[9] and the theory appears to have strongest predictive power in Case 4.

It is encouraging, for two reasons, that the best result is obtained for Case 4. First, a change in price expectations is evidently (from Appendix I) an important parameter change in practice, and secondly, because although overseas hedging business is said by traders to be net short, and Australian business is said to be net long, the latter predominates. Most traders would appear to under-hedge and/or over-hedge, and hence the theory predicts well for a large single group of traders.

IV

More significant of the predictive power of the theory is an analysis by individual. First, however, a comment is necessary on the effective size of the sample. For some individuals (traders nos. 8, 9, 14, 16), two or less answers to prediction questions were received, either because the traders thought the questions were not meaningful for them, or because they were unable to answer for some other reason; *e.g.*, some individuals refused to answer questions about selling futures on the grounds that their business is essentially long hedging; also some individuals said that their willingness to take risk never altered, and hence had no answers to offer for Section II of the 'Changes in Factors Affecting Behaviour' part of the questionnaire. Because a proportion of such individuals is to be expected for any sample of traders, however, it is not proposed to make any adjustment to the sample for the presence of these individuals, even though for some respondents data are available for only one prediction in six.

If we use the arbitrary number of at least five predictions correct as a criterion of success, ten cases fulfil this requirement. They are:

	Trader No.	$\frac{\partial R(x)}{\partial x}$	Business
Six predictions correct	1	< 0	Floor Member
	11	< 0	Speculator
	15	< 0	Floor Member
	19	< 0	Merchant
	25	< 0	Floor Member
Five predictions correct	3	< 0	Floor Member
	18	$= 0$	Broker
	21	< 0	Broker-merchant
	22	< 0	Merchant
	24	< 0	Merchant

In addition, a reasonable degree of success (four out of six predictions correct) was recorded for four other traders:

Trader No.	$\frac{\partial R(x)}{\partial x}$	Business
6	$= 0$	Textile manufacturer
13	$= 0$	Floor Member
20	< 0	Speculator
23	$= 0$	Broker

Apart from traders for whom data on two or less predictions were available (nos. 8, 9, 14 and 16), there were five traders for whom the theory predicted poorly. The results for these five traders are:

Trader No.	Predictions Correct / No. Made	$\frac{\partial R(x)}{\partial x}$	Business
2	1/6	= 0	Floor Member
4	0/4	= 0	Textiles
7	0/6	= 0	Merchant-textiles
10	1/6	= 0	Merchant
12	2/6	= 0	Textiles

For the other two respondents (nos. 5 [merchant-textiles] and 17 [brokers]) the theory was only moderately successful in predicting their behaviour: three of five and three of six predictions correct. Both of these respondents claimed to have constant $R(x)$ functions.

Two important results appear to emerge. First, in the group of traders for whom at least five predictions are correct, all but one are risk-averters. This group contains three of the five Floor Members interviewed (including trader no. 15, who claims to be responsible for half of the business done in some periods) and one of the two pure speculators interviewed. Secondly, all the traders for whom the theory predicted poorly have constant $R(x)$ functions, and, with the exception of trader no. 2 (Floor Member), they are all textile manufacturers or merchants.

V

As a preliminary to the conclusions it should be noted that although the sample size is small the information and results obtained may be representative of the market because the sample includes more than half of the Floor Members, as well as several associate members, and all transactions must go through a Floor Member.

The main conclusions of the study appear to be as follows. First, the pure speculators, most Floor Members and some merchants in the sample are risk-averters in the sense that their willingness to take risk is a decreasing function of commitments.

Secondly, for a minority of Floor Members, some merchants and all textile manufacturers in the sample, willingness to take risk is constant with respect to commitments. No respondent was risk-loving in the sense that his willingness to take risk was an increasing function of commitments, although some traders (20 per cent of respondents)[10] were risk-loving in the sense that they were willing to take a market position where the subjective estimate of the risk of loss exceeded 0.5.

Thirdly, the theory predicts well for traders with decreasing $R(x)$ functions, and poorly for traders with constant $R(x)$ functions. Some of the traders with constant $R(x)$ functions claimed to be chart theorists. If so, this is consistent with the results obtained, *e.g.*, a chart theorist would adjust his market position in response to a change in the current futures price only if he thought a new trend were being established, and not because his estimate of the risk of loss associated with his current market position had changed.

It is suggested that the major implications of these conclusions are as follows. First, although most respondents claim to form price expectations, less than one quarter claim to estimate the subjective probability of a price change. It is clear, however, from the results obtained for the six hypotheses tested that the majority of respondents behave *as if they do* (for each of the six hypotheses: see Appendix II).

Secondly, since all respondents have $\frac{\partial R(x)}{\partial x} \leqslant 0$, it would appear that the market equilibrium is stable in the Marshallian and Walrasian senses. For a predominance of risk-loving individuals in the sense of having $\frac{\partial R(x)}{\partial x} > 0$, this theory predicts that the market equilibrium would be unstable in both the above senses, since the market demand function for futures would be upward sloping, and the supply function downward sloping.

Thirdly, recent work on the supply of storage of commodities has employed the Nerlove Adaptive Expectations hypothesis, where the revision of price expectations for the next period is in proportion to the error of the expectation for the current period:[11]

$$EP_{t+1} - EP_t = \beta(P_t - EP_t)$$

that is

$$EP_{t+1} = (1 - \beta)\, EP_t + \beta P_t$$

which can be written

$$EP_{t+1} = \beta \sum_{t=0}^{\infty} (1 - \beta)^i\, P_{t-i}$$

where $0 < \beta < 1$, P_t is the spot price in period t, and EP_t is the expected spot price for period t.

The evidence obtained in this study suggests that traders revise expectations for a change in the state of the economy in general, for a change in the current state of the market for the particular commodity, and for the receipt of new information relating to that commodity, even though the expectations formed last period were correct. These factors may react upon traders' expectations about the future, causing them to respond in a variety of different ways.

To the extent that these factors have already affected current prices (the release of information, of course, may affect current prices) their effect upon expectations is already incorporated in the adaptive model. These factors however, may have an effect on expectations over and above their impact on current prices: this is possible for the first two factors as well as for the third, although perhaps more likely for the third factor in practice. It is this additional effect on expectations which is not taken into account by the adaptive model, and which may be represented in an expectations function by proxy or dummy variables.

Finally, it is suggested that the approach adopted in this paper is not limited to futures markets, but may be applicable to other markets with speculative elements, where price expectations and willingness to take risk are important determinants of the individual's market position.

APPENDIX I

Questionnaire for the individual trader and summary of replies

	Ans.	*Yes*	*No*	*Sometimes*
I *Expectations*				
1. If you are trading in futures contracts do you form expectations about:				
(a) the futures price	25	21	3	1
(b) the spot price	25	19	3	3
(c) contango or backwardation, relating to a later date?	24	16	7	1
2. Given the current futures price, do you estimate the percentage chance:				
(a) that it will rise, or				
(b) that it will fall?	25	6	18	1
3. Do you estimate the price that you think most likely?	25	19	6	
4. (a) Do you estimate the amount by which you expect the futures price to differ from the most likely price?	25	12	13	
(b) Please give an idea of the size of this 'margin or error'.				
5. Do you estimate the range within which you expect the futures price to lie?	24	17	7	
6. Do you estimate a point at which you think there is a 50-50 chance of the price going either way?	24	13	10	1
II. *Willingness to Take Risk*				
Please consider your estimation of the risk of loss in relation to the size of your investment in the market.				
1. Are you willing to take more risk the greater your investment in the market?	25		25	

APPENDIX I—*continued*

	Ans.	*Yes*	*No*	*Sometimes*
2. Are you willing to take less risk the greater your investment in the market?	25	14	11	
3. Does the size of the risk you are willing to take have no effect on the amount of your investment?	25	11	14	
4. What is the maximum risk of loss that you are willing to take?	23	17 (<50%)	5 (>50%)	1 (other)
III. *Selection of Change-Over Point Buying to Selling*				
1. Is there some level of futures price, or some level of odds of a price change, at which you will change from buying to selling of futures or vice versa?	24	15	7	2
2. (a) Is this price the same as the most likely price? or	11	4	1	6
(b) At what odds do you make the change: *i.e.*, what are the odds at which you will do nothing?				
3. If the current futures price exceeds this point do you buy or sell futures?	14	12 (Sell)		2 (Sell)
IV. *Buying and Selling Futures*				
1. If you are selling futures and the futures price rises (and nothing else changes) do you sell more or less futures?	25	14 (More)	8 (Const.)	3 (Less)
2. If you are buying futures and the futures price falls (and nothing else changes) do you buy more or less futures?	25	17 (More)	7 (Const.)	1 (Less)
V. *Limitation of Capital*				
1. Does the amount of capital you have available limit the extent of your dealing in the market?	25	12	13	
2. If so, do you deal up to the maximum point allowed by this limit?	11	7	4	

APPENDIX I—*continued*

	Ans.	*Yes*	*No*	*Sometimes*
3. If not, what other factors limit the extent of your dealing?	18*	8 Discretion 11 Production Requirements 3 Company Rules 4 Other		
Changes in Factors Affecting Behaviour				
I. *Expectations*				
1. (a) Do you ever revise upwards or downwards:				
(i) the price you think most likely,	25	24	1	
(ii) the general level of your expectations of the futures price?	25	24	1	
(b) What factors would cause you to do this?	24*	13 Market 11 New Information 8 Economy 6 Other		
2. Suppose you revise upwards: (i) the price you think most likely, and (ii) the general level of your expectations. The current futures price is assumed to be unchanged.				
(a) If you were a seller of futures, would you sell more or less contracts?	19	12 Less 5 More 2 Constant		
(b) If you were a buyer of futures, would you buy more or less contracts?	23	17 More 5 Less 1 Constant		
II. *Willingness to Take Risk*				
1. (a) Does your willingness to take risk (at any one level of investment) ever increase or decrease?	23	14	9	
(b) What factors would cause this?	14*	7 Market 5 Profit and Loss 3 Psychology 3 Other		

APPENDIX I—*continued*

	Ans.	*Yes*	*No*	*Sometimes*
2. Suppose that you become generally more willing to take risk.				
(a) If you were a seller of futures, would you sell more or less contracts?	17	15 More 2 Constant		
(b) If you were a buyer of futures, would you buy more or less contracts?	18	17 More 1 Constant		
III. *Change in Capital Available*				
1. Does the amount of capital available for your dealings ever change?	25	12	13	
2. Does an increase in capital available affect the quantity of futures contracts you would buy or sell:	10			
(a) at all prices, or		2		
(b) at very high selling prices, or (c) at very low buying prices, or		5		
(d) not at all?		3		

* Several respondents gave more than one factor.

APPENDIX II
Predictions correct

Prediction	*No. Made*	*No. Correct*	*Proportion Correct*
1. Shape of supply curve	22	14	.6364*
2. Shape of demand curve	22	15	.6818*
3. Supply response to expectations change	19	13	.6842*
4. Demand response to expectations change	23	18	.7826*
5. Supply response to $R(x)$ change	17	13	.7647*
6. Demand response to $R(x)$ change	18	12	.6667*

* Significant at half-per-cent level of significance.

NOTES

1 Jerome L. Stein, 'The Simultaneous Determination of Spot and Futures Prices?', *American Economic Review*, vol. 51, 1961 and 'The Opportunity Locus in a Hedging Decision: A Correction', *American Economic Review*, vol. 54, 1964; M. H. Peston and B. S. Yamey, 'Inter-Temporal Price Relationships with Forward Markets: A Method of Analysis', *Economica*, vol. 27, 1960; Leland L. Johnson, 'The Theory of Hedging and Speculation in Commodity Futures', *Review of Economic Studies*, vol. 27, 1959–60.

2 Since the aim is to present a method of analysis and to assess its empirical validity, the model is restricted to analysing the market position of an individual who speculates in futures only. It can be applied to the case of an individual who speculates in spot only or to that of an individual who under-hedges or over-hedges. The analysis can be extended by introducing other speculators, with expectations either homogeneous or heterogeneous, and by introducing hedgers who are net long or net short and arbitrage. These extensions, however, are not considered here.

3 The extent of commitments is measured by the number of contracts bought or sold. In simplifying assumption (3) it is assumed that $R(x)$ is linear. This *is* only for simplicity: a concave or convex $R(x)$ function will not cause a change in the sign of the first derivative of the individual's supply or demand function.

4 We ignore costs of dealing. This point is discussed in detail by B. S. Yamey, 'Short Hedging and Long Hedging in Futures Markets: Symmetry and Asymmetry', *Journal of Law and Economics*, vol. 14, 1971. Yamey points out (p. 424) that in practice the actual commodity normally commands a premium over the maturing future.

5 It is assumed that the individual, when buying futures, must pay a deposit at the time of purchase and, when selling, must deposit a stake with the market authority at the time of sale.

6 Respondents in groups 2, 3 and 4 were all Associate Members.

7 In a similar study on the London Metal Exchange, one respondent replied by mail and gave unduly brief replies.

8 *E.g.*, C. A. Moser, *Survey Methods in Social Investigation*, London, 1959, p. 227.

9 Each proportion was tested against the hypothesis $H_0 = 0.33$, which is the proportion expected by chance if there are three possible answers to the questions asked (increase, decrease, or no change).

10 See Appendix I.

11 M. Nerlove, 'Adaptive Expectations and Cobweb Phenomena', *Quarterly Journal of Economics*, vol. 72, 1958. This hypothesis was used for estimation purposes by M. J. Brennan, 'The Supply of Storage', *American Economic Review*, vol. 48, 1958.

Section Four
Price Movements

11 Measurement of a Random Process in Futures Prices

ARNOLD B. LARSON

This paper presents the results of application of a new method of time-series analysis, which appears to give the first really satisfactory answer to the question of whether commodity futures markets facilitate excessive daily price fluctuations. The method uses an entirely new test statistic, the index of continuity, rather than autocovariance as do virtually all other methods. In order to show why the new statistic is needed, I will first sketch the current status of the relevant area of time-series analysis, and demonstrate the failure of existing methods to solve the problem at hand.

RECENT TRENDS IN TIME-SERIES ANALYSIS

From the viewpoint of the economist engaged in research into economic relationships, progress in development of time-series analysis can be gauged by the kinds of 'cycles' which can be detected. These may be true sine waves of fixed period and amplitude, or the apparent cycles which occur in series with purely random movements, or they may be intermediate types such as the disturbed cycles of autoregressive schemes. Usually the processes which generate the cycles embody or reveal interesting economic relationships, and the parameters of the processes can be given economic interpretation.

Much of the early work in time-series analysis was concerned with the decomposition of a series into trend, seasonal or other cyclic, and random components. Often the cycle so isolated was of indeterminate character. Among the first procedures which at least by implication addressed themselves to the question of the type of process which generates cycles was the periodogram. It tested for cycles of fixed period against the counter hypothesis of a purely random series. A systematic development of the theory of stationary stochastic processes, beginning in about 1930,

* Reprinted from *Food Research Institute Studies*, vol. I, no. 3, 1960, with the permission of the publishers, Stanford University Food Research Institute

permitted the formulation of a large sample theory for the harmonic, autoregressive, and moving average processes. The parameters of even high order processes can be estimated, although the methods are quite cumbersome and almost require the use of electronic computers. These three processes – harmonic, autoregressive, and moving average – are thought to correspond to many real processes, including many of those in operation in economic situations.

There appear to be many difficulties involved in applying the methods of analysis of stochastic processes to economic data, in spite of the seemingly satisfactory state of the theory. Since many economic series are short, the large-sample estimates are of doubtful validity. The process in operation in the series may not be stationary, and in fact may be intermittent or at times completely obscured by random factors. Most of the methods of parameter estimation depend fundamentally on the correlogram, that is, the graph of successive autocorrelation coefficients. Empirical correlograms have been shown to have highly autocorrelated terms, and to depend heavily on the particular sample drawn. Results of correlogram analysis of economic time series have been generally disappointing to date, being both inconclusive and of doubtful validity.[1] Usually only the first one or two terms of the correlogram have been used, and even these often have not differed significantly from zero. However, it must be granted that the possibilities have not been exhausted for successful application of correlogram methods.

Often in time-series analysis greater interest attaches to the *type* of process in operation than to the particular values of the parameters of a process once specified. The type of process is interesting to the scientist because it determines the nature of the mechanism in operation, and the mechanism may be basically unaltered under a wide range of parameter values. Furthermore, the type of process may be genuinely in doubt. Tests of significance, which in general help us choose between alternative parameter values, are in consequence not as important as are tests of goodness of fit, which choose between alternative specifications of process type. Sometimes more than one specification is acceptable on the basis of the test of goodness of fit. Procedures for choosing among the acceptable specifications can be devised, but one can never determine by purely statistical means that *the* true process has been found. All statistical investigation encounters this problem, of course, but it is of special importance here.

THE THEORY OF ANTICIPATORY PRICES

A time series, such as a commodity futures price series, can be analyzed in one of two ways. First, one may apply formally and naively the methods for estimating each of several processes, and choose the best fitting process as the one which is presumably in operation in the series. This will normally involve some *a posteriori* rationalization of the existence of such a process in the series. The test of goodness of fit will not ordinarily provide conclusive evidence that this is the true process, but quite possibly the rationale will be sufficiently plausible so that the results may be accepted.

The second approach, which seems preferable because of the lack of power of the tests of goodness of fit, is to determine the type of process which is implied by the structure of the market, or other institution being studied. Then only the order of the process and certain parameters need be estimated by statistical means. It is still necessary that the data fit the specification satisfactorily, but acceptance of the hypothesis rests primarily on its *a priori* probability, based on economic considerations.

Something close to the first approach is most often used in economic analyses. A process of one of the well developed types is fitted after the most casual theorizing, just to see if it gives a good fit. It may be that more sophisticated and realistic theories do not ordinarily lead to stochastic processes of one of the standard types. But if this is true, a conscious process of simplification with an eye to retaining the essential features of the economic structure in the stochastic process would be more likely to yield valid results.

In this study the second course is pursued and an attempt is made to derive the stochastic processes implied by two theories of market price formation, and to subject the theories to empirical test by estimating the implied processes. The two theories are not mutually exclusive, but they do present opposing views about the probable existence and importance of excessive price fluctuations generated in futures markets. No attempt is made at complete expositions of either theory. Rather only those facets which touch upon the implied stochastic process and the central question of excessive fluctuation are developed at all fully.

The first theory is that of Professor Taussig[1]. He held that the equilibrium price is only roughly determinate, and that the market price is free to fluctuate within a penumbra of uncertainty about the equilibrium price. At the edge of the penumbra there would be a reaction, or at least a check, presumably caused by equilibrating forces asserting themselves, returning the price toward equilibrium.[2] Since no one knows just where within the penumbra the price should be, it moves in this zone in response to the slightest impulse, which may be completely unrelated to market information. Furthermore, and this is perhaps Taussig's main point, movements away from equilibrium in the penumbra of uncertainty will not necessarily call forth an immediate return to equilibrium, but may well produce further movement in the same direction. Taussig assigns a big role to the market manipulator who, for example, may sell in hopes of inducing further sales and an artificially low price, at which he buys and awaits the return of price to equilibrium. The timing of the reversal of price movement varies, and sometimes the manipulator fails in his objective.

Taussig's theory unfortunately cannot be reformulated as a stationary stochastic process, at least without considerable simplification. A Markov chain with reflecting barriers corresponding to the edges of the penumbra might be an approximate model. The analogy is far from complete, however. For instance Taussig's theory apparently differentiates between price changes caused by manipulation and those caused by market information, and hence one cannot apply the same transition probabilities, which imply the same probable subsequent course of events, to the two situations. The probabilities to be assigned should perhaps depend on the path previously taken, which would make the process non-Markovian and make analysis much harder.

Even the correlogram implied by the theory is not clear. Presumably there would be numerous short runs of various lengths, many but not all of them followed by abrupt reactions. This might imply rather high negative correlation coefficients for several days' lag, for a series of price changes. Or if the runs are of several days' duration there may be positive correlations followed by negative ones. The correlogram, which completely describes the autoregressive and the moving average schemes, appears to tell little about this kind of process.

It would evidently be difficult or impossible to test Taussig's theory by standard statistical methods, because it fails to conform to any of the well developed stochastic processes. But maybe it is wrong anyway. Past prices have had to stand the test of market clearing and presumably cannot be grossly in error very long. The primary task of the traders in the market is thus reduced from the formidable one of estimating the correct price *level* to the much more modest one of gauging the price *changes* appropriate to changes in the demand and supply conditions. This they might well be able to do. So maybe the penumbra is not there.

Holbrook Working has developed a theory of anticipatory market prices which reflects quite a different view of market behavior [2]. He argues that anticipatory prices depend on expectations regarding the future course of events affecting demand and supply of the commodity being traded. Traders base their expectations on market news, which in broad and highly organized commodity markets, he suggests, tends to be generally accurate, timely, and relevant.

In an ideal market, existing knowledge of market conditions would be reflected in current price, and any new information, showing altered conditions, would produce a price movement. Truly new information emerges randomly, and so price movements would tend to be random. Working's model of price movement in an ideal market is thus a random walk; that is, price is the cumulation of random movements. Equilibrating forces restrain the random walk, of course, but during the life of any one future the random movements predominate. These random movements, far from being blind stumbling around in a penumbra, would be movements to accurately estimated new equilibrium prices.

No actual market behaves exactly like an ideal market. Many commodity futures markets approach the ideal, and differ principally in that traders react with varying skill to varying sources of information, and so some of the response to price-making forces is delayed. The initial response is inadequate, and subsequent corrective response is in the same direction. The delayed response is a rather small fraction of the

TABLE 1

Autocorrelograms of close-to-close price changes, corn futures prices, Chicago, 1922–31 *and* 1949–58

Lag	*1922–31*	*1949–58*	*Lag*	*1922–31*	*1949–58*
1	−.017	.012	31	−.003	−.020
2	.008	−.086[a]	32	.012	−.004
3	.008	.037[b]	33	−.001	.034[c]
4	.022	−.000	34	.016	−.024
5	.035[b]	.033[c]	35	.056[a]	−.010
6	−.026	.013	36	.006	.016
7	−.023	−.070[a]	37	−.017	−.034[c]
8	−.009	.030[c]	38	−.030[c]	.014
9	.038[b]	.013	39	−.023	.003
10	.009	−.018	40	.018	.018
11	−.007	.036[c]	41	.029[c]	.011
12	.052[a]	.018	42	−.006	−.008
13	−.000	−.011	43	.003	.002
14	.027[c]	.008	44	−.013	.014
15	.015	−.022	45	−.014	.004
16	.009	−.010	46	−.006	−.031[c]
17	.008	.018	47	.016	−.006
18	−.006	.021	48	−.000	.014
19	−.006	.034[c]	49	−.008	−.002
20	.028[c]	.021	50	.021	.010
21	−.012	−.012	51	−.005	.037[b]
22	−.002	.020	52	.014	.013
23	.005	.029	53	−.005	.030[c]
24	.021	.021	54	−.050[a]	−.022
25	.023	.021	55	−.003	−.018
26	.010	−.021	56	.032[c]	−.006
27	.017	−.001	57	−.034[c]	−.023
28	.037[b]	.018	58	−.020	.028
29	−.032[c]	.030[c]	59	−.008	.034[c]
30	−.012	.003	60	.032[a]	−.022

[a] Significant at 1 per cent level.
[b] Significant at 5 per cent level.
[c] Nearly significant.

total, and is dispersed over a considerable number of days, in a highly variable pattern.

This completes the essential economic argument, but for mathematical reasons, to reduce the number of parameters to be estimated, it is further specified that the average pattern of dispersion is approximately rectangular; that is, a constant percentage of the delayed price response occurs on each day of the dispersion span. This is a gratuitous assumption, and as a matter of fact we will modify it shortly, but even major changes in the specified pattern do not seem to call for revision of the economic interpretation.

With this assumption, Working's theory of anticipatory prices leads directly to a moving average stochastic process of order equal to the length of dispersion span and with uniform weights. Price changes are a moving average of the price changes which would have occurred had the market been perfect. The process is not quite stationary, since the

CHART 1

Autocorrelograms of close-to-close price changes, corn futures prices, Chicago, 1922–31 and 1949–58

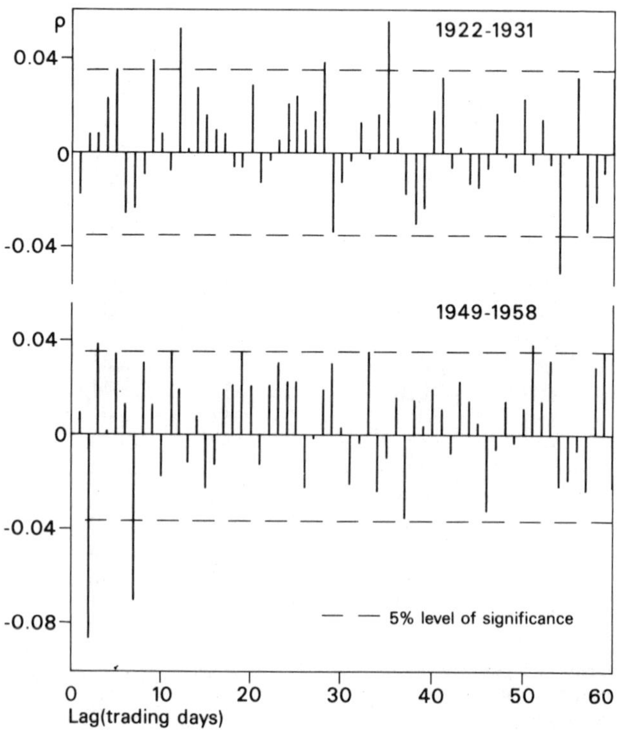

variance of price influences varies over time, but this is not likely to be a serious discrepancy.

For large dispersion span and low per cent dispersed, the weights of the moving average process are very low. A moving average stochastic process which generates a series is completely determined by the mean and variance of the series and by the correlogram equal in length to the order of the process. The very low weights, with resulting low values of correlation coefficients, coupled with the difficulties mentioned above, make estimation of the process from the empirical correlogram extremely difficult.

The correlograms of the series of changes in closing prices of corn futures on the Chicago Board of Trade for two ten-year periods,

CHART 2
Distribution of close-to-close price changes, Chicago corn futures, 1922–31 *and* 1949–58, *compared to normal distribution*

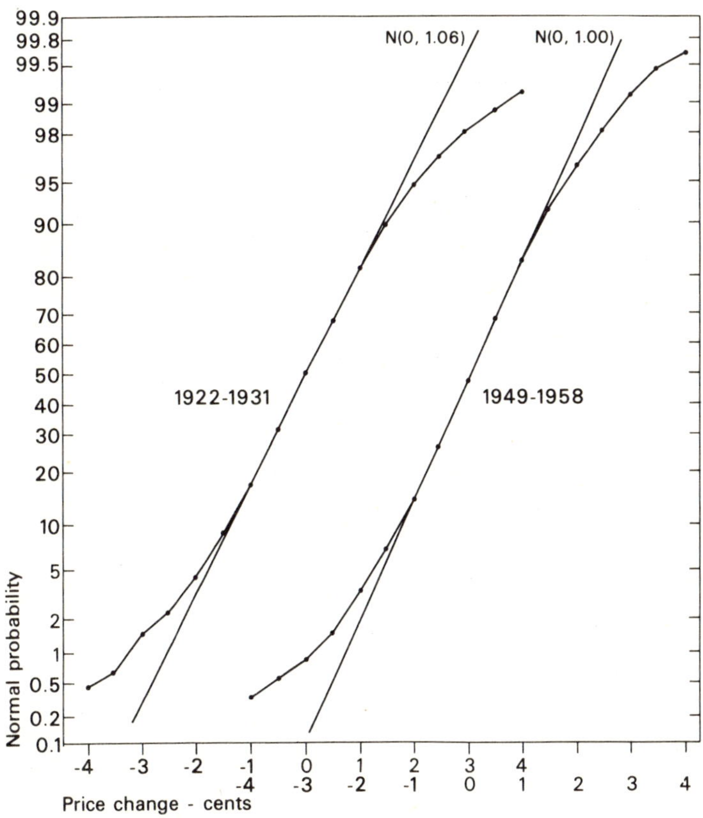

1922–31 and 1949–58, up to lag 60, are shown in Table 1 and Chart 1. Several of the coefficients of correlation are significantly different from zero, but no clear pattern emerges. For instance, significant values seem to be as likely at high orders of lag as at low. Also, high positive coefficients frequently occur adjacent to high negative values. Moreover, there appears to be no correspondence between the correlograms for the two periods. The general appearance of the correlograms virtually rules out the possibility of a low-order process of any sort, and strongly suggests that the series is indeed a random walk. Because the correlogram method lacks power to detect moving average processes with very low weights, we should not accept this negative conclusion on the basis of this evidence.

The erratic patterns in the correlograms may arise in part from the nature of the distributions of price changes shown in Chart 2. The distribution for each 10-year period has mean near zero, and is symmetrical and very nearly normally distributed for the central 80 per cent of the data, but there is an excessive number of extreme values. Also, some of these are quite extreme, being 8 or 9 standard deviations from the mean. If these extreme values occur randomly the estimates of correlation coefficients are consistent, but the confidence intervals shown are somewhat too narrow. Indeed, the cross-product of two of the higher extreme values would be of the same order of magnitude as the autocovariances found in the study. Examination of the pattern of occurrence of all price changes in excess of three standard deviations from zero, and of the cross-products of these changes, indicated that they have no special autocorrelation properties, and it is assumed that the data are essentially homogeneous and that underestimation of the variance of the autocorrelation coefficients is probably the only problem arising from presence in the data of an excessive number of extreme values.

THE INDEX OF CONTINUITY

Holbrook Working developed the test of the index of continuity specifically to analyze anticipatory prices. The index is based on the ratio of the range of a series on an interval to the sum of the ranges of the subintervals within the interval. The subintervals are of equal length and non-overlapping. The series of values of index of continuity, designated H, for one-day subintervals and interval lengths of 2, 4, 8, . . . , 256 days, trace a curve which forms the basis for estimation procedures. Positive values of H occur when the range of the series tends to exceed the expected range of a random-walk series over intervals of a given length. Positive values of H thus imply movement of the series predominantly in one direction; in other words, relatively long, but perhaps interrupted, runs and positive autocorrelation. Negative values of H imply an excessive number of reversals in the series, so that the range tends to be less than that of a random-walk series. Autocorrelations between members of a series at any lag within the interval length tend to affect the index of continuity for that interval length similarly. Hence the index of continuity test relaxes the assumption of rigid lag between initial and corrective movements, and substitutes the more realistic assumption that the correction occurs sometime within a given interval of time.

Since the index of continuity is based on the range, i.e., the difference between maximum and minimum, it is rather difficult to treat analytically. With the assistance of two associates,[3] Working has determined the approximate distribution of H for a random series, thus providing a test of the hypothesis that a series is random. Some of the basic mathematical work on the test remains to be done, but enough has been done to make the test usable.

The parameters of a 'rectangular-tailed' dispersion pattern, and hence the weights of the particular type of moving average stochastic process postulated in Working's theory, have been estimated by Monte Carlo methods, dispersing a random-walk series in ways corresponding to several moving average processes [3]. Such dispersions give rise to a family of curves of H-values which can be approximated by a family of logistic curves depending on the parameters of dispersion. In this way the parameters of dispersion can be estimated from the empirical H-curves for one-day subintervals.

Empirical H-curves for the two ten-year periods of corn prices, and the logistic curves fitted to them, are tabulated below, and are shown in Chart 3A:

Interval length	*1922–31 Period*		*1949–58 Period*	
	Empirical	*Fitted*	*Empirical*	*Fitted*
2	−.006	.001	.012	.001
4	−.022	.002	.008	.003
8	−.033	.006	−.007	.009
16	−.032	.017	−.003	.023
32	.005	.038	.030	.051
64	.048	.074	.082	.100
128	.133	.112	.181[a]	.164
256	.148	.139	.253[b]	.220

[a] Significant at 5 per cent level.
[b] Significant at 1 per cent level.

These fitted curves correspond to dispersion parameter estimates of 14 per cent dispersed over 36 days for the 1922-31 period, and 22.5 per cent dispersed over 52 days for the 1949–58 period.

CHART 3

Comparison of empirical and fitted curves of index of continuity

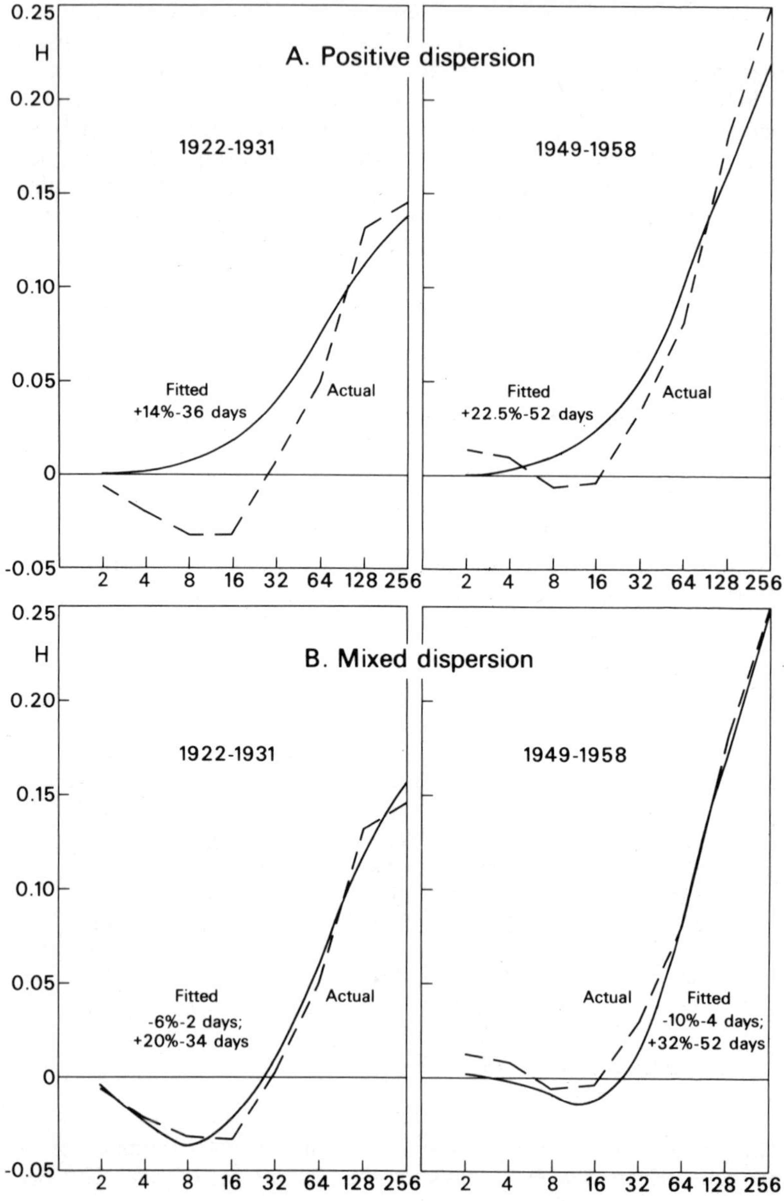

The fit is fairly good. The general character of the empirical curve conforms rather well to the fitted theoretical curve. The negative H-values at low interval lengths are definitely anomalous, however. A much better fit is achieved if it is assumed that the weights of the lower portion of the dispersion span are negative. This might result from profit-taking by quick-turn traders, or if some group of traders tends to regard most price movements as somewhat excessive. This is compatible with the rest of the theory of anticipatory prices, even though it does introduce an element of trading that is not immediately motivated by market information. The modification results in a moving average process with four parameters; a negative per cent dispersed over a short span, and a positive per cent dispersed over a longer span. The curve of H-values resulting from this mixed dispersion pattern is approximately the sum of the curves which result from the two dispersions taken separately. The parameter estimates for the mixed dispersion patterns for the two periods are: −6 per cent dispersed over 2 days and +20 per cent dispersed over 34 days, for 1922–31, and −10 per cent dispersed over 6 days and +32 per cent dispersed over 52 days, for 1949–58. The actual and fitted curves are tabulated below and shown in Chart 3B:

Interval length	*1922–31 Period*		*1949–58 Period*	
	Empirical	*Fitted*	*Empirical*	*Fitted*
2	−.006	−.005	.012	.001
4	−.022	−.023	.008	−.002
8	−.033	−.036	−.007	−.007
16	−.032	−.024	−.003	−.011
32	.005	.010	.030	.015
64	.048	.063	.082	.082
128	.133	.118	.181[a]	.172
256	.148	.156	.253[b]	.256

[a] Significant at 5 per cent level.
[b] Significant at 1 per cent level.

The degrees of freedom are reduced, but the improvement in fit seems to be sufficiently pronounced to warrant the introduction of the more complex pattern of dispersion.

The two periods yield strikingly similar patterns of continuity, and may be combined to yield a single estimate of −8 per cent dispersed over 4 days and +27 per cent dispersed over 45 days. This implies that 81 per cent of the price effect of demand and supply influences occurs on a single day, presumably the day the influences occur and/or the day they become known to the majority of traders in the market. There is then some reaction away from this price movement, even though the initial movement had been insufficient to bring the price to equilibrium. Finally corrective movements occur, resulting in total movement which is just appropriate. If this is a true picture of the operation of the corn futures market, then it approaches very closely the ideal.

We do not yet have a mathematically determined test of goodness of fit, whereby we can evaluate the fit achieved. Other specifications of process might yield an even better fit than is obtained here, though this does not seem very likely. But the most plausible alternative hypothesis – the Taussig theory – can be rejected simply on the basis of the general character of the curve of indexes of continuity.

If the dominant source of price movement were the bounding of price up and down between the edges of a penumbra, the index of continuity should have high positive values at low interval lengths and high negative values at longer interval lengths. If most movements result from over-excited response to minute stimuli and what might be called panicky reactions to previous movements, whether or not consciously manipulated, the index of continuity would have high negative values at *all* interval lengths. Movements of the type Taussig speaks of may occur, occasionally, and the empirical content of the theory consists in saying that these are the dominant sources of movement, or that they occur often enough to have adverse effects on traders and on the resource allocation function of the market. This is disproved by the high *positive* values of the index of continuity at long interval lengths.

The test of continuity seems to demonstrate the existence of a moving average stochastic process of the type postulated by Working's theory of anticipatory prices. At the same time it disproves the theory of Taussig and other critics of futures markets. Correlogram analysis failed to do either of these things. We cannot on this account dismiss the correlogram test completely, however. In order that we may accept the moving average process, it is necessary to show that the empirical correlogram is not inconsistent with the theoretical correlogram which is implied by such a process.

Theoretical correlograms for the moving average processes estimated by the index of continuity method were computed for the two 10-year periods. (The negative dispersion span for 1949–58 was increased from 6 days to 7 days in order to include the second large negative correlation coefficient.) The empirical correlation coefficients over the spans so determined were then averaged and the empirical and theoretical correlograms compared. The results are shown in Chart 4. There is one major discrepancy, for the negative dispersion span for the 1922–31 period. Other than that, the agreement is close. This analysis lends further support to the hypothesis that the moving average is the true type of process in operation.

CHART 4
Comparison of the theoretical correlograms associated with the estimated dispersion patterns and the empirical correlograms averaged over the dispersion spans

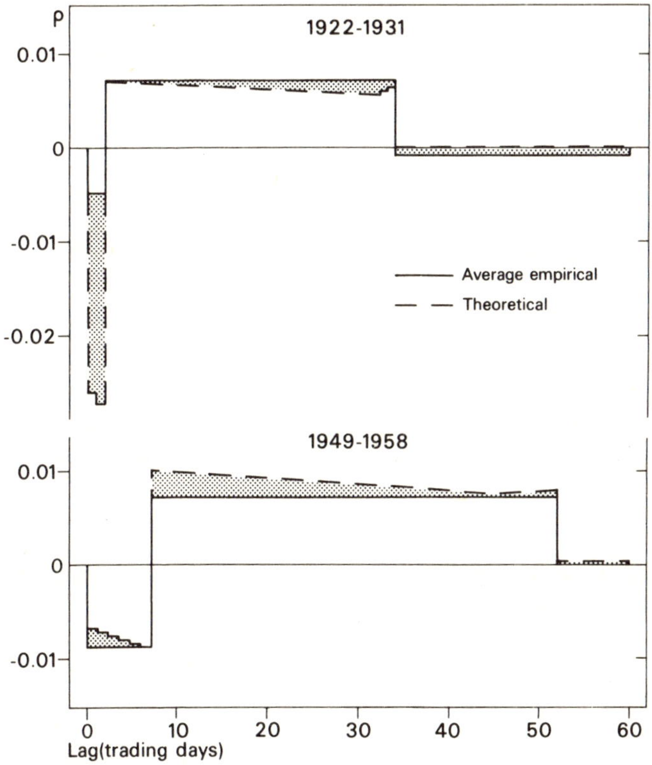

Perhaps an estimating procedure based on the smoothed correlogram could be constructed. Moving average processes of simple types, such as the rectangular, have associated with them correlograms which are also rather simple and reflect the pattern of the weights of the process. Autoregressive processes have correlograms which are damped oscillatory. The empirical correlogram may have a pattern of one of these types, hidden by random elements which smoothing would eliminate. It is surprising to find virtually no discussion of correlogram smoothing in the literature of time-series analysis, in view of the importance of smoothing in this field. There are hazards in the use of the smoothed correlogram, and there may be insurmountable obstacles, but it is an intriguing possibility.

SUMMARY AND CONCLUSIONS

Analysis based on the index of continuity has demonstrated the existence of a high-order, low-weight moving average stochastic process generating price changes, as envisioned by Working's theory of anticipatory prices. At the same time it has denied the existence of the excessive fluctuation supposed to occur by many critics of futures markets. Autocovariance analysis appeared unable to do either.

These statistical results can be given the economic interpretation that market price changes are closely tied to market news, which tends to be a true reflection of changing demand and supply conditions. But this interpretation rests on the assumption that price can not wander away from equilibrium and remain away for long. For if it could, price movements could be oriented about misinformation or pure guesses, provided only that the misinformation or guesses be random. Taussig and Working both assume that equilibrating forces soon assert themselves, but other critics of futures trading may disagree, and to them much of the argument of this paper may appear tautological. Whatever interpretation one places on the moving average process, it is not to be taken as the only imperfection possible in futures markets.

The potential scope of application of the index of continuity cannot be accurately predicted at this time. It may be that few markets are as near the ideal as are the corn and wheat futures markets, and that any further departure from the ideal introduces factors which will have to be detected and analyzed by other means. On the other hand, the index may prove to be a versatile tool for the analysis of time series from many fields of study, and may be capable of detecting some processes other than the moving average.

NOTES

1 See Gerhard Tintner, *Econometrics*, 1952, for a number of applications and discussions of the results.

2 This phenomenon resembles in many respects the 'support' and 'resistance' levels of chart traders, although the support and resistance seems often to be attributed to more esoteric causes than equilibrating forces. If we grant that they are the same, we would conclude that price does not immediately bounce off the edge of the penumbra and continue toward the center, but rather remains near the edge for some time.

3 Phillipe Berthet and Claude S. Brinegar.

REFERENCES

[1] F. W. Taussig, 'Is Market Price Determinate?' *Quarterly Journal of Economics*, May 1921, pp. 394–411.

[2] Holbrook Working, 'New Ideas and Methods for Price Research,' *Journal of Farm Economics*, Dec. 1956, pp. 1427–36, and 'A Theory of Anticipatory Prices,' *American Economic Review*, May 1958, pp. 188–99.

[3] Arnold B. Larson, 'Evidence on the Temporal Dispersion of Price Effects of New Market Information' (diss. Stanford University, Calif., 1960).

12 Testing the Efficient Markets Theory on the Sydney Wool Futures Exchange

P. D. PRAETZ

I. INTRODUCTION

The efficient markets theory is most commonly associated with Sharpe [16], Lintner [13, 14], Fama [5] and Fama and Miller [6]. In simple terms it states that a market in which prices fully reflect all available information is regarded as efficient. To make this proposition testable, it is necessary to specify a model of price formation in terms of expected returns, which depend on the risk vis-a-vis other securities and are conditional on an information set (S). This can be formalized by

$$E(p_{t+1}|S) = [1 + E(r_{t+1}|S)]\, p_t$$

where E is the expectation operator, p_t is the price of a security at time t, r_{t+1} is the one-period return and p_t and r_t are random variables. The information set, S, is fully utilized in equilibrium expected returns and therefore in the price.

These assumptions imply that trading systems using only information in S cannot have returns greater than equilibrium expected returns. Thus the excess return x_t, defined by

$$x_t = r_t - E(r_t|S)$$

must have expectation zero, i.e. it is a 'fair game' with respect to S. This was used by Samuelson [15], who proved that properly anticipated prices would fluctuate randomly. This is consistent with empirical studies which showed price changes or returns behaving like random walks. In fact the random walk model is an important special case of the efficient markets model, as if successive returns are independent and if the returns are identically distributed, they will constitute a random walk.

Prices would fully reflect available information if there were no transactions costs, all information were costlessly available to all

* From *Australian Economic Papers*, vol. 14, 1975, pp. 240–49. Reprinted by permission.

participants and they agreed on the implications of current and future information for prices. Even though these conditions are not fulfilled in practice, they should approximate efficiency if enough investors have access to information, if disagreement over information is not systematically exploitable and if all available information is utilized even though transactions costs exist.

Formal testing of the efficient market theory has been confined to security markets, but it is a natural extension to consider commodity cash and futures markets, because earlier studies there have tested the random walk model using statistical or financial tests. In terms of Fama's [5] division of empirical testing into weak, semi-strong and strong form tests, this study is a weak form one as it is concerned with past price data.

The plan of this paper is as follows. Section Two reviews the recent research on the statistical analysis of commodity prices and makes some critical comments on their interpretation. Then, in Section Three, wool futures price changes are studied for independence, using runs tests, serial correlations, spectral analysis and filter tests. Finally, Section Four draws some conclusions from the analysis of earlier sections about the market efficiency of the Sydney wool futures exchange. This paper is the first to use a number of complementary tests on any commodity exchange over a considerable period of time (2000 daily prices) using statistical methods which do not suffer from any of the defects which have been present in earlier work. In this way, we can see more clearly if this market approximates to an efficient one. The Sydney wool futures market is one of the major commodity futures markets in the world and one of only three outside the U.S.A. and London (see Labys and Granger [9]).

II. CURRENT RESEARCH ON THE STATISTICAL ANALYSIS OF COMMODITY PRICES

Larson [11] studied corn price futures in the U.S. and was unable to detect any dependence in the price changes using serial correlation coefficients. However, using an Index of Continuity, he claimed to find a small amount of dependence but this is dubious as his Index is an *ad-hoc* statistical tool whose sampling properties are unclear. Working [21] has found a small amount of dependence in some U.S. commodity spot and future prices using the Index of Continuity. Smidt [17], using a mechanical trading rule to seek dependence in U.S. soybeans futures prices, generally felt that his results supported independence in price changes.

Labys and Granger [9] used spectral analysis on thirteen futures and six spot price series of major U.S. commodities on a monthly basis from 1950–1965. Most of the future price changes had flat spectra and so supported the independence of price changes, but there was a little evidence of an annual component and its harmonics. For the spot series, the situation was similar except the seasonality was a little stronger. Even stronger support for independence was obtained from weekly and daily prices.

Copper spot and futures prices on the London metal exchange were examined by Labys *et al* [10] monthly from 1953 to 1958 using spectral methods. In general, they found only a small four month cycle apart from randomness of price changes. The spot and futures prices were coincident but there was some evidence of other exchanges lagging behind London. Both these studies sought peaks in the spectra outside confidence limits rather than formally testing all points outside these limits as evidence against independence.

Leuthold [12] has investigated the independence of price changes for the live beef cattle futures market in the U.S.A. using filter tests and spectral analysis from 1965 to 1970. He claims that his results cast serious doubt on the principle that the prices fluctuate randomly and that profitable trading is possible using mechanical rules. His spectral results support randomness much more strongly than he asserts because he has classified spectra as random if all points are within the limits, non-random if there is a peak outside the limits and otherwise almost random. This is not consistent with normal sampling variation as, with 50 lags, we expect $2.55 = .05\ (50 + 1)$ points outside the limits. Using Poisson probabilities, there must be six or more points outside the limit to be significant at the 95 per cent level. In addition, he seems to have used the Fama and Blume [4] procedure for filter tests. Dryden [2] has shown that returns derived from their procedure are biased upwards. More importantly, Leuthold provides no buy-and-hold rates for comparison, so it is logically impossible to distinguish between independent and dependent price changes, so his work gives no real evidence against randomness.

Stevenson and Bear [19] have studied U.S. corn and soybeans futures prices, daily over 1951–68, seeking dependence with serial correlations, runs tests and filters. The statistical measures do not provide strong evidence for dependence, and on the basis of some large filter profits, they conclude that the random walk hypothesis can be rejected. This seems unwarranted as the overall average returns in their study were much less for filters than for buy-and-hold and what they were rejecting was normal sampling variation.

Tier and Kidman [20] studied weekly price movements in the wool, wool tops and yarn spot and futures markets in Australia, the U.K. and Japan over 1962–70 using spectral methods. Their results are extremely unclear as they present no evidence on their methodology at all except a few brief comments on their spectra and cross-spectra. In particular, in the wool and wool futures price series, there was some evidence of seasonality in the Australian data. They also felt most of the medium to short term movements in each series had been random, with the main exception being a seven week seasonal in Australian wool prices. Cross-spectral analysis produced no evidence of any series leading or lagging the others. Apart from Tier and Kidman, the only other statistical research on the Sydney greasy wool futures market seems to be by Snape [18] and Goss [7]. These are mainly concerned with testing certain theories about futures markets, although Snape found some evidence of a small seasonal in futures prices less spot prices.

III. STATISTICAL TESTS ON PRICE CHANGES

(a) *Treatment of price changes*

The price data has not been analysed directly, but transformed to a log price change (x_t); where

$$x_t = \ln p_{t+1} - \ln p_t \tag{1}$$

and p_t is price at time t. This is because the theory is in terms of price changes and the change in log prices is a return, under continuous compounding, from holding a contract.

The data consisted of daily prices over 18 months of contracts maturing in July, October and December for 1966 to 1972, a total of 21 series with approximately 390 members. Also, daily prices over 1965–72 inclusive (2000 observations) were studied at durations 12 months, six months and zero months (spot) from maturity. Prices were closing buyer prices in cents per kg., cents per lb. and pence per lb. of clean wool and were transformed to cents per lb. The three fixed duration from maturity series were based on the nearest contract to 12, six and zero months.

The mean ($\bar{x}$) and standard deviation (s) of daily log price changes are given in Table I. The means of the 18 month futures reflect the history of the period well. Prices moved erratically over 1965–68, fell heavily in 1969–70, were fairly stable in 1971 and rose sharply in 1972. Thus the $\bar{x}$ values for July 1966 to December 1969 contracts oscillate over small positive and negative values, the 1970 and 1971 contracts show larger negative values of $\bar{x}$ and the 1972 contracts have large positive values. The variability of the period is also clear in the standard deviation figures as until the October 1970 contract, s was very stable at around half a percent, but from then on increased to about 2 percent. Spot, six and 12 months all have similar means and their standard deviations vary from 1.1 to 1.4 percent, for daily price changes over the eight year period.

(b) *Independence of price changes*

Independence is important in price changes as, if it is true, a knowledge of past price changes will not help to predict future price changes and prices. If independence does not hold, it is possible that the dependence or imperfections present could be used to provide profits for speculators. We test for independence using serial correlation tests, runs tests, spectral analysis and filter tests. Spectral analysis provides a non-parametric test in the frequency domain for general dependence, whereas the others are time domain tests. Serial correlations and runs tests measure associations of adjacent price changes parametrically and non-parametrically, and filters measure non-linear 'financial-type' dependencies. Thus each test complements the others in a general search for dependence in price changes.

(c) *Serial correlation tests*
The sample serial correlation coefficient is defined by r_a, $a = 1,2,3, \ldots$

$$r_a = \sum_{i=1}^{n-a} (x_{i+a} - \bar{x})(x_i - \bar{x}) / (n - a)\, s^2$$

When the x_i values are independent, then var $(r_a) = 1/(n - a)$ and $E(r_a) = 0$ approximately, so 95 percent limits for r_a are given by + and − .044 and .100 for the eight year and 18 month series respectively. Values of r_a have been calculated for a = 1,20 and are given in Table I, for $a = 1$. Clearly spot, six months, all 1968, July 1970 and July and October 1971 are significant. However, this significance is mainly due to large sample size as the coefficients are all so low as to offer no appreciable explanation. The largest, − .17, explains only 2.89 percent of the total variation involved and is hardly exploitable. The situation was similar when other values of a, from 2 to 20, were studied.

(d) *Runs tests*
An alternative method of seeking out dependence in price changes is to study the number of runs. A run is a sequence of price changes of the same sign, which can be +, − or 0. The test involves comparing the total number of runs of all signs, assuming price changes are independent. The actual number of runs, r, has mean and variance defined by

$$E(r) = n + 1 - \sum m_j^2 / n$$

$$\text{var}(r) = \left\{ \sum m_j^2 \left(\sum m_j^2 + n^2 + n \right) - 2n \sum m_j^3 - n^3 \right\} / (n^3 - n)$$

where m_j, j = 1,2,3 are the total +, 0 and − price changes. Values of $Z = (r - E(r)) / (\text{var}(r))^{\frac{1}{2}}$ are given in Table I. At the 5 percent significance level, it is obvious that the 12 months, December 1970 and all 1971 futures are significant. As Z is negative, this means less runs than expected and thus positively correlated price changes. Only July and October 1971 are significant in both tests so far. The amount of correlation present is very small as $Z = -3.5$ (July 1971) has 185 runs against an expected 218.

(e) *Spectral analysis*
The spectrum of any non-autocorrelated series is a constant which does not depend on frequency. When the spectrum is estimated at a number of frequencies, it can be compared with its theoretical value by including confidence limits for the spectrum, following the procedure of Granger [8]. Table I has values of *ns*, the number of spectral values outside the 95 percent confidence limits. The number of spectral values estimated were 100 for the eight year series and 40 for the 18 month series, which implies an expected number of points outside the limits of five and two. Poisson probabilities give that 12 or seven points outside the limits is a significant departure from randomness for the price changes at the 1 percent level.

TABLE 1
Values of mean ($\bar{x}$), standard deviation (s), serial correlation coefficient (r_1), spectral points (ns) and runs test statistic (Z) for daily price changes of wool futures contracts

Future	$\bar{x}$ ($\times 10^5$)	s(%)	r_1	ns	Z
Spot	24	1.4	−.06	25	−1.8
6 months	27	1.3	−.15	47	−1.7
12 months	20	1.1	.04	43	−4.6
July 66	44	0.5	−.02	2	.0
October 66	20	0.5	.04	3	− .1
December 66	0	0.5	−.01	1	.3
July 67	− 37	0.6	.06	0	−1.2
October 67	− 33	0.6	−.03	4	−1.0
December 67	− 28	0.6	−.08	2	− .8
July 68	− 8	0.7	−.12	2	− .9
October 68	8	0.6	−.17	8	− .5
December 68	− 3	0.6	−.14	8	.1
July 69	− 12	0.5	−.05	3	1.1
October 69	7	0.5	−.06	2	− .9
December 69	− 24	0.5	.01	4	.4
July 70	− 73	0.5	.13	6	−1.6
October 70	−160	0.9	−.09	11	−1.3
December 70	−154	1.3	.09	11	−2.3
July 71	−122	1.1	.16	15	−3.5
October 71	− 66	1.2	.13	4	−3.5
December 71	− 79	1.2	.04	1	−2.4
July 72	81	1.2	−.05	5	−1.4
October 72	194	1.8	−.03	5	−1.4
December 72	247	2.1	−.03	6	−1.8

Clearly, spot, six and 12 months and October and December for 1968 and 1970 all have an excessive number of points outside of the confidence limits, which is not completely consistent with independence of price changes. The eight year series have significant peaks in their spectra corresponding to cycles of 20, 8, 5, 3.3 and 2.5 days of market time approximately. This would seem fairly close to a monthly cycle and its harmonics, although the 5 and 2.5 day peaks could be part of a weekly cycle. In the eighteen month series, it is difficult to observe any cycles except the short ones. However, cycles of length 5, 3.2 and $2\frac{1}{2}$ days were observed a number of times. Thus, although all of the eight year and five of the 21 eighteen month series showed departures from the strict independence assumptions, the amount of dependence found was not at all large. We cannot say much about business cycles or seasonal components as the 18 month series are too short and the eight year series are probably best studied as monthly averages for spectral purposes here.

(e) *Filter tests*

Filter tests are a financial method of seeking dependence in prices, by proposing a strategy which 'filters out' small price fluctuations and attempts to exploit large price movements. In order to approximate the trading rules devised by chartists, Alexander [1] devised the filter test. A filter trading rule is used to 'filter out' unimportant movements in the price of a future and to identify the significant movements. Thus, using an 'X' percent filter, if a futures price rises by X percent from a previous low, buy that contract. If subsequently the future falls by X percent from a previous high, sell it and go short in it until the next X percent rise. This necessarily assumes that movements persist sufficiently to enable excess profits to be made, as the chartists claim. If the market is a fair game, however, this trading rule will not provide a higher return than simply buying and holding throughout any period. In essence, then, it is an attempt to discover whether there is any information coveyed by prices which can be used to construct a particular trading rule which will guarantee higher returns than the naive buy and hold policy. If the rule is successful, the market is clearly not efficient – there is available unused information which can be utilized profitably.

If p_0 is the price at which a transaction is initiated and p_1 is the price at its conclusion, then the annual rate of return (r) is given, Dryden [2], by

$$(2) \qquad p_0 (1 + r)^n = p_1 \qquad \text{(long)}$$

$$(3) \qquad = p_0 + (p_0 - p_1) \qquad \text{(short)}$$

where n is the time in years between p_0 and p_1. If a filter generates a series of m individual returns, r_j, $j = 1, m$, each over n_j years, then the return over this whole period (r) is given by

$$(1 + r)^N = \prod_j (1 + r_j)^{n_j} \tag{4}$$

where N is the total time in years. The rate of return on buy-and-hold, with which the filter returns are compared, is given by equation (2), where p_0 and p_1 are the opening and closing prices of the first and last completed transaction respectively.

Equations (2) and (3) are illustrated by a transaction over 2 years with $p_0 = 100$ and $p_1 = 144$. The long rate of return is given in

$$100\ (1 + r)^2 = 144, \text{ i.e. } r = 20\%$$

and the short rate of return in

$$100\ (1 + r)^2 = 56, \text{ i.e. } r = -25.2\%$$

The overall return from long transactions (*RL*) is given by (4) when *j* runs over long positions only. The return from short transactions (*RS*) is defined similarly in (4) when *j* runs over short positions. The overall filter return (*RF*) is given by (4) with *j* including long and short positions. The overall return from a buy-and-hold strategy (*RBH*) is given by (2).

The 24 filter sizes used in this study have been (percentages) ½, 1, 1½, 2, 2½, 3, 3½, 4, 4½, 5, 6, 7, 8, 9, 10, 11, 12, 13, 14, 15, 16, 18, 20, 25.

In Table II, we have results expressed as annual rates of return for *RL* (long positions), *RS* (short positions), *RF* (filters – long and short) and *RBH* (buy-and-hold) for the eight year and 18 month series averaged over the 24 filter sizes to 25 percent, as larger filters often are not initiated. Table III presents annual rates of returns for the filter strategy (*RF*) and buy-and-hold (*RBH*) for various filter sizes, averaged over the 18 month and eight year series. In 12 of the 21 contracts of 18 month length and all three eight year series, *RBH* is greater than *RF*, the average differences being 0.1 percent and 2 percent respectively. So there is no evidence to suggest that filter returns are larger than buy-and-hold.

In ten of the 24 filter sizes for the 18 month contracts and all sizes for the eight year period there are *RBH* values larger than *RF*, the average differences being 0.8 percent and 1.0 percent respectively. The grand total of 441 comparisons has only 206 times when *RF* was greater than *RBH*, which lends no support to *RF* being systematically larger than *RBH*.

Thus, these three summaries of the filter strategy provide no evidence for its superiority over a buy-and-hold approach. Clearly, there were certain times when certain filter sizes were more profitable than buy-and-hold, but it is doubtful if they would persist in the future in any predictable manner. In particular, they involved mainly small filters with many transactions, whose superiority would be removed if transactions costs were included.

TABLE II

Returns, averaged over filter size, for long (RL), short (RS), filter (RF) and buy-and-hold (RBH) strategies for various contracts. (Percentages)

Contract		*RL*	*RS*	*RF*	*RBH*
Spot		9.6	− 5.8	1.0	1.0
6 months		9.4	−12.3	−2.1	1.6
12 months		7.4	− 4.6	−1.5	1.0
July	1966	0.3	− 8.2	−0.1	0.5
October	1966	4.0	−18.1	−4.9	2.6
December	1966	− 1.2	0.3	−1.3	− 1.1
July	1967	− 9.9	− 4.2	−1.7	− 0.8
October	1967	−13.3	2.7	−0.8	− 1.6
December	1967	−13.7	3.8	−0.8	− 1.7
July	1968	− 5.4	− 9.8	−2.0	− 0.2
October	1968	− 1.5	−10.5	−6.2	1.9
December	1968	− 0.7	− 8.8	−5.8	1.6
July	1969	− 2.0	− 5.0	−1.4	− 0.7
October	1969	− 1.0	0.0	−0.8	− 0.8
December	1969	− 2.5	12.1	3.5	− 2.6
July	1970	−27.5	16.3	0.8	− 3.6
October	1970	−30.6	35.2	2.9	− 7.2
December	1970	2.6	47.6	5.0	− 9.1
July	1971	−25.3	34.6	1.7	− 7.3
October	1971	−26.0	14.5	−0.3	− 4.4
December	1971	−28.0	16.3	−2.1	− 5.6
July	1972	13.2	−23.1	−7.8	4.3
October	1972	31.2	−25.7	7.7	11.3
December	1972	67.7	−60.5	2.9	15.5

The filters have not been re-run with transactions costs included because of their complexity and as the evidence in favour of filter rules can only diminish compared with buy-and-hold, due to the number of transactions. In fact, the charges were on both a variable and a fixed cost basis, neither of which were constant over 1965–72. In addition, traders operated on margin (deposit) which had to be increased if price movements were adverse. Thus, calculation of exact returns to include this plus the varying costs is difficult to incorporate in a program and was not attempted. If these returns were available, they could not be directly compared with a buy-and-hold return because the latter is a much less risky process due to the very large leverage effects achieved by the margin. In terms of the risk–return tradeoff derivable from the

TABLE III

Returns for various filter sizes from filter (RF) and buy-and-hold (RBH) strategies, averaged over 8 year and 18 month contracts. (Percentages)

Filter Size (%)	*18 months*		*8 years*	
	RF	*RBH*	*RF*	*RBH*
25	0.6	2.1	−0.2	2.4
20	−1.9	−0.6	−0.6	1.8
18	−8.7	0.3	−0.2	1.4
16	−5.9	1.6	−0.3	0.8
15	−3.5	0.9	−0.4	0.8
14	−2.9	0.6	−0.3	0.7
13	0.4	−1.9	−0.5	0.7
12	0.1	−1.0	−0.6	0.7
11	0.4	0.1	−0.9	0.7
10	−4.1	0.8	−0.1	0.8
9	−3.2	0.9	0.5	0.9
8	−2.0	0.7	−0.1	0.9
7	−0.7	0.7	−0.3	0.9
6	1.3	0.3	−0.2	0.9
5	0.7	−0.1	0.1	0.9
4½	0.1	−0.2	0.5	0.9
4	1.6	−0.3	0.6	1.0
3½	1.3	−0.6	0.0	1.0
3	1.3	−0.6	0.5	1.1
2½	1.1	−0.6	0.6	1.0
2	1.2	−0.4	0.5	1.1
1½	0.7	−0.3	0.3	1.0
1	0.9	−0.3	−0.1	1.2
½	0.9	−0.5	0.6	1.1

efficient markets model, returns with unequal degrees of risk cannot be compared directly and would need adjustment for the differences in risk. The returns we have used in Tables II and III all have equal degrees of risk and so can be directly compared with each other without adjustment.

IV. CONCLUSIONS

The evidence on the independence of price changes from all four tests is remarkably consistent in its support for the efficient markets theory. The statistical tests, correlation coefficients, runs tests and spectral analysis all provide only small departures from a model in which price changes are uncorrelated. Clearly, this model stands as a good first approximation to the underlying stochastic process generating price changes. Spectral analysis provides some insight into the non-randomness we have found, which may be due to the harmonics of a weak seasonal movement. The evidence from the financial filter-type tests is even more strongly in favour of the efficient markets model. There is a large amount of non-stationarity in the returns which can be seen from the way the standard deviations in Table I vary from 0.5 per cent to 2.1 percent.

All our results have been developed for daily price changes, but the effects we have observed should persist over longer intervals. Thus the task of prediction of price changes will be an extremely difficult one, given the lack of success of Labys and Granger for U.S. commodity prices. They found that the best predictor was a random walk, so finding a better one is akin to medieval alchemy.

The exact reason why the Sydney wool futures market seems to be efficient appears to lie in the presence of many well informed traders who all agree on the worth of all current and expected future information concerning the market. Obviously the market is not fully efficient, but there appear to be enough informed participants to reduce the size of any imperfections which occur to about the size of transactions costs.

REFERENCES

[1] S. Alexander, 'Price Movements in Speculative Markets: Trends or Random Walks', *Industrial Management Review*, vol. 2, 1961.

[2] M. Dryden, 'A Source of Bias in Filter Tests of Share Prices', *Journal of Business*, vol. 42, 1969.

[3] E. Fama, 'The Behaviour of Stock Market Prices', *Journal of Business*, vol. 38, 1965.

[4] E. Fama and M. Blume, 'Filter Rules and Stock Market Trading', *Journal of Business*, vol. 39, 1966.

[5] E. Fama, 'Efficient Capital Markets: A Review of Theory and Empirical Work', *Journal of Finance*, vol. 25, 1970.

[6] E. Fama and M. Miller, *Theory of Finance*, Holt, Rinehart and Winston, New York, 1972.

[7] B. Goss, 'Trading on the Sydney Wool Futures Market: A Test of a Theory of Speculation at the Level of the Individual', *Australian Economic Papers*, vol. 11, 1972.

[8] C. Granger, *Spectral Analysis of Economic Time Series*, Princeton University Press, 1964.

[9] W. Labys and C. Granger, *Speculation, Hedging and Commodity Price Forecasting*, Heath–Lexington, Lexington, Mass., 1970.

[10] W. Labys, H. Rees and C. Elliott, 'Copper Price Behaviour and the London Metal Exchange', *Applied Economics*, vol. 3, 1971.

[11] A. Larson, 'Measurement of a Random Process in Futures Prices', *Food Research Institute Studies*, vol. 1, 1960.

[12] R. Leuthold, 'Random Walks and Price Trends: The Live Cattle Futures Market', *Journal of Finance*, vol. 27, 1972.

[13] J. Lintner, 'The Valuation of Risk Assets and the Selection of Risky Investments in Stock Portfolios and Capital Budgets', *Review of Economics and Statistics*, vol. 47, 1965.

[14] J. Lintner, 'Security Prices, Risk, and Maximal Gains from Diversification', *Journal of Finance*, vol. 20, 1965.

[15] P. Samuelson, 'Proof that Properly Anticipated Prices Fluctuate Randomly', *Industrial Management Review*, vol. 6, 1965.

[16] P. Sharpe, 'Capital Asset Prices: A Theory of Market Equilibrium Under Conditions of Risk', *Journal of Finance*, vol. 19, 1964.

[17] S. Smidt, 'A Test of the Serial Independence of Price Changes in Soybeans Futures', *Food Research Institute Studies*, vol. 5, 1965.

[18] R. Snape, 'Price Relationships on the Sydney Wool Futures Market', *Economica*, vol. 35, 1968.

[19] R. Stevenson and R. Bear, 'Commodity Futures: Trends or Random Walks?', *Journal of Finance*, vol. 25, 1970.

[20] T. Tier and P. Kidman, 'Price Movements in and Between the Wool, Wool Tops and Worsted Yarn Spot and Futures Markets', *Quarterly Journal of Agricultural Economics*, vol. 23, 1970.

[21] H. Working, 'Speculation on Hedging Markets', *Food Research Institute Studies*, vol. 1, 1960.

13 Does Futures Trading Reduce Price Fluctuations in the Cash Markets?

MARK J. POWERS

One of the recurring arguments made against futures markets is that, by encouraging or facilitating speculation, they give rise to price instability. This argument, in various versions, has been made throughout past Congressional hearings on onion and potato futures. The theoretical literature available on the subject of futures trading and price stability is rather scanty and inconclusive. Most of the evidence has been gathered on onion and potato prices. It suggests that: a) the seasonal price range is lower with a futures market because of speculative support at harvest time; b) sharp adjustments at the end of a marketing season are diminished under futures trading because they have been better anticipated; and c) year-to-year price fluctuations are reduced under futures trading because of the existence of the futures market as a reliable guide to production planning. See Roger Gray, and Holbrook Working (1958, 1960, 1963).

These conclusions are most valid for seasonally produced storable commodities. They probably do not hold for other commodities, particularly those that are continuously produced and semi- or non-storable. A more general approach to the study of the impact of futures trading on cash prices is needed.

The statistical evidence assembled in support of the above three conclusions has always dealt with the total seasonal variation in cash prices. This paper concerns itself with an analysis of the impact of futures trading on the fluctuations of the separate elements of a price series. It focuses mainly on the effect futures trading has on the random element.

Working (1934 p. 11–24) and Arnold Larson (p. 313–24) have provided evidence that an anticipatory price series may be thought of as

* From *American Economic Review*, vol. LX, 1970, pp. 460–4. Reprinted by permission.

describing a random walk. Paul Cootner and others in analyses of stock market prices have done additional work on the hypothesis. Hendrik Houthakker (p. 164–72) questions the applicability of the random-walk hypothesis to futures prices, particularly in the short run. He argues that futures price series are composed of both a random element and a systematic component. None of these studies considers the application of the random-walk hypothesis to the cash price series.

If one were to accept Working's and Larson's results as being applicable to a cash price series, then a measure of the total variation in the series would also be a measure of the random element in the series. On the other hand, if their evidence on futures price series is not relevant to cash price series, then a measure of the total variation in the cash series would be a measure of more than just the random element. Since cash price series are not entirely anticipatory and no evidence is available that they do or do not describe a random walk, it is assumed that the latter is correct and that the cash price series considered here are composed of both a systematic and a random component.

The first part, the systematic component of the time-series, is the part of the price series that is representative of fundamental economic conditions and varies with those conditions. Fluctuations in this component are not only desirable but necessary in a free market economy where prices allocate resources and distribute outputs. The second part of the price series, the random component, cannot be explained by underlying economic forces. Random fluctuations are undesirable in a price series because they act only to distort the price message and, thus, really represent a 'noise' factor in the price system.

To illustrate, consider:

(1) $$P_t = S_t + E_t$$

The variance of the series is

(2) $$V(P_t) = V(S_t) + V(E_t)$$

and the covariance is

(3) $$\text{cov}\ (S_t E_t) = 0$$

where

P_t = time-series of prices
S_t = the systematic component associated with fundamental economic conditions
E_t = the error or random component which represents noise and disturbance in the price system.

One would expect that $V(S_t) \neq 0$, implying that changes in economic conditions result in price changes, and it would be desirable that $V(E_t) = 0$, i.e., that there be no random fluctuations.

Given the above, then the real concern with the pricing system is to improve its efficiency as a communications and allocative device by reducing the noise factor, the random elements in the prices, while maintaining the responsiveness of the systematic component of fundamental economic conditions.

Since a price series is composed of systematic and random parts, the question arises: What would happen to these two components if a viable futures market were introduced into the pricing system? Consider $V(S_t)$ first.

One possibility is that the introduction of futures trading would have no effect on $V(S_t)$. A second and more likely result might be that $V(S_t)$ would be reduced. Gray (p. 273–75) and Working (1958 and in Congressional hearings) support this contention. This might occur because of a close relationship between expected (futures) prices and economic fundamentals.

In general, however, there have been few studies of the impact of futures trading on $V(S_t)$, since most studies do not distinguish between $V(S)$ and $V(E)$. Important questions with respect to $V(S_t)$ remain unanswered, suggesting further research is needed in this area.

The main focus of this paper, however, is $V(E_t)$, the second element of variance in the price series. What happens to $V(E_t)$ when a futures market is injected into the marketing system for a commodity?

To seek an answer to this question an analysis of two commodities, pork bellies and live cattle, was undertaken. For purposes of conducting the study it was hypothesized that $V(E_t)$ would be lower during time periods with futures trading than during time periods without futures trading.

To analyze the data and test the hypothesis it was desirable to use a technique which would isolate and estimate the random element in a variable which is changing over time. The technique ultimately selected was the *Variate Difference Method*, developed by Gerhard Tintner.

I. THE VARIATE DIFFERENCE METHOD

Although several different techniques might be used for determining the random variations in a time-series, the variate difference method fits our purpose best, mainly because it is a statistical method that does not require the specification of a rigid model and it isolates and estimates the random element without affecting the systematic component.

The variate difference method starts from the assumption that an economic time-series consists of two additive parts. The first is the mathematical expectation or systematic component of the time-series. The second is the random or unpredictable component. The assumption is that these two parts are connected by addition but are not correlated. It is further assumed that the random element is not autocorrelated and has a mean of zero; that the random element is normally distrubuted; and that the systematic component is a 'smooth' function of time.

The steps involved in the analysis are essentially three. First, the random element is isolated in the time-series. This is accomplished by finite differencing. Successive finite differencing of a series will eliminate or at least reduce to any desired degree the systematic component without changing the random element at all. The random component cannot be reduced by finite differencing because it is not ordered in time.

Second, the variance of the random element is calculated. The calculation of the variance for the original series is as follows:

$$V_0 = \frac{\sum_{i=1}^{N} (W_1 - \overline{W})^2}{N - 1}$$

where $\overline{W}$ = the mean of the original series.

The estimate of the variances of the higher differences is as follows:

$$V_k = \frac{\sum_{i=1}^{N-K} (\Delta^{(k)} W_i)^2}{(N - K)_{2k}C_k}$$

where ${}_{2k}C_k$ is the binomial coefficient of the Kth difference equal to the number of combinations of $2k$ things taken k things at a time.

When a finite difference of the order K_0 is found such that the variance of the $K_0{}^{th}$ difference is equal to the variance of the $(K_0 + 1)^{th}$ difference and equal to that of the $(K_0 + 2)^{th}$ difference, and equal to the $(K_0 + 3)^{th}$ difference etc., it is reasonable to assume that the mathematical expectation has been eliminated to a reasonable degree by taking K_0 differences and that the remaining variance is attributable to the random element. The variances are considered to be approximately equal, from a probability standpoint, when the differences between the variances for successive finite differences are less than three times the standard error.

To determine whether or not there is a statistically significant difference in the random variance for price series in different time periods, a standard-error-difference formula for testing the difference between two variances was used.[1]

II. THE ANALYSIS

Weekly cash prices for pork bellies and live beef were collected for eight years, fours year preceding the start of futures trading and four afterwards.[2] The four-year periods considered for pork bellies were 1958 through 1961, and 1962 through 1965. For beef, the four-year periods were 1961 through 1964, and 1965 through 1968. The cash prices used

TABLE 1
Random variances of cash prices of live choice grade cattle and pork bellies, four-year basis[a]

Commodity	*Four-Year Period Without Futures Trading*	*Four-Year Period With Futures Trading*	*Difference*
Pork Bellies	1.040	.62	−.420*
Beef	.086	.041	−.045*

* Difference significant at 5 percent level.
[a] Original data in cents/pound.

for choice live steers represented the average weekly prices paid for choice steers at Chicago. The pork belly prices, obtained from the National Provisioner, represented 12–14 pound bellies in Chicago. The data were analyzed on the basis of four-year and two-year time periods.

The analysis of the data on the four-year basis indicates that the variance of the random element in live beef prices was reduced from .086 or about 30 cents per cwt. during the four years without futures trading to .041 or about 20 cents per cwt. during the four years with futures trading.[3] The difference between these variances was significant (5%). Similarly, during the four years without futures trading in pork bellies, the variance in the random element was 1.040 or a little more than $1.00

TABLE 2
Random variances of cash prices of live choice grade cattle and pork bellies, two-year basis[a]

Period and Commodity	*Period Without Futures Trading*	*Period With Futures Trading*	*Difference*
Beef			
1	.101	.045	−.560*
2	.073	.041	−.032*
Pork Bellies			
1	.62	.38	−.240*
2	1.29	.85	−.440*

* Difference significant at 5 percent level.
[a] Original data in cents/pound.

per cwt., while in the four-year period with futures trading the random variance declined to .62 or about 78 cents per cwt. These differences in variance were also significant at the 5 percent level. See Table 1.

The results of the two-year analyses parallel those for the four-year analysis as seen in Table 2. In each of the two-year periods considered in live beef, the random fluctuations were significantly lower than in each of the two-year periods without futures trading. Likewise for pork bellies the analysis indicates that for similar years in the price cycle the random fluctuations were significantly lower when there was futures trading than when there was not. On this basis the variances in the random element in pork bellies were .38 and .85 with futures trading compared to .62 and 1.29 in the corresponding periods without futures trading.

It should be noted that in the case of the beef data, the prices represent different years in essentially the same price cycle, while the pork belly data represent years in different cycles. The most logical comparison would be on the basis of corresponding years in successive price cycles. This was not possible in beef. Nevertheless, it was assumed that any changes in random fluctuations that might be related to the upswings or downswings in a cycle would not be major. In any case it would be unrealistic to attribute the nearly 50 percent reduction in random beef price fluctuation to changes in the price cycle.

In summary the evidence suggests that during the time periods considered for pork bellies and live beef the variance of the random element in cash prices for these commodities was significantly lower when futures trading occurred then when it did not.

The question remains 'Can this reduction in the variance of the random element be attributed to futures trading?' If so, what logic suggests it? Answers to these questions are not easily found. Part of the difficulty arises from the usual problems associated with the *ceteris paribus* assumption.

The most logical explanation for random variations in prices rests on the degree to which market participants are informed of fundamental supply and demand conditions. The more informed are market participants, the greater the likelihood that the prices arrived at in the market will represent true supply and demand; the less informed they are, the greater the likelihood that prices will deviate from the true equilibrium price, or, the larger the random element will be. On this basis one would expect the fluctuations in price that cannot be explained by fundamental supply and demand conditions to be reduced when market participants are more informed than when they are less informed.

III. THE INFORMATION ROLE OF THE FUTURES MARKET

Information is the key to competition. Market information has a particularly important place among the factors that determine what is offered for sale and what is demanded, and hence among the factors that determine prices. As markets become more decentralized, information concerning current and future demand and supply conditions must be carefully collected and interpreted.

Commodity future exchanges have been termed clearing centers for information. Information relative to supplies, movements, withdrawals from storage, purchases, current production, general supply and demand conditions, cash and futures prices, and volume of futures trading, is collected, collated, and distributed by the exchange, its members and the institutions such as brokerage houses, which serve the exchange. This information is used not only by current and potential traders in futures, but it is also carefully evaluated by cash market operators.

The existence of futures trading in a commodity should increase the speed with which information is disseminated, the area over which it is disseminated, and the degree of saturation within the area. It should tend to equalize the flows of information to current and potential futures and cash market participants.[4] The result should be more informed decision making and prices that are more closely representative of basic supply and demand conditions; prices whose random element is less than it would be without futures trading; price messages that are more sharply defined and less distorted by noise or the random element.

During the time periods considered in this study the only major changes in information flows for these commodities were those resulting from futures trading. Perhaps then, the answer to the first question posed above is, yes, part of the reduction in the variance in the random element can be attributed to the inception of futures trading in these commodities. In answer to the second question, the relationship between the reductions in random price fluctuations and futures trading is explained in part by the improvements in the information flows fostered by futures trading.

This conclusion is necessarily quite tentative. The results of the data analysis are quite significant although they represent a rather small sample of commodities. The impact of the futures market on the market information system and on decisions made by potential and current market participants needs empirical verification.

This conclusion with respect to $V(E_t)$ in the above analysis implies nothing about the effect futures have on $V(S_t)$. Further work needs to be undertaken to determine the effect futures trading has on $V(S_t)$. It may be that $V(S_t)$ may be greater, less than, or the same when futures trading is in effect than when it is not. Further, it may be that futures trading has a different effect on $V(S_t)$ when the commodity considered is storable and seasonally produced than when the commodity is non- or semi-storable and continuously produced.

To further test the hypothesis developed in this paper and other hypotheses on the effect of futures trading on price fluctuations more studies need to be conducted on a wider range of commodities. The recent genesis of futures trading in a number of other commodities should offer ample opportunity for such research in the years immediately ahead.

NOTES

1 See any basic statistics text for the standard-error-difference formula for testing the difference between two variances. An *F*-test at the 5 percent level was used to determine the significance of the difference.

2 Four-year periods were considered in order to hold to a minimum the changes that occurred in the structure of the markets concerned.

3 The variance is measured in $(\text{cents/cwt})^2$. Thus a variance of .041 $[\text{cents/cwt}]^2$ is equivalent to $[.20\ \text{cents/cwt.}]^2$.

4 In the long run both the quality and quantity of information may also be increased.

REFERENCES

P. H. Cootner, ed., *The Random Character of Stock Market Prices*, Cambridge, Mass. 1964.

R. Gray, 'Onions Revisited,' *Journal of Farm Economics*, vol. 45, 1963.

H. S. Houthakker, 'Systematic and Random Elements in Short-Term Price Movements,' *American Economic Review*, vol. 51, 1961.

A. Larson, 'Measurement of a Random-Process in Futures Prices,' *Food Research Institute Studies*, vol. 1, 1960.

G. Tintner, *The Variate Difference Method*, Bloomington, 1940.

H. Working, 'A Random-Difference Series for Use in the Analysis of Time-Series,' *Journal of American Statistical Association*, vol. 29, 1934.

———, 'A Theory of Anticipatory Prices,' *American Economic Review*, Proceedings, vol. 48, 1958.

———, 'Price Effects of Futures Trading,' *Food Research Institute Studies*, vol. 1, 1960.

———, 'New Concepts Concerning Futures Markets and Prices,' *American Economic Review*, vol. 51, 1961.

———, 'Futures Markets Under Reserved Attack,' *Food Research Institute Studies*, vol. 4, 1963.

U.S. Congress. House Subcommittee on Agriculture. 'Prohibit Trading in Irish Potato Futures on Commodity Exchange,' *Hearings on H.R. 904*, 88th Cong., April 8–10, 1963.

———. Senate. *Hearings Before a Subcommittee of the Committee on Agriculture and Forestry*, 85th Cong., 1st sess., Aug. 12, 1957.

———. Senate. *Hearings Before the Committee on Agriculture and Forestry*, 85th Congress, 2nd sess., Mar. 22–26, 1958.

Bibliography

(referred to in Introduction)

BAKKEN, 1970. H. H. Bakken (ed.), *Futures Trading in Livestock – Origins and Concepts*, Madison, Wisc.: Mimir Publishers.

BAUER and YAMEY, 1968. P. T. Bauer and B. S. Yamey, *Markets, Market Control and Marketing Reform*, London: Weidenfeld and Nicolson.

BAUMOL, 1957. W. J. Baumol, 'Speculation, Profitability, and Stability', *Review of Economics and Statistics*, vol. 39.

BAUMOL, 1959. W. J. Baumol, 'Reply', *Review of Economics and Statistics*, vol. 41.

BLAU, 1944. G. Blau, 'Some Aspects of the Theory of Futures Trading', *Review of Economic Studies*, vol. 12.

BRAND, 1964. S. S. Brand, 'The Decline in the Cotton Futures Market', *Food Research Institute Studies*, vol. 4.

BRENNAN, 1958. M. J. Brennan, 'The Supply of Storage', *American Economic Review*, vol. 48. Reprinted partly in this book.

BRINEGAR, 1970. C. S. Brinegar, *A Statistical Analysis of Speculative Price Behaviour*, *Food Research Institute Studies*, vol. 9, supplement.

CHEUNG, 1969. S. Cheung, 'Transactions Costs, Risk Aversion, and the Choice of Contractual Arrangements', *Journal of Law and Economics*, vol. 12.

COOTNER, 1960. P. H. Cootner, 'Returns to Speculators: Telser vs Keynes' and 'Rejoinder', *Journal of Political Economy*, vol. 68.

COOTNER, 1964. P. H. Cootner (ed.), *The Random Character of Stock Market Prices*, Cambridge, Mass: M.I.T. Press.

COWING, 1965. C. B. Cowing, *Populists, Plungers, and Progressives: A Social History of Stock and Commodity Speculation, 1890–1936*, Princeton, N.J.: Princeton University Press.

DANTWALA, 1937. M. L. Dantwala, *Marketing of Raw Cotton in India*, Bombay: Longman, Green.

DEMSETZ, 1967. H. Demsetz, 'Towards a Theory of Property Rights', *American Economic Review*, vol. 57.

DEMSETZ, 1968. H. Demsetz, 'The Cost of Transacting', *Quarterly Journal of Economics*, vol. 82.

DOMINGUEZ, 1972. J. R. Dominguez, *Devaluation and Futures Markets*, Lexington, Mass. and London: Lexington Books.

DOMINION OF CANADA, 1931. *Report of the Commission to enquire into Trading in Grain Futures*, Ottawa: The King's Printer.

DOW, 1940. J. C. R. Dow, 'A Theoretical Account of Futures Markets', *Review of Economic Studies*, vol. 7.

DOW, 1941. J. C. R. Dow, 'The Inaccuracy of Expectations', *Economica*, vol. 8.

DUMBELL, 1927. S. Dumbell, 'The Origin of Cotton Futures', *Economic History*, vol. 1.

DUSAK, 1973. K. Dusak, 'Futures Trading and Investor Returns: An Investigation of Commodity Market Risk Premiums', *Journal of Political Economy* vol. 81.

EHRICH, 1966. R. L. Ehrich, 'The Impact of Government Programs on Wheat Futures Markets, 1953–1963', *Food Research Institute Studies*, vol. 6.

EHRICH, 1969. R. L. Ehrich, 'Cash-Futures Price Relationships for Live Beef Cattle', *American Journal of Agricultural Economics*, vol. 51.

EMERY, 1896. H. C. Emery, *Speculation on the Stock and Produce Exchanges of the United States*, New York: Columbia University.

FARRELL, 1966. M. J. Farrell, 'Profitable Speculation', *Economica*, vol. 33.

FEDERAL TRADE COMMISSION, 1954. *Economic Report of the Investigation of Coffee Prices*, Washington: U.S. Government Printing Office.

FRIEDMAN, 1953. M. Friedman, *Essays in Positive Economics*, Chicago: University of Chicago Press.

FURUBOTN and PEJOVICH, 1972. E. G. Furubotn and S. Pejovich, 'Property Rights, Economic Decentralisation and the Evolution of the Yugoslav Firm', *Journal of Law and Economics*, vol. 16.

FUTRELL, 1970. G. A. Futrell, 'Do Live Cattle Futures differ from other existing Futures Contracts?' in Bakken, 1970.

GEORGESCU-ROEGEN, 1958. N. Georgescu-Roegen, 'The Nature of Expectations and Uncertainty', in Mary J. Bowman (ed.), *Expectations, Uncertainty and Business Behaviour*, New York: Social Science Research Council.

GLAHE, 1966. F. R. Glahe, 'Professional and Nonprofessional Speculation, Profitability, and Stability', *Southern Economic Journal*, vol. 33.

GLAMANN, 1974. K. Glamann, 'European Trade 1500–1750', in C. M. Cipolla, *The Fontana Economic History of Europe*, vol. 2, London: Collins/Fontana Books.

GOSS, 1972*a*. B. A. Goss, *The Theory of Futures Trading*, London: Routledge & Kegan Paul.

GOSS, 1972*b*. B. A. Goss, 'Trading on the Sydney Wool Futures Market: A Test of a Theory of Speculation at the Level of the Individual', *Australian Economic Papers*, vol. 11. Reprinted in this book.

GRAF, 1953. T. F. Graf, 'Hedging – How Effective is it?' *Journal of Farm Economics*, vol. 35.

GRAY, 1960*a*. R. W. Gray, 'The Importance of Hedging in Futures Trading; and the Effectiveness of Futures Trading for Hedging', in *Futures Trading Seminar*, vol. 1, Madison, Wisc.: Mimir Publications.

GRAY, 1960*b*. R. W. Gray, 'The Characteristic Bias in Some Thin Futures Markets', *Food Research Institute Studies*, vol. 1.

GRAY, 1961*a*. R. W. Gray, 'The Search for a Risk Premium', *Journal of Political Economy*, vol. 69. Reprinted partly in this book.

GRAY, 1961*b*. R. W. Gray, 'The Relationship among Three Futures Markets', *Food Research Institute Studies*, vol. 2.

GRAY, 1963. R. W. Gray. 'Onions Revisited', *Journal of Farm Economics*, vol. 45.

GRAY, 1964. R. W. Gray, 'The Attack upon Potato Futures Trading in the United States', *Food Research Institute Studies*, vol. 4.

GRAY, 1967. R. W. Gray, 'Price Effects of a Lack of Speculation', *Food Research Institute Studies*, vol. 7, Supplement.

GRAY, 1970. R. W. Gray, 'The Prospects for Trading in Live Hog Futures', in Bakken, 1970.

GRAY, 1972. R. W. Gray, 'The Futures Market of Maine Potatoes: An Appraisal', *Food Research Institute Studies*, vol. 11.

GRAY and TOMEK, 1971. R. W. Gray and W. G. Tomek, 'Temporal Relationships among Futures Prices: Reply', *American Journal of Agricultural Economics*, vol. 53.

HACCOÛ, 1947. J. F. Haccoû, *Termijnhandel in Goederen*, Leiden: Stenfert Kroese.

HAUSER, 1974. W. B. Hauser, *Economic Institutional Change in Tokugawa Japan*, London: Cambridge University Press.

HAWTREY, 1940. R. G. Hawtrey, 'Mr. Kaldor on the Forward Market', *Review of Economic Studies*, vol. 7.

HEIFNER, 1966. R. G. Heifner, 'The Gains from Basing Grain Storage Decisions on Cash-Futures Spreads', *Journal of Farm Economics*, vol. 48.

HEIFNER, 1971. R. G. Heifner, 'Temporal Relationships among Futures Prices: Comment, *American Journal of Agricultural Economics*, vol. 53.

HICKS, 1953. J. R. Hicks, *Value and Capital*, London: Oxford University Press. One section reprinted in this book.

HOFFMAN, 1932. G. W. Hoffman, *Futures Trading upon Organized Commodity Markets in the United States*, Philadelphia: University of Pennsylvania Press.

HOUTHAKKER, 1957. H. S. Houthakker, 'Can Speculators Forecast Prices?', *Review of Economics and Statistics*, vol. 39.

HOUTHAKKER, 1959. H. S. Houthakker, 'The Scope and Limits of Futures Trading', in M. Abramovitz *et al.*, *The Allocation of Economic Resources*, Stanford, Calif.: Stanford University Press.

HOUTHAKKER, 1967. H. S. Houthakker, *Economic Policy for the Farm Sector*, Washington: American Institute for Public Policy.

HOUTHAKKER, 1968. H. S. Houthakker, 'Normal Backwardation', in J. N. Wolfe (ed.), *Value, Capital and Growth; Papers in Honour of Sir John Hicks*, Edinburgh: Edinburgh University Press.

HOWELL, 1948. L. D. Howell, *Analysis of Hedging and Other Operations in Grain Futures*, Washington: U.S. Department of Agriculture.

HOWELL and WATSON, 1938. L. D. Howell and L. J. Watson, *Relation of Spot Cotton Prices to Prices of Futures Contracts and Protection afforded by Trading in Futures*, Washington: U.S. Department of Agriculture.

INTERNATIONAL CHAMBER OF COMMERCE, 1956. *Obstacles to the Operation of Futures Markets*, Paris, I.C.C.

IRWIN, 1935. H. S. Irwin, 'Seasonal Cycles in Aggregates of Wheat-Futures Contracts', *Journal of Political Economy*, vol. 43.

IRWIN, 1937. H. S. Irwin, 'The Nature of Risk Assumption in the Trading on Organized Exchanges', *American Economic Review*, vol. 27.

IRWIN, 1954. H. S. Irwin, *Evolution of Futures Trading*. Madison, Wisc.: Mimir Publishers.

ISLAM, 1966. T. Islam, 'Cotton Futures Markets In India: Some Economic Studies', Ph.D. thesis, University of London.

ISLAM, 1973. T. Islam, 'Structure of Futures Contract, Difference System and Hedging Effectiveness', *Indian Economic Journal*, vol. 20.

JOHNSON, 1972. A. C. Johnson, 'Whose Markets? The Case for Maine Potato Futures', *Food Research Institute Studies*, vol. 11.

JOHNSON, 1957. L. L. Johnson, 'Price Instability, Hedging and Trade Volume in the Coffee Futures Market', *Journal of Political Economy*, vol. 65.

JOHNSON, 1960. L. L. Johnson, 'The Theory of Hedging and Speculation in Commodity Futures', *Review of Economic Studies*, vol. 27. Reprinted in this book.

KALDOR, 1939. N. Kaldor, 'Speculation and Economic Stability', *Review of Economic Studies*, vol. 7. Reprinted in N. Kaldor, *Essays on Economic Stability and Growth*, London: Duckworth, 1961. Reprinted partly in this book.

KALDOR, 1940. N. Kaldor, 'A Note on the Theory of the Forward Market', *Review of Economic Studies*, vol. 7.

KEMP, 1963. M. C. Kemp, 'Speculation, Profitability and Price Stability', *Review of Economics and Statistics*, vol. 45.

KEYNES, 1930. J. M. Keynes, *A Treatise on Money*, vol. 2, London: Macmillan.

KEYNES, 1936. J. M. Keynes, *The General Theory of Employment, Interest and Money*, London: Macmillan.

KLEIN, 1972. L. R. Klein, 'The Treatment of Expectations in Econometrics', in C. F. Carter and J. L. Ford (eds.), *Uncertainty and Expectations in Economics: Essays in Honour of G. L. S. Shackle*, Oxford: Blackwell.

KOFI, 1973. T. A. Kofi, 'A Framework for Comparing the Efficiency of Futures Markets', *American Journal of Agricultural Economics*, vol. 55.

LABYS and GRANGER, 1970. W. C. Labys and C. W. J. Granger, *Speculation, Hedging and Commodity Price Forecasts*, Lexington: D. C. Heath & Company.

LARSON, 1960. A. B. Larson, 'Measurement of a Random Process in Futures Prices', *Food Research Institute Studies*, vol. 1. Reprinted in this book.

LARSON, 1961. A. B. Larson, 'Estimation of Hedging and Speculation Positions', *Food Research Institute Studies*, vol. 2.

LERNER, 1944. A. P. Lerner, *The Economics of Control*, London: Macmillan.

LIVERPOOL COTTON ASSOCIATION, 1957. *Liverpool Raw Cotton Annual*, 1957.

LIVERPOOL COTTON ASSOCIATION, 1958. *Liverpool Raw Cotton Annual*, 1958.

LONDON METAL EXCHANGE, 1958. *The London Metal Exchange*, prepared and published by the Economist Intelligence Unit.

MCKINNON, 1967. R. I. McKinnon, 'Futures Markets, Buffer Stocks, and Income Stability for Primary Producers', *Journal of Political Economy*, vol. 75.

MARSHALL, 1932. A. Marshall, *Industry and Trade* (third ed. reprinted), London: Macmillan.

MILL, 1848. J. S. Mill, *Principles of Political Economy*. London.

MILLS, 1962. E. A. Mills, *Price, Output, and Inventory Policy: A Study of the Economics of the Firm and Industry*, New York: Wiley.

MINGER, 1970. W. W. Minger, 'Financing Live Beef Cattle Futures Contracts', in Bakken, 1970.

MIRACLE, 1972. D. S. Miracle, 'The Egg Futures Market: 1940 to 1966', *Food Research Institute Studies*, vol. 11.

NAIK, 1970. A. S. Naik, *Effects of Futures Trading on Prices*, Bombay: Somaiya Publications.

NATU, 1962. W. R. Natu, *Regulation of Forward Markets*, London: Asia Publishing House.

NERLOVE, 1958. M. Nerlove, 'Adaptive Expectations and Cobweb Phenomena', *Quarterly Journal of Economics*, vol. 72.

OI and HURTER, 1965. W. Y. Oi and A. P. Hurter, *Economics of Private Truck Transportation*, Dubuque, Iowa: Wm. C. Brown Company.

OZGA, 1965. S. A. Ozga, *Expectations in Economic Theory*, London: Weidenfeld and Nicolson.

PAUL, 1970. A. B. Paul, 'The Pricing of Binspace – A Contribution to the Theory of Storage', *American Journal of Agricultural Economics*, vol. 52.

PAUL and WESSON, 1966. A. B. Paul and W. T. Wesson, 'Short-run Supply of Services – The Case of Soybean Processing', *Journal of Farm Economics*, vol. 48.

PAVASKAR, 1965. M. G. Pavaskar, 'Accuracy of Futures Market Price Forecasts', *Journal of the University of Bombay*, vol. 34.

PAVASKAR, 1968. M. G. Pavaskar, *Effects of Futures Trading on Short-Period Price Fluctuations* (mimeo.), Bombay: University of Bombay.

PAVASKAR, 1969. M. G. Pavaskar, *Hedging Efficiency of the Cotton Futures Market*. Bombay: University of Bombay.

PESTON and YAMEY, 1960. M. H. Peston and B. S. Yamey, 'Inter-temporal Price Relationships with Forward Markets: A Method of Analysis', *Economica*, vol. 27, Reprinted partly in this book.

POOLE, 1970. W. Poole, 'McKinnon on Futures Markets and Buffer Stocks', *Journal of Political Economy*, vol. 78.

POWERS, 1967. M. J. Powers, 'Effects of Contract Provisions on the Success of a Futures Contract', *Journal of Farm Economics*, vol. 49.

POWERS, 1970. M. J. Powers, 'Does Futures Trading Reduce Price Fluctuations in the Cash Markets?', *American Economic Review*, vol. 60. Reprinted in this book.

PRAETZ, 1975. P. D. Praetz, 'Testing the Efficient Markets Theory on the Sydney Wool Futures Market', *Australian Economic Papers*, vol. 14. Reprinted in this book.

RADI, 1957. M. A. Radi, 'The Structure of the Cotton Market in Egypt', M.Sc. (Econ.) thesis, University of London.

REES, 1972. G. L. Rees, *Britain's Commodity Markets*, London: Paul Elek.

REES and JONES, 1975. G. L. Rees and D. R. Jones, 'The International Commodities Clearing House Limited', *Journal of Agricultural Economics*, vol. 26.

RICHARDSON and FARRIS, 1973. R. A. Richardson and P. L. Farris, 'Farm Commodity Price Stabilization through Futures Markets', *American Journal of Agricultural Economics*, vol. 55.

ROCKWELL, 1967. C. S. Rockwell, 'Normal Backwardation, Forecasting, and the Returns to Commodity Futures Traders', *Food Research Institute Studies*, vol. 7, Supplement. Reprinted partly in this book.

RUTLEDGE, 1972. D. J. S. Rutledge, 'Hedgers' Demand for Futures Contracts:

A Theoretical Framework with Applications to the United States Soybean Complex', *Food Research Institute Studies*, vol. 11.

SAMUELSON, 1957. P. A. Samuelson, 'Intertemporal Price Equilibrium: A Prologue to the Theory of Speculation', *Weltwirtschaftliches Archiv*, vol. 79.

SAMUELSON, 1972. P. A. Samuelson, 'Economic Problems concerning a Futures Market in Foreign Exchange', in *The Futures Market in Foreign Currencies*, Chicago: Chicago Mercantile Exchange.

SANDOR, 1973. R. L. Sandor, 'Innovation by an Exchange: A Case Study of the Development of the Plywood Futures Contract', *Journal of Law and Economics*, vol. 16.

SCHIMMLER, 1974. J. Schimmler, *Spekulation, spekulative Gewinne und Preisstabilität*, Meisenheim am Glan: Anton Hain.

SHARP, 1940. M. W. Sharp, 'Allied Wheat Buying in relationship to Canadian Marketing Policy, 1914–18', *Canadian Journal of Economic and Political Science*, vol. 6.

SIMON, 1958. H. A. Simon, 'The Role of Expectations in an Adaptive or Behavioural Model', in Mary J. Bowman (ed.), *Expectations, Uncertainty and Business Behaviour*, New York: Social Science Research Council.

SMIDT, 1965. S. Smidt, *Amateur Speculators*, Ithaca, N.Y.: Cornell University Press.

SMITH, 1776. A. Smith, *The Wealth of Nations*.

SMITH, 1922. J. G. Smith, *Organised Produce Markets*, London: Longmans, Green.

SNAPE, 1962. R. H. Snape, 'Protection and Stabilization in the World Sugar Industry', Ph.D. thesis, University of London.

SNAPE, 1968. R. H. Snape, 'Price Relationships on the Sydney Wool Futures Market', *Economica*. vol. 35

SNAPE and YAMEY, 1965. R. H. Snape and B. S. Yamey, 'Tests of the Effectiveness of Hedging', *Journal of Political Economy*, vol. 73.

STEIN, 1961*a*. J. L. Stein, 'The Simultaneous Determination of Spot and Futures Prices', *American Economic Review*, vol. 51. Reprinted partly in this book.

STEIN, 1961*b*. J. L. Stein, 'Destabilizing Speculative Activity can be Profitable', *Review of Economics and Statistics*, vol. 43.

STEIN, 1964. J. L. Stein, 'The Opportunity Locus in a Hedging Decision: A Correction', *American Economic Review*, vol. 54.

STEINMANN, 1970. G. Steinmann, *Theorie der Spekulation*, Tübingen: J. C. B. Mohr.

STEWART, 1949. B. Stewart, *An Analysis of Speculative Trading in Grain Futures*, Washington: U.S. Department of Agriculture.

TELSER, 1955. L. G. Telser, 'Safety First and Hedging', *Review of Economic Studies*, vol. 23.

TELSER, 1958. L. G. Telser, 'Futures Trading and the Storage of Cotton and Wheat', *Journal of Political Economy*, vol. 66.

TELSER, 1959. L. G. Telser, 'A Theory of Speculation relating Profitability and Stability', *Review of Economics and Statistics*, vol. 41.

TELSER, 1960. L. G. Telser, 'Returns to Speculators: Telser vs Keynes: Reply', *Journal of Political Economy*, vol. 68.

TELSER, 1967. L. G. Telser, "The Supply of Speculative Services in Wheat, Corn, and Soybeans', *Food Research Institute Studies*, vol. 7, Supplement.

TELSER and YAMEY, 1965. L. G. Telser and B. S. Yamey, 'Speculation and Margins', *Journal of Political Economy*, vol. 73.

TEWELES *et al.*, 1968. R. J. Teweles, C. V. Harlow and H. L. Stone, *The Commodity Futures Trading Guide*, New York: McGraw-Hill Book Company.

TOMEK and GRAY, 1970. W. G. Tomek and R. W. Gray, 'Temporal Relationships among Prices on Commodity Futures Markets', *American Journal of Agricultural Economics*, vol. 52.

UNITED STATES DEPARTMENT OF AGRICULTURE, 1958. *The Economic Importance of Futures Trading in Potatoes*, Marketing Research Report, no. 241, Washington: U.S. Government Printing Office.

VENKATARAMANAN, 1965. L. S. Venkataramanan, *The Theory of Futures Trading*, London: Asia Publishing House.

VICZIANY, 1975. A. M. Vicziany, 'The Cotton Trade and the Commercial Development of Bombay, 1855–1875', Ph.D. thesis, University of London.

WARD, 1971. R. W. Ward, 'Futures Contract for Frozen Concentrated Orange Juice', Bureau of Economics and Business Research, University of Florida, *Economic Leaflets*, vol. 30.

WARD, 1974. R. W. Ward, 'Market Liquidity in the FCOJ Futures Market', *American Journal of Agricultural Economics*, vol. 56.

WARD and FLETCHER, 1971. R. W. Ward and L. B. Fletcher, 'From Hedging to Pure Speculation', *American Journal of Agricultural Economics*, vol. 53.

WILSON, 1966. R. B. Wilson, 'Merchandising and Inventory Management of Commodities', in E. A. Gaumnitz (ed.), *Futures Trading Seminar*, vol. 3. Madison, Wisc.: Mimir Publishers.

WISEMAN and YAMEY, 1956. J. Wiseman and B. S. Yamey, 'The Raw Cotton Commission, 1948–52', *Oxford Economic Papers*, vol. 8. Reprinted in Bauer and Yamey, 1968.

WORKING, 1948. H. Working, 'Theory of the Inverse Carrying Charge in Futures Markets', *Journal of Farm Economics*, vol. 30.

WORKING, 1953*a*. H. Working, 'Futures Trading and Hedging', *American Economic Review*, vol. 43. Reprinted partly in this book.

WORKING, 1953*b*. H. Working, 'Hedging Reconsidered', *Journal of Farm Economics*, vol. 35.

WORKING, 1954. H. Working, 'Whose Markets? – Evidence on Some Aspects of Futures Trading', *Journal of Marketing*, vol. 19.

WORKING, 1960*a*. H. Working, 'Price Effects of Futures Trading', *Food Research Institute Studies*, vol. 1.

WORKING, 1960*b*. H. Working, 'Speculation on Hedging Markets', *Food Research Institute Studies*, vol. 1.

WORKING, 1962. H. Working, 'New Concepts concerning Futures Markets', *American Economic Review*, vol. 52.

WORKING, 1963. H. Working, 'Futures Markets under Renewed Attack', *Food Research Institute Studies*, vol. 4.

WORKING, 1967. H. Working, 'Tests of a Theory concerning Floor Trading on Commodity Exchanges', *Food Research Institute Studies*, vol. 7, Supplement.

WORKING, 1970. H. Working, 'Economic Functions of Futures Markets', in Bakken, 1970.

YAMEY, 1951. B. S. Yamey, 'An Investigation of Hedging on an Organised Produce Exchange', *Manchester School*, vol. 19. Reprinted in Bauer and Yamey, 1968.

YAMEY, 1954. B. S. Yamey, 'Futures Trading in Cocoa, Rubber and Wool Tops', *Three Banks Review*, no. 23.

YAMEY, 1959. B. S. Yamey, 'Cotton Futures Trading in Liverpool', *Three Banks Review*, no. 41. Reprinted in Bauer and Yamey, 1968.

YAMEY, 1968. B. S. Yamey, 'Addendum' to 'An Investigation of Hedging. . .', in Bauer and Yamey, 1968.

YAMEY, 1971. B. S. Yamey, 'Short Hedging and Long Hedging in Futures Markets', *Journal of Law and Economics*, vol. 14.

Index of Authors

Page numbers followed by the letter n indicate that the reference is to a note or bibliographic entry. The abbreviation ps refers to the Postscript to the Introduction, pages 47–9.

Index of Commodities